FAMILY
MIRRORS

Books by Elizabeth Fishel

Sisters
The Men in Our Lives
Family Mirrors

Elizabeth Fishel

FAMILY MIRRORS

What Our Children's Lives Reveal about Ourselves

Houghton Mifflin Company · Boston · 1991

For information about permission to reproduce selections from
this book, write to Permissions, Houghton Mifflin Company,
2 Park Street, Boston, Massachusetts 02108.

Library of Congress Cataloging-in-Publication Data

Fishel, Elizabeth.
Family mirrors : what our children's lives reveal about ourselves
/ Elizabeth Fishel.
p.   cm.
Includes bibliographical references and index.
ISBN 0-395-44261-3
1. Family — Psychological aspects.   2. Parenting — Psychological
aspects.   3. Intergenerational relations.   4. System theory.
I. Title.
HQ518.F47   1991   91-2005
306.874 — dc20   CIP

Printed in the United States of America

MP 10 9 8 7 6 5 4 3 2 1

"Where Is the West" is from *Tamsen Donner: A Woman's Journey* by Ruth Whitman. Reprinted
by permission of alicejamesbooks, Cambridge, Massachusetts. "The Purgatory of Loving"
and "Mother, the Same Witch Haunts Us," by Judith W. Steinbergh, © 1983 by Judith
W. Steinbergh, were first published in *Motherwriter*, available from Talking Stone Press,
99 Evans Road, Brookline, Massachusetts 02146. "That Moment" is from *The Gold Cell* by
Sharon Olds, © 1987 by Sharon Olds. Reprinted by permission of Alfred A. Knopf, Inc.
"The Envelope" is from *Our Ground Time Here Will Be Brief*, by Maxine Kumin, © 1982
Maxine Kumin. Used by permission of Viking Penguin, a division of Penguin Books USA
Inc. "This Be the Verse" is from *High Windows* by Philip Larkin. Copyright © 1974 by
Philip Larkin. Reprinted by permission of Farrar, Straus and Giroux, Inc. "It May Be,"
by Alfonsina Storni, is reprinted by permission of the translator, Mark Smith-Soto. "Sce-
nario," by Barbara Eve, is reprinted from *Prairie Schooner* by permission of University of
Nebraska Press. Copyright © 1973 University of Nebraska Press. "The Writer" is from *The
Mind-Reader*, copyright © 1971 by Richard Wilbur. Reprinted by permission of Harcourt
Brace Jovanovich, Inc. "Generations of Swan," is from *The Great Ledge* by Peter Davison,
© 1989 by Peter Davison. Reprinted by permission of the author.

The quotations from *A Good Enough Parent*, by Bruno Bettelheim, copyright © 1987 by
Bruno Bettelheim, are reprinted by permission of Alfred A. Knopf, Inc. Quotations from
Clinical Studies in Infant Mental Health, by Selma Fraiberg, © 1980 by Selma Fraiberg, are
reprinted by permission of Basic Books, a division of HarperCollins Publishers.

To my sons, Nate and Will,
and to the memory of my father-in-law,
James Houghteling

ACKNOWLEDGMENTS

Above all I would like to thank the 160 parents from all over the country who generously shared their time and their family stories either in personal interviews or on questionnaires. Without their willingness to take time from the bustle of family life and their thoughtful concern and insights, this book would not have been possible.

Special thanks to my editor, Janet Silver, whose incisive questions and provocative responses enlarged my own vision and helped shape the book at every stage. Erica Landry's technical expertise and Peg Anderson's careful copy-editing were also most welcome as the book reached completion. Thanks also to Larry Kessenich, whose original excitement kindled my own, and to Katrina Kenison, who helped guide the manuscript at a pivotal stage. Joy Harris, my agent, has been an unflappable source of support and enthusiasm throughout this project's circuitous journey. My great appreciation to her as well.

During my four years of work on this book, many astute clinicians contributed crucial ideas to its development. I would especially like to thank Sheri Glucoft Wong, L.C.S.W., who gave generously of her wisdom, wit, and clinical expertise about families. I am greatly indebted to her. I would also like to thank Ronnie Wong, who helped me develop the original questionnaire.

Special thanks as well to Leah Potts Fisher, L.C.S.W., and Helen Neville, pediatric advice nurse at Oakland's Kaiser Hospital, who organized and led the Berkeley, California, parents' group that I taped and participated in, and to Marsha Greenstein, clinical psychologist, who co-led the Newton, Massachusetts, parents' group with me. I would also like to thank the parents who participated in these groups for sharing their candid discussions with me. Their contributions — which, of course, appear anonymously — broadened my understanding and added depth to my work.

I am also deeply grateful to my sister, Anne Fishel, a clinical psychologist at Massachusetts General Hospital in Boston and in private practice. Her sophisticated understanding of family systems theory and her wise clinical insights were invaluable resources for this book. With each of us juggling an infant and a toddler, our countless cross-country phone conversations were a bit of a high-wire act, but this book has been enriched by the information shared.

A number of people read drafts of various chapters, and their compelling comments and questions helped hone the finished book. I would especially like to thank Dusky Pierce, Carol and Zick Rubin, Merry Selk, Steve Seligman, Betty and Don Stone, and again, Leah Potts Fisher and Sheri Glucoft Wong.

For their careful assistance transcribing interview tapes and typing portions of the manuscript, I thank Lucy Collier, Mary Strads, and Kara Adams, who also painstakingly prepared the notes and bibliography.

Clearly, no book called *Family Mirrors* would be possible without the cooperation and inspiration of the writer's family. My parents, Edith and James Fishel, were my first and best models for the joys of life as a family; my mother-in-law and father-in-law, Fiora and James Houghteling, helped extend that earliest vision.

And although there were days when I lamented to my husband that this book would progress a lot faster if I didn't have children, the obvious and most heartfelt truth is that I couldn't possibly have written it without them. My beloved boys, Nate and Will, were an unlimited source of inspiration — and provided just enough interruptions to help me keep my perspective. My husband, Robert Houghteling, knew when to keep the boys out of my hair and, as always, made writing this book and being a family together a happy and satisfying time.

CONTENTS

— *Introduction* —

My Mother's Alphabet,
Letters for My Sons

WHERE IS THE WEST

If my boundary stops here
I have daughters to draw new maps on
   the world
they will draw the lines of my face
they will draw with my gestures my
   voice
they will speak my words thinking they
   have invented them.

they will invent them
they will invent me
I will be planted again and again
I will wake in the eyes of their
   children's children
they will speak my words

    Ruth Whitman, in the voice of pioneer
    woman Tamsen Donner

Beginning this book, I searched beneath the skin of the words I first learned as a child, the words I grew up on, the words I would pass along to my sons. These words are the mother tongue, whose cadences we first hear dimly in the womb, whose syllables we learn at our mother's and father's knee, whose messages we transmit and translate from the moment we first coo to our own newborns. And bringing back my earliest memories of learning the mother tongue, I remembered the game of letters that my mother taught me, long before I could read, and that I am now teaching my sons.

In that quiet, receptive time between day and evening, my mother stretches out on her bed, and I sit next to her, expectant as a baby bird, mouth open for the worm. My mother is resting, but she is also playing with me, guiding me through the game. Her back is my slate, and her languishing arms await my scribbles. As she alternately dozes and focuses, I write letters up and down her back and along her arms, as she has taught me, and she tries to name them. "A," she guesses, then "V." Finally she gets it: "H. H for 'head,' 'heart,' and 'happy,' " she tells me, teaching me gently the sounds of words, of language, her language. "H for 'hamburger' and 'Aunt Harriet.' "

Sometimes my mother stirs to greater wakefulness and writes letters on me. Her fingers, with their polished and pointed nails, are more like the fine point of a pencil or pen than my stubby, crayonlike fingers. Though her letters are precisely formed, my guesses are erratic. I grope to make sense of the letters, which are still pictograms to me, mysterious hieroglyphics, not the second nature they will become. But our game makes language more tangible, the abstract more physical. And even at this early age I know that my mother's letters, her words, have the weight and sheen and texture of the beads of her necklaces. They carry powerful messages, a text and subtext I am just beginning to decode.

I cannot pinpoint the moment when I first taught this game to my son, just as I cannot pinpoint the moment when the lullabies my mother sang to me came to my lips. But in that quiet, receptive time between night and morning, my older son crawls into bed with my husband and me, and I find myself teaching him this game. Now I am the giant stretched out on the bed, and Nate is the small and eager scribe beside me. He is poised expectantly, waiting to make contact, to learn, to be entertained. I am still halfdozing, in that pleasant stupor between dreams and wakefulness. But this is a game I can almost play in my sleep. Indeed, as my role in the game has shifted from student to teacher, I see that one of its beauties is that it can be played effortlessly, lying down. I can rest and teach, relax and entertain at the same time. Taking my place as parent of the new generation — well-intentioned but too often weary — I have new respect for my mother's ingenuity.

Now I am my son's human blackboard but hardly a blank slate. Beneath my skin, the old messages are hidden; my pores still hold the letters and lessons from my past. "V," I guess, as he scratches the letters on my arm, "no, H," then finally I get it, "A. A for 'alligators,' 'apples,' and 'alphabet,' " I teach him. "A for 'astronaut' and 'Aunt Anne.' " Then I stir to greater wakefulness and tickle out the letters on his arm, the old letters, exactly the way I learned them, but in new combinations that I am choosing to pass along.

After we have played the game many times the way I first learned it, my son comes up with his own version. "Let's write whole words," he suggests, and this we gamely try, bouncing into the far reaches of imagination, since Nate, only five, cannot write or read conventionally and invents his own idiosyncratic spelling as he goes along. But this is how the game is refined and changed, how the generations learn from each other, how the mother tongue is passed along.

Beginning this book, I took the alphabet game as a symbol for my search, and its subtext as the first text for my book. My objectives were at least threefold. First, I wanted to explore how we learn our own family's particular language — our mother's and father's tongue — at our parents' side and then how we translate and transform it for our own children. Which messages and lessons, values and ideas do we repeat, which do we alter, which avoid? And if we hope to change the messages we pass along, how do we bring to consciousness the old words and stories, the old memories and games?

Second, I wanted to examine the loop of influence between the generations: between ourselves and our children, our children and our parents, our parents and ourselves. How do our children, hearing our words, give them back to us in a different form? And then how do we, now parents ourselves, speak to our parents in a new way? How does our children's pivotal presence redefine the balance between our parents and ourselves?

And finally, I wanted to focus on the mutuality of growth in children and parents. How, in the process of guiding and teaching our children, do we ourselves change and grow? What mysteries about ourselves and our own childhoods do our children help us uncover? And how can we nurture our children's dreams without dreaming through them and define our own dreams without insisting that our children live them out?

In chapters 1 through 5 of this book, I explore these questions within the framework of family systems psychology. Chapter 1, "Ghosts in the Nursery," grounds the book in what Freud called the "unrememberable and unforgettable" terrain of infancy, the exhausting and exhilarating time when our infants' cries bring us back to our own. Chapter 2, "Becoming a Family," examines the complexities of adding a new member to the trio of mother, father, and first child. This chapter uses the language of the family systems perspective — an approach that views the family as a complex and interdependent system, experiencing stresses and opportunities for mutual growth as it moves through each transition of the life cycle. Chapter 3, "Family Snapshots," explores some of the changes, both emotional and sociological, from our parents' generation to our own. Three family portraits in this chapter introduce key images of what makes contemporary families work well — and what issues provide intergenerational stumbling blocks.

Why we repeat old family patterns and how we can begin to change them is the focus of Chapter 4, "Cycles of Pain, Strategies for Change." And four parenting styles of repetition and change are the subject of Chapter 5, "Traditionalists, Rebels, Compensators, and Synthesizers."

With my first son's birth, my identity both as a woman and a writer forever shifted. Although all of my work explores the unfolding of identity against the background of family, in my first two books I was the daughter looking back at the imprint of the past. In *Sisters* I looked through the lens of sisters' impact on each other; in *The Men in Our Lives*, through the lens of fathers' influence on daughters.

Now, as a mother and writer, I am at the midpoint between generations. I look back once again to the secrets and puzzles of childhood, but this time from a parent's perspective. I also look forward at the emerging personalities of my two sons, born into my family's crucible yet increasingly separate from us. These two little powerhouses (five and two as I write) fulfilled my earliest fantasies and also took me places I had never dreamed of; they are dynamic and physical where I had imagined docile and cerebral, insistent where I dreamed of mellow. They arouse feelings of pride, love, frustration, and outrage fiercer than any I had imagined or experienced before.

As I stand between my parents and my children, between my own past and my children's future, I watch my identity balance between being the child of my parents and being the parent of my children. This is the territory poet Judith Steinbergh calls "the purgatory of loving," and here I reposition myself between my memories of my childhood self and my memories of my parents, between my commitment to my husband and my alliance with the values of our generation.

As I watch my children's struggles and breakthroughs, I remember and relive my own disappointments and joys. Easing their rough edges gives me another chance to polish my own. Guiding my children through the choppy waters of their challenges teaches me to improve my own strokes.

And in teaching them, I learn from them as well, the child being father to the man in this way, as in others. This is the paradox Erik Erikson calls "the dependence of the older generation on the younger one," when he names "generativity versus stagnation" as the seventh of his "eight ages of man." "Mature man needs to be needed, and maturity needs guidance as well as encouragement from what has been produced and must be taken care of," he says in *Childhood and Society.* Elsewhere he points out that "it is as true to say that babies control and bring up families as it is to say the converse. A family can bring up a baby only by being brought up by him." I watch myself, my husband, and our children develop together and marvel at how each stage brings leaps of growth for the two of them *and* for the two of us.

As I struggle over my decisions as a parent (how much to stay, how much to go, what to limit, what to permit), I make my choices against the scrim of my parents' choices, differentiating myself from them in the light of my new family. Yet even as I distance myself from my parents, I see their choices with a new compassion, bringing us closer. I am disengaging from them at the same time that I identify more closely with them.

And as my husband and I merge and accommodate our histories, we, too, hammer out a new identity as a couple. For if there are said to be four extra spirits dancing over the marriage bed (his parents and hers), so too in the nursery. There is the way his mother burped her babies and the way my mother did it, the way his father jounced a baby on his knee and the way my father did it. Whose way shall we choose? Or shall we produce a new amalgam through trial and error, memory and merger?

My husband and I identify ourselves as part of a new generation of parents with mores, values, and viewpoints specific to our time.

Where our mothers bottle-fed us because medical wisdom then held that method most modern, healthy, and convenient, we breast-feed our babies for much the same reasons. Where our fathers were most often the family's sole breadwinner, today mothers and fathers often share both the breadwinning and the family's daily maintenance, as this era demands. Such choices are personal, but they are also social and generational. As parents, we surge and stumble forward with our peers, while looking over our shoulder at the wisdom and practices of our parents.

Moving beyond my own extended family, I began to share experiences with other parents of my generation, in kitchens and on playgrounds, in parents' groups and discussion groups, in interviews and questionnaires. I began to see our confrontation with internal dilemmas, with the words and puzzles of our own childhoods, as the most complex challenge of parenthood. Unexamined, these internal collisions of past and present can stand in the way of our being the best parents possible at each different stage. But examined and synthesized, these confrontations can generate exhilarating breakthroughs when new insights are revealed and new choices defined.

The tough issues are different for each parent. With each child, at each age, different topics may arise or recede as old dramas are replayed, shuffled, resolved, or shelved. Listening to these parents talking about their tender spots with their children touched a nerve with me and encouraged me to write this book.

"What single issue gives you the most trouble with your child?" I asked parents in my first interviews for this book.

"Separation," said one, a first-time mother in her forties. Looking for child care outside her home for her one-year-old daughter, she was struck by how "bereft" she felt. "I find it much harder separating from my daughter than she finds it separating from me. When I take her to visit these day cares, she likes them all, and I like none of them." Weeks of mournfulness sent her looking back to her own past, to a mother who had such difficulty separating from *her* daughter that in their house "no door was ever closed, not even when I was a teenager."

"Privacy," said another mother, speaking about a door she preferred to keep closed. She remembered being a very private child, one whom classmates called aloof, a snob. "Sharing emotions was like currency," she felt, "and I didn't want to give it away." Now her bright and verbal five-year-old was starting to close the door on her. "When I ask him about his day at school or what happened in drama class, he says, 'I don't want to talk about it.' I have to respect his sense of privacy, but how I'd love to know what goes on in those classes! And I also worry about other kids thinking he's aloof the way they labeled me — I know too well the price he's going to have to pay."

"Anger," said a father of two school-age daughters. "My own expression of anger was curtailed by my very domineering parents during my childhood and adolescence. When my younger daughter rages, part of me wants it to stop immediately and part lets it go on maybe too long, often becoming angry myself. What's repression, I ask myself, and what's supporting and teaching self-control?"

"Self-esteem," said the mother of a demanding ten-month-old infant. "My long-standing issue left over from childhood is the sense that I'm not doing enough, not accomplishing enough, not keeping busy enough. My baby plays right into this with his demands and protestations. I try one thing to amuse him, to comfort him or calm him down. That works for about ten seconds, and then he pushes me to try something else. Never lets me rest, read a book, just do nothing." Recalling the intensity of her own childhood as the only child of parents who lost a baby after they had her, she wonders, "Did I feel I had to make it up to them, always keep moving, never just rest and be however I was?"

"Performance and perfectionism," said a father of two rambunctious and athletic boys. "When I take my seven-year-old to the playground, and he loses it completely, crying uncontrollably because he hasn't hit the ball far enough or well enough, I see myself again at thirteen in disgrace on the tennis court. Through my son's tears, I see myself again throwing my racket into the net, against the fence, even breaking it once in half, so enraged was I at my less than perfect performance."

Separation and closeness. Anger and limit setting. Success and self-esteem. Exploring these topics provides the second part of my book, chapters 6, 7, and 8. As I observed my own conflicts with my children and listened to other parents brooding about theirs, these themes came up again and again. These were the areas of

transition, intensity, or stress where reverberations from generations back were most likely to show up. And in the psychological
literature, as well as in poems, stories, and novels, I came upon
these issues again and again, as writers in every era circled around
the complex territory of children's and parents' unfolding identities.

As in my previous work, my research for this book began with
personal experience and memory. I then wove together readings in
fiction, poetry, and psychological literature, interviews with parents
and with professionals trained to work with parents, and answers
to questionnaires that traced connections across three generations.
During the two years I spent on research, I heard from 160 parents
around the country and consulted with 35 parenting experts in the
helping professions with a variety of perspectives.

Much of the richest material came from my lengthy, intense, and
detailed personal interviews with eighty-five parents. Their stories
cover a range of ages, occupations, economic and social back-
grounds, geography, and family size and composition. I talked with
seriously troubled families as well as healthy ones, poor families as
well as the financially secure, nuclear families and extended families
under one roof, families struggling with alcoholism or abuse or the
serious needs of a handicapped child and families coping with
the garden-variety hassles of everyday life. But the majority of the
parents I interviewed were from basically healthy, well-functioning
families and were in their thirties and forties, white, professional,
and middle class, like myself. Since this is the group of parents I
know best, I chose to concentrate on them.

Looking for subjects, I followed leads from friends and neighbors,
from professional colleagues and people in the helping professions,
from readers familiar with my previous books, and people who
volunteered to be interviewed after hearing me lecture about my
earlier work. At times a provocative newspaper or magazine story
led me to a particularly distinguished — or anguished — parent,
whom I then contacted for an interview.

We arranged these conversations around the schedules and needs
of our children. Some interviews took place at kitchen tables when
children were asleep; some in offices, restaurants, or living rooms
while children were at day care or school. When need dictated, the

tape recorder hummed while babies nursed or toddlers danced their interruptions around parents' feet. But mostly we managed to find a quiet space, removed from children's demands, to reflect thoughtfully on our shared experience of being parents. My subjects and I savored the opportunity to make the leaps between our own and our children's childhoods that are at the heart of this book.

At times our conversations had the charged quality of phone calls between two parents at their wits' end, trying to help each other pick up the pieces at the end of a frazzling day. At other times the interviews were supportive or illuminating, like a parents' group comparing notes and searching for a common thread. Still other conversations had the intensity and self-discovery usually reserved for a more clinical setting, as parents tried to dovetail childhood memories with the predicaments of their current family life.

Sometimes these memories were little more than a fleeting image, a sensory impression, which we followed from there. "In my mother's house, her vacuum was always on," remembered a woman grappling now with combining family and career. "Please be quiet because mother is tired," was a recurring phrase remembered by a woman struggling with the decision to have a second child.

I listened the way a therapist might for the subtext of these stories, for the revealing gap between what is remembered and reported and what may indeed have happened. But while making my own interpretations, I also trusted the emotional truth of my respondents. When, for example, one young mother described her mother smiling "only ten times" from her early childhood to her wedding day, I may have doubted the exact tally of smiles, but I didn't question for a moment their chilling emotional impact on her childhood and on her later resources as a mother learning to nurture her own children.

At times my interviewees surprised me — and themselves — with the clarity and immediacy of their childhood memories, with the vehemence of the influence of the past on the present. At other times their memories were hidden by the cloudiness of repression or distraction, denial or uncertainty. Believing in the palimpsest quality of the past, I searched with my subjects through the layers of truth beneath the present. Like novelist Margaret Atwood, I "began to think of time as having a shape, something you could see, like a series of liquid transparencies, one laid on top of another. You don't look back along time but down through it, like water. Sometimes this comes to the surface, sometimes that, sometimes nothing. Nothing goes away." Even when time had washed away the particulars, I searched with my subjects for the residue of emotional truth left behind, like the stain left on the porcelain after the bath water has drained away.

My second source of information came from a questionnaire I distributed through an ad in *Parenting* magazine, a letter in my local parenting newspaper, *Parents Press*, and a variety of parenting classes, workshops, and lectures. (The questionnaire is reproduced in the Appendix.) The completed questionnaires comprise sixty of my subjects. Although I advertised for responses by both mothers and fathers, most came from mothers. Even in these changing times, mothers still seem to be the family reporters, guardians both of the hearth and of the truths of the family's emotional life, gatekeepers between the family and the outside world.

The questionnaire was lengthy, specific, and quite emotionally demanding, but my respondents rose to the challenge with an outpouring of memory and insight across generations. The format was open-ended, aimed at unearthing feelings, impressions, and memories from the respondent's family of origin and connecting them with incidents and themes in present family life. My goal was to generate anecdotal rather than statistical data and to widen and deepen my cross-section of views beyond the scope of my interviews.

As with the responses to questionnaires for my previous books, I was impressed with the commitment, care, and depth of feeling shown by the parents who wrote to me, people who would remain strangers to me and anonymous to readers except in the shared intimacy of their stories. (I have indicated pseudonyms either by using a first name alone or by italicizing the full name the first time it appears.) Reading these heartfelt responses from all over the country reminded me of the need all parents have to share our stories. In a society like ours, where geography often separates us from kin, where extended families are shrinking, where each family often feels like a tub on its own bottom, contributing to a book like this one seemed to help close the communication gap. I hope that reading it will have the same effect.

Chapter 5 will explore the four parenting styles revealed by the questionnaires, but a brief sampling of responses to a question about what parents most like or dislike about parenting illustrates the respondents' typical willingness to probe beneath the bustling surface of everyday life. Wrote a forty-two-year-old mother of two young girls:

▶ What I enjoy most about parenting is observing our kids learn, grow, change. Also the sheer physical and emotional closeness I share with my daughters; we hug a lot; they still sit on my lap, hold hands — it feels sweet. I also love reliving my childhood pursuits with them like going to the Ice Capades, ballet, walking and talking, going out for ice cream, to the zoo. I least like having to civilize them! Repeating thousands of times 'Brush your teeth,' 'Wash your face,' 'Use your fork, not fingers!' It seems to take years for manners and civilized behavior to sink in, and Mom gets to do the teaching.

Wrote another mother, forty-six, with two young teenagers:

▶ Best part: witnessing the miraculous unfolding of a personality in all its complexity.
Worst part: being too tired to notice or to respond as I would like to ideally.
My parents enjoyed the spontaneity and originality, but were put off when their children didn't turn out to be exactly like them in tastes, temperaments, way of life.

And this, from a twenty-five-year-old mother of an infant, sums up the feelings of many mothers who responded:

▶ Things learned from becoming a parent:
1. That having a child is a tremendous responsibility, and my outlook has changed because of it. She's my first consideration.
2. That having a child brings out the best and the worst in a person whether s/he likes it or not.
3. That it's dark as hell at 3 AM.
I recognized that the complexity of the subject required respondents

to delve into deeply hidden, often unconscious areas that even the most intimate interview could not always reach. To explore this material, I collaborated on two parents' groups that focused on the key questions of this book. The first was a short-term discussion group in Boston, where I lived for a year during the research phase of this book. I led this group with Marsha Greenstein, a clinical psychologist who specializes in family issues. The second was a long-term parents' therapy group in Berkeley, led by Leah Potts Fisher, a social worker and a founder of the pregnancy and child-birth resource center Birthways, and Helen Neville, a pediatric advice nurse at Oakland's Kaiser Hospital and coauthor of *No-Fault Parenting*. I sat in on this group occasionally, but with the group's permission, all of the sessions were taped. I listened to the tapes carefully after the sessions, taking notes and consulting with the leaders about unfolding issues and themes. The members of these groups comprise fifteen of my subjects.

In the context of these two groups — and with anonymity and confidentiality guaranteed — participants were able to explore still troubling childhood memories as well as questions and problems of day-to-day family life. In an open-ended, free-associative way, parents could pursue their inquiries into past and present with a sense of attention and privacy simply not possible in an interview setting. "I'm so afraid I'm going to be a depressed person for my child the way my mother was for me," lamented one mother. "How can I change?" "I hated being pushed to succeed all the time by my parents," confided another parent, "but now that I have a child, of course I want him to do well. How can I strike a balance?" "I felt securely loved by my full-time mother," remembered a third. "Will my daughter feel as securely loved by me even if I work part-time?"

The questions that concerned these parents were both purely personal and broadly social, both steeped in the past and recon-noitering with the future. Where internal and external, past and future collided, we struggled to invent new answers. Sounding out the resonances of the past, sharing the idioms of the present, we were also listening to the new language our children were sharing with us.

FAMILY
MIRRORS

Ghosts in the Nursery

THE PURGATORY OF LOVING

Tonight
I hold my daughter at her window
while we trace the heat of sunset
colored like her chapped cheeks.
She rubs hers against mine
to cool them
to weave herself into me
to keep me in the room
and put off sleep.

Downstairs, my mother sleeps.
I have grown too large for her arms
too wise to risk words on.
She has diminished some.
I seem to look down
shrink back
wanting to have hatched from an egg.

I am in the purgatory of loving
between my mother and my child.
We move up the rungs
into lesser loving as we grow,
and my daughter
who hangs now
from my elbows
will stand behind me
on the second from the top rung
and want
desperately
to push.

Judith Steinbergh

I yearned for a child long before I had one, yearned through miscarriages and uncertainty and the countless baby showers of friends. I would cross the street to avoid a pregnant woman or two mothers pushing their baby strollers, chatting together, lost in the world of diapers and two A.M. feedings I so ached to join. I would rush past the racks of baby clothes in department stores, fingering the soft cottons as I ran, so powerful was the attraction, so stern the defense. And while I tried and lost and counted out the months and tried again, I had longer than many to think about what exactly I yearned for. For it was both a baby and so much more than a baby — a new stage, a new identity, a new lifetime.

I dreamed of my baby's birth and with it my own rebirth.

Above all, my fantasy was a sensual one. I saw a pink and pudgy little person, an endless reservoir of smiles and coos and cuddles. We were embracing in a rocking chair singing long-forgotten lullabies whose words I intuitively remembered. We were lolling on a blanket in the back yard, playing in the dappled sun. We were splashing in a warm bathtub. Were these memories or daydreams? They lingered just before consciousness, just before words. The world I imagined with this baby was a world of touch and sweet smells and preverbal pleasure, a release from the world of words and intellect I labored in as a writer every day.

Just as this imagined baby would reconnect me to my past, so too would she enliven the meaning of the present. She would provide a new identity, a second chance at childhood (and this time I would get it right, of course, no temper or anxieties, just a mellow even keel). He would be a mirror of my own face and my husband's (his slim nose, my red hair, his athletic prowess, my love of words). But deeper than that, this baby would reflect our inner lives, mirroring our strengths and magically erasing our insecurities. The baby would also be a continuous affirmation of married love.

Most valuable of all, the baby would vault us into the future. He would advance us up the generational ladder, moving us finally from the tight cocoon of coupledom against which we had begun to chafe and toward the place where adulthood truly started: parenthood. How we longed for those magnetic alphabet letters on our refrigerator, that net bag of plastic toys hanging over the bathtub, the daily paraphernalia of parenthood.

Like many parents of our generation who postponed having children and then found that babies did not come immediately and easily, we obsessed together about our fantasy child and ogled other people's children like shameless voyeurs. "Baby lust," I have heard it called, and surely our mooning over a curly red-headed toddler waddling down the beach or a contented baby dozing in a backpack was as intense as any adolescent crush and seemed as unattainable.

But if we hungered together for our yet-to-be-born child, I also dreamed my private dreams of *becoming a mother*. The two desires were interwoven, yet different. Having a baby would be the *new* relationship: pure, playful, pleasurable. But in becoming a mother,

I would join forces with all those mothers who had gone before me. In particular, I would reconnect with my own mother, renew our bond. When I became her equal I would alter forever the balance between us. With the gift of a grandchild, I would give her that tantalizing peek at immortality. As mothers we would share a new focus, replenishment for both of us. When my friends compared notes about how their new babies had mellowed their relationships with their mothers, I mourned doubly for what I was missing.

Indeed, after the ecstatic birth of my first son, when my first visitor, a photographer and mother of three, appeared in my hospital room, she brought her lyrical book of photographs of mothers and babies. In it she inscribed, "Welcome to the sisterhood of motherhood." Knowing my history and my hopes, she had correctly linked my themes.

"This is like having a second life," glows my husband as we stand, bedazzled and besotted, staring at our firstborn son in his bassinet, watching his every move, appraising his every mood. Like all new parents, we spend hour after hour staring at our baby's face — at his huge, silky brown eyes (M and M's, we call them, or Italian olives), his button nose and shell-like ears, his downy skin with the three freckles scattered on one cheek like a new constellation. Hour after hour, we lose ourselves in his firmament.

"It takes both of our full attention to feed the baby," confesses a friend, an older mother of an adopted baby she and her husband waited many years for. "One of us to hold his bottle and the other to worship him!"

At times I croon to my son about what I see as I worship him, and without thinking the words come out: "I love my big, big eyes, I love my sweet, sweet skin . . ." And though I think I mean "my *son's* big, big eyes," dropping his name to fit the tune, the unconscious wish remains. Gazing at his face gazing at me, I search for my own face, my new face, my best face reflected as if in a flattering and rejuvenating mirror.

My husband and I search for the idiosyncrasies we've passed on (Bob's olive eyes, my fair skin), the family resemblances that bind generation to generation. Sifting through the boxes and albums of old baby pictures, we trace the continuities of flesh and family —

my father-in-law's forehead, my father's profile, the distinctive shape of my brother-in-law's head. Linked through our son to the past, we see ourselves reflected but also amplified. What psychologists call "engrossment" we also experience as becoming bigger than we were before.

But deeper than these physical reflections is the emotional mirror our baby presents to us. "Who's the fairest parent of them all?" we ask in countless different ways, gazing into the mirror of his face as the moods flicker across it faster than the dancing bears on his mobile. Can we make him smile or, better still, giggle, those wonderful pure and pearly pebbles of baby laughter? Seeing him happy, we sigh deeply in our contentment that we are good parents, lively and responsive. But when the tears come, when the little face buckles in frustration, anger, or fatigue, then what we see in his mirror chills and saddens us. In self-punishing recriminations, we fear that we are hapless parents after all. "Our judge you may become," wrote the German poet Wildgans to his newborn. "You are he already."

Nor can we always tell where our baby's reality ends and our own projections begin. At times our own moods or doubts, wishes or fantasies — or simply mind-numbing fatigue — distort our ability to see our baby as he really is. Our needs or desires for our child billow across his face like a gauzy curtain obscuring the mirror. Infant researcher Robert Emde corroborates this distortion in an experiment where mothers are shown photographs of babies' faces both happy and sad. Despite the objective reality of black-and-white photography, certain mothers see happiness in sad faces, sadness in happy ones, so strong are their internal interferences.

Another example of this distorting phenomenon is the story I'm told in an interview about a new baby brought to a family gathering who begins to cry as he's passed from relative to relative. "Overstimulated," says Grandma. "Frightened," says Grandpa. "Manipulative," says Auntie. "Antisocial," says Uncle. Each relative interprets the baby's crying according to his own inner history. Each hears it distorted by his own projections. And were the relatives to pause and listen to themselves listening to the new baby, they would also learn something new about their own psyches.

*   *   *

All the while we are rediscovering ourselves and the world in our baby's face, he is intensely discovering *himself* and the world in our faces. Such is the life-giving mutuality of infancy that in the hours spent gazing, smiling, cooing, and imitating we are slowly learning to be parents and our baby is ever so subtly and gently learning to become a person. I can remember eagerly, anxiously asking our pediatrician what toys would be best — for our month-old infant, no less. He replied, "The most engaging, exciting toy right now and for many months to come is your face."

As our faces appear over his bassinet at the first sound of crying, our baby learns to trust that his needs will be acknowledged and answered. As we reflect and help integrate his flickering moods, he learns to feel understood and protected. And as we offer up "the world in small doses" — in the magical phrase of British infant psychiatrist D. W. Winnicott — he learns to cope with these small doses and feel secure. And from every look and every touch, he learns that he is loved. As he watches us watching him, our baby also comes to learn the most enduring lesson, the lesson of his own identity.

The "good enough mother" — again in Winnicott's provocative phrase — reflects her baby's feelings out of her deep empathy with her infant and helps him find himself as she sees him. The *not* good enough mother, according to Winnicott, is so preoccupied with her own feelings or agenda that she fails to reflect back her baby's face and feelings. In this case, the baby is left worried and isolated, with a sense of foreboding. The mirroring function of the mother's face both enriches the infant's sense of self and the world and protects him from the potential menace of the unknown.

Never is the play of mirrors between parent and child as intense as in infancy: the parent looks into the baby's face to find herself reborn and redefined; the baby looks into the parent's face to find the contours of self and world. But my premise is that this interplay of mirrors continues through every stage of childhood and through every incarnation of parenthood. For while we are teaching our children about themselves and about the world, they are also educating us. While we provide mirror and reference point for them, they provide the same for us.

From the moment we hold them adoringly in our arms as new-

borns to the first deafening noes of toddlerhood, from the challenges
and escapades of their school years through the maddening struggles
of adolescence and the advances and retreats necessary to letting
them go — at every stage our children reflect our own strengths
and foibles, our doubts and demons, our childhood memories, pleasurable or menacing, resolved or unresolved. What we cherish or
criticize about our children will depend in large part on what we
are comfortable or shaky with about ourselves. And which of our
children's issues, events, and stages are easy or difficult for us will
depend on the inner struggles we are currently contending with
and the peace we've made with our own past.

Different parents need to see different reflections in their children's mirrors, according to their own unfinished business. One
parent needs, above all, a happy baby, an optimistic child to fend
off her own dark shadows of depression. As long as the baby gurgles
and the child giggles, all is well with mother. But when this mother
sees her baby's brow furrow, hears her adolescent storm moodily
to her room, she can't accept the normalcy of these mood shifts.
Instead, she blames herself that her own depression is poisonous
and mourns that her child has not saved her from herself, has not
become that buoyant, optimistic person she wished she could be
herself.

Another parent needs, above all, a responsive baby and a child
who does everything first. This parent's sense of self-worth is so
shaky that he needs his child's accomplishments to patch up his
inner holes. As long as his child is out on the front lines — the
first to walk and talk and write his name — this parent is content.
But should his child's reflection be less flattering — first steps and
words late, early scribbles illegible — this parent tenses. He fears
that his own inadequacies have been passed along and mourns that
his child will not grasp the brass ring he covets for himself.

So the mirrors our children present to us reveal not only the
antics of the present but also the goblins of the past. In our baby's
howls our own, answered or unanswered, echo back to us; in our
teenager's rages our own storms are replayed.

In a poem titled "Mirror," Sylvia Plath writes of the tender and
painful relationship between mothers and daughters. The voice of
the mirror seems to be the voice of the poet as well as the voice of
the daughter:

I am silver and exact. I have no preconceptions.
Whatever I see I swallow immediately.
Just as it is, unmisted by love or dislike.
I am not cruel, only truthful.
. . . .
Now I am a lake. A woman bends over me,
Searching my reaches for what she really is.
Then she turns to those liars, the candles or the moon.
I see her back, and reflect it faithfully.
She rewards me with tears and agitation of hands.
I am important to her. She comes and goes.
each morning it is her face that replaces the darkness.

In me she had drowned a young girl, and in me an old woman
Rises toward her day after day, like a terrible fish.

The eminent psychoanalyst Therese Benedek writes about the
positive and negative mirroring phenomenon between parent and
child in psychoanalytic terms. Here she describes how the child
can provide a flattering reflection of his parents, amplifying their
sense of themselves:

> The imitating child holds up a mirror image to the parent. Thus
> the parent responding to the mirror image may recognize and even
> say to the child: "This is your father; this is me in you." If the
> child's imitating behavior shows the positive aspect of their rela-
> tionship, the parent will like what he sees and consequently feel that
> both child and parent are lovable. Imitation then reinforces the pos-
> itive balance of identities.

But the child may throw back negative images of the parents, exposing a side of themselves more painful to acknowledge:

> It can also happen that the child shocks the parent by exposing the
> representation of hostile experiences in the past and in the present.
> In this even the parent feels the child's rejection and withdraws from
> the child (even if just for a moment), since the unloved self equals
> the unloved child. Imitation, externalizing what has been internal
> from early infancy on, brings the child sometimes closer to the
> parent; at other times it pushes the child away.

Throughout the life cycle, our children show us things about ourselves we may be proud or puzzled to recognize, unwilling or un-
ready to accept. As Stendhal once observed about the ideal novel,
our children provide "a mirror that strolls along a highway. Now
it reflects the blue of the skies, now the mud puddles underfoot."
Reflecting back our own inner lives, our children expand our knowledge of ourselves and give us new opportunities to grow.

Looking into the mirror of my children's lives and listening to
other parents talk about their children, I see one more glassy truth
reflected. Beyond the fleeting images — the conundrums of our
past, the quirks of our present — lies the reality that our children
are unique and separate personalities. Their mirror also shows us
their crucial differences, their capabilities that may not match our
own or may go way beyond us. The measure of these differences,
the gap between our idiosyncrasies and theirs, can be enlightening,
sometimes maddening, often comforting, sometimes healing.

My older son, for example, is braver, more daring, and more
assertive than I am now or ever was as a child. When, rattled with
frustration as he scampers in front of me on the street, I inadvertently accuse him of causing Willy's stroller wheels to jam, Nate
draws himself up with awesome dignity and asserts, "I did not do
that. That was not my fault." My jaw drops in admiration at an
audacity I would never have dared with my own mother. But when
he answers my motherly directives with a "don't order me around,"
I yearn for a little more compliance — while acknowledging (to
myself) that compliance was a childhood mode that frequently made
my life miserable.

Sometimes he unfurls his feistiness on my own parents, his grandparents, and that, too, changes the intergenerational chemistry. At
a big family gathering, my son chats with my mother, while my
father — across the wide restaurant table — strains to catch every
precious word. "What was that?" my father asks, the patriarch
keeping tabs on his progeny. "You don't have to know everything!"
retorts my son, a brassy impudence I would never have risked.
Amid the laughter at naming the game, we all shift in our seats
and grow imperceptibly as well. In this way our children alter as

well as mirror our own struggles, enlarging our options as we dig deep in ourselves to grow to meet them.

Five years have passed since our first child's birth. Our cuddly infant has become a spunky toddler, a chattering preschooler, and now, suddenly, is ready for school — to leave us! — for the world. In those five years the reflections he has offered us have been dazzling and daunting. Walking outside in late April, on the afternoon of his fifth birthday, I experience again, as in the weeks right after his birth, the sweet softness of the world reborn, the rose bushes bursting with color, the jasmine pouring forth scent. I remember the gift of his newness, the gift of seeing myself and the world anew.

But five years later there is another dimension beyond the purity and exhilaration of birth and rebirth. More and more complexities, more and more challenges have been revealed. Looking into the mirror of my son's life, I have found unexpected depths, unexpected ghosts from my past, unexpected quirks of personality — both things I pride myself on and things I would prefer to hide. No meditation, no self-evaluation cuts to the heart of the matter as quickly, or as mercilessly, as the reflections offered by our children's lives. Over and over in my interviews, parents describe lambasting their children for some fault, some flare of temper, some show of idleness, only to realize with a shudder that they are guilty of the same.

So I smile with pleasure when I hear my language echoed in my son's — the "actually"s, the contemplations, the oddball images he apes intuitively (flying across the country to visit grandparents, he sees in the cloud formations dinosaurs, castles, seals, and kangaroos). But then I wince with recognition at his intensity, his stubborn determination, his wanting, wanting, wanting to be first. "It's the fun of playing the game," we always say, "not who wins or loses," but our actions must belie our words, and our son's Geiger counter picks this up. Watching him dissolve in tears when the Oakland A's lose a crucial game in the World Series, my husband and I exchange sheepish glances. Do we secretly feel just as heartbroken but are too adult to show it?

Then again, my heart swells when I hear my son singing to

himself with masterful recall of the lyrics or carrying on elaborate conversations with himself in fantasy play, as I passed hours of my childhood doing (never mind that his terrain is dinosaurs and knights, and mine was dolls and more dolls). And when I hear him speak tenderly to a stuffed bear, or his little brother, I appreciate that my nurturing has been received and carried on.

But then I reel again when the tantrums strike, when he falls apart at the seams (the two of us periodically dissolved in tears during the terrible twos), when my own emotions are rubbed raw by his throbbing insistence on having his own way. And always the issues that provoke me are the ones left hanging from my own past, like yarn dangling off an unfinished baby's blanket, not yet incorporated into the weave.

Among clinicians skilled in healing family breaches, in working with infants and parents to interrupt the generational repetitions of pain, and to educate parents in healthier, more empathetic parenting skills, the work of child psychotherapist Selma Fraiberg has been especially influential. Fraiberg is the author of the popular child-rearing text *The Magic Years* and was the innovator and director of infant mental health and child development projects first at the University of Michigan and later at the University of California in San Francisco. My copy of her seminal essay "Ghosts in the Nursery" has become dog-eared from being passed from friend to friend. Its wisdom provides the groundwork for this chapter and in large part for this book. She explains:

> In every nursery there are ghosts. They are the visitors from the unremembered past of the parents; the uninvited guests at the christening. Under all favorable circumstances the unfriendly and unbidden spirits are banished from the nursery and return to the subterranean dwelling place. The baby makes his own imperative claim upon parental love and, in strict analogy with the fairy tales, the bonds of love protect the child and his parents against the intruders, the malevolent ghosts.

According to Fraiberg there are three different types of ghosts, and the intensity of their mischief varies. One is an occasional ghost who "break[s] through the magic circle in an unguarded moment," causing parent and child to "reenact a moment or a scene from another time with another set of characters," but ultimately causing no lasting damage. When I take my older son to nursery school for the first time, I feel the stomach-sinking wrench of separation, remembering the weeks of tearful clinging to my mother's skirts during my first nursery school year. Seeing that my son is undaunted at the separation, eagerly and confidently scoping out the scene, I mark the "occasional" ghost who has for a moment obscured our path.

Another is a selective ghost who does mischief "according to a historical or topical agenda, specializing in such areas as feeding, sleep, toilet training or discipline, depending upon the vulnerabilities of the parental past." When my older son picks at his dinner and rejects it for the fourth night in a row or my younger son stands upright on his changing table, making diapering difficult if not impossible, I feel an overwhelming — surely overblown — rage boil up. Then, in a calmer moment, I contemplate the "vulnerabilities" of my past around mealtime or diaper changing and note the "selective" ghost who has added freight to what are rather normal developmental rebellions.

The third and most malevolent, suggests Fraiberg, is the ghost so possessive it has been present for two or more generations, burdening the new baby from the moment he enters the world with "the oppressive past of his parents." This ghost condemns the parent "to repeat the tragedy of his own childhood with his own baby in terrible and exacting detail." It is the parents possessed by this ghost who are Fraiberg's clinical population. These are seriously dysfunctional families whose lives have been disrupted by social and internal disorder, by the extra stresses of poverty, drugs, or alcohol. Their stories — and the lessons learned by Fraiberg and her successors to break the debilitating intergenerational cycle — are explored in Chapter 7, on anger.

But my primary focus here is not on extreme cases but on the everyday, on the ways our very ordinary infants bring us back to our own infancy to confront the hidden ghosts still hovering from our beginnings. This is the terrain Freud dubbed "the unremembered and the unforgettable." We move through it when we feed our babies and when we diaper them, when we rock them to sleep and when we sit bolt upright to their two A.M. cries, when we hold them close to us and when we feel the first stirrings of their independence.

The process of reviewing the way we were parented often begins in pregnancy and continues in earnest once the baby arrives and day-to-day demands begin. Consciously or unconsciously the questions simmer, haunting us whether we bring them to therapy or pursue them in conversations with mates or friends, aloud or in the privacy of journals, dreams, or daydreams.

First there are the questions of identity. How will I define myself against the image of my parents? Will I be more or less patient, more or less feisty, more or less controlled or controlling? Which of my parents' choices will I repeat, which hope to avoid or change? And when all the cards are in, will my children's childhood be as happy as mine — or will I be unable to live with myself unless it is happier?

Then there are the questions of social mores. If my mother was a full-time mother, must I be one too, or can I comfortably leave my baby to go to work? If I felt that my father worked too much of the time, how can I spend more time with my children? And if my parents divided their labors traditionally, how will my mate and I share the load, given our own changes and the changing demands of our times?

Nagging questions about our own dependencies and needs surface as we grapple with those of our babies. Did I get enough of what I needed as a child — time and cuddles, limits and freedom — to feed that nourishment to my own children? How will my own needs be met while I am taking care of my child's? And will my mate and I ever have time for each other again?

No matter how keenly anticipated and well prepared for, the constancy of a new baby's presence and the unrelenting nature of his demands come as a surprise to most parents, a shock to many, and a nightmare to more than a few. The complete transformation of a new parent's identity can be a source of exhilaration but also of frustration, disappointment, and, at times, grief. One interpretation of the post-baby blues is that it is a mourning for the old identity before the new one has fully settled in. Support from partner, family, friends, or baby-sitters lightens the emotional load just as surely as isolation intensifies it. And for new parents whose image of their own parents is a troubled one, the transition to parenthood can be especially stressful. Here the thirty-nine-year-old working mother of a ten-month-old speaks of the psychic upheaval of becoming a parent. Her postpartum struggles were intensified by memories of her own mother's periodic bouts of depression:

> ▶ I never dreamed in my wildest imagination or nightmare how much having a baby would completely change my life, my inner world, my physical reality, my career, my values, my worry level, my stress level. I felt for months like I had died and am just now beginning to feel like there is a life that can be managed. But it is still very precariously balanced, and I get depressed very easily (suspiciously like my mother, and she didn't even work).

Suspiciously like my mother — in moments of great stress as well as tenderness we hear the unforgettable echoes of our mothers' voices in our own. As early as the lullabies we croon to our infants, the words we rage at wit's end from exhaustion, we feel our mothers' mothering spirits pass into our voices, our touches, our tears, the ways we cope and the ways we unravel at the seams. Asked in interviews how they are similar to or different from their own mothers as mothers, many women think first of the echo of their mother's voice in their own. Observes a mother of four daughters who was herself one of six:

> ▶ I hear my mother's voice in mine when I talk to babies. I also have her high-pitched angry voice and her iron grip. Like her I balance between being a wife and a mother — but I also work outside the home. I have lots of kids like her — and the ability to do three things at once.

Another mother is helped through a time of potential crisis by acknowledging her mother's echoes in her voice and in her nurturing style. Newly separated from her husband, this mother was left with the full-time care of a ten-month-old son. But her positive identification with a mother who coped with eight children helps her manage the stresses of single parenthood fairly comfortably:

> ▶ I was the third child of eight and the youngest daughter, so I absorbed a lot of my mother's style. My mother is very businesslike; I've never seen her cry. But with small babies, she's very animated, affectionate, speaks in a falsetto. I speak to my baby in that voice, too. I learned from my mother that you can't be too much of a perfectionist. You have to kid your children out of a bad mood. Sometimes I sing crazy songs while my baby is crying madly — I maintain detachment. I learned that from observing my mother in the chaos of eight children — things aren't the crisis for me that they would be for other first-time mothers. I was used to living with much background noise.

Fathers, too, report that words, phrases, and tunes from their parents come unbidden to their lips as they comfort or cajole their infants. "Snoodledorfer" and "geschlopskadoodle" are "nonsense Yiddish" names a young father of two calls his girls, as his mother called him. A father of daughters now grown recalls in gory detail the macabre nursery rhymes with which his father titillated him and with which he, in turn, teased his young daughters. My own husband and both his brothers comfort their children with the same singsong, wordless version of "Go Tell Aunt Rhodie" that their father sang to them. "Nee, na, na, na, na," I hear my husband croon in the stillness of the night, just as my mother-in-law and my sisters-in-law heard their husband croon to their babies.

At no time is our double identification with our parents and our children as poignant as in this earliest period of parenting. And just as the unforgettable echoes of our parents' voices may either help or hinder us as we care for our babies, so, too, our identification with our infants' cries — and the unrememberable echoes of our own early cries — may aid or impede us as caretakers. If our own infant cries were quickly heeded, if our own needs were predictably met, we may find — without knowing their origin — more resources to comfort our infants' cries and tend to their unrelenting needs with a minimum of conflict. A new mother reported watching her mother cuddle and coo to her newborn son with rapt devotion. She hugged her mother with appreciation, exclaiming, "No wonder I turned out so well if that was the way you talked to me."

But if our own infant cries were not reliably answered, we will certainly be more agitated during the demanding months of infancy. The nonstop hours of soothing and holding, of interpreting and answering baby's cries, of diaper changing and nursing and diaper changing again — all these ministrations can be labors of love joyfully offered or merely labors, repetitive and draining. Early nurturing that was steady, comforting, and competent can be a great source of strength during our children's infancies, just as an early deficit can deplete our confidence and competence with our own babies.

During the course of a long interview, a divorced mother of an eight-year-old girl confronts a ghost from her infancy. As this mother pieces together her mother's regrets and her own memories, she hears some painful reverberations:

▶ My mother once admitted that she had regrets about not being a good enough mother to me. "I was so busy with the house and with the two older kids," she confided sadly, "that I didn't pick you up enough or give you enough attention. And the house was so big, sometimes I didn't even hear you when you cried."

But as this daughter got older, and as her two older sisters became independent, self-involved teenagers, her mother at last turned her attention to her youngest. The attention she had missed as a baby was lavished on her in her middle years. Reflecting on the ebb and flow of maternal attention, the youngest daughter, now the mother of an eight-year-old, describes the impact this way:

▶ Maybe this was why, even though I really wanted a baby, I found infancy hard. All that holding. Sometimes at the end of a holding period, I'd get really uncomfortable. But as my daughter became older, it was a lot easier, and now even though she's almost eight, I can hold her on my lap for long periods of time and not mind it.

For a totally helpless and dependent infant, nothing is more frightening than the wavering of a parent's attention, the falling away of a parent's love, a prolonged separation. The memory of such an early separation may be so painful that the child buries it in order to handle the developmental challenges facing him at the time. But the demands of new parenthood will often jar loose the shaky stones in that early foundation. Our infants' persistent cries revive the memory of our own sobs that were never answered, and a family ghost gets tangled in the nursery curtain.

For a mother now in midlife with two young teenagers, the ghost intruded not in her first child's infancy, for he was a mellow baby, easily consoled and distracted, but in her second child's. This baby's inconsolable crying evoked her own long-muffled and neglected cries, and the force of her buried rage surprised her:

> ▶ When my second child, a daughter, was four or five months old, and the crying I hoped would stop at three months didn't, I had a nightmare that there was a killer leopard in our house. I knew I was the killer leopard when I woke in the morning. I had had fantasies of putting a pillow over her face so I'd never have to hear her cry again. For the first six months, she cried unless she was asleep, eating, or in motion. I carried her *all* the time, but she screamed during every diaper change, when I sat on the toilet or paused to load the laundry, plus whenever I took her off my back to change my clothes or drive in the car. As soon as she turned six months old and could crawl, she stopped crying. I felt in danger of hurting her and went into therapy because I found the feeling so frightening.

The history she remembered, the ghost she uncovered, was this: when she was nine months old, her mother was hospitalized for a year with tuberculosis. Even when her mother returned, in that pre-antibiotic era she was concerned and anxious about contagion. The daughter puzzled:

▶ It took me years in therapy to figure out a big mystery in my life. Something felt out of sync. Since my mother got better and returned, why did I feel so bereft? Finally I got in touch with the fact that my "first" mother never did return. She was a hugger of babies, and the "second" mother who returned a year later from the hospital was afraid to be close for fear of infection.

As an infant she had suffered two traumatic losses: first the year-long separation from her mother and then the bitterly disappointing reunion with a mother who no longer held and cuddled her. More sobering yet were the memories — the most agonizing, deeply buried, and hardest to reach — of the shocking fact that her cries had not only gone unanswered but that she had actually been abused by her substitute caretakers:

▶ Only in recent therapy have I gotten in touch with the memories of being hit by caretakers trying to get me to stop crying when my mother was in the hospital.

For this woman, the shattering memories of early separation, loss, and abuse remained hidden until her infant daughter's demands forced her to confront them. Her despair that she couldn't console her baby reawakened her despair that she hadn't been consoled as a baby herself. And her fear of her own potential rage — the killer leopard loose in her house — revived her fear of the abusive rage unleashed by her caretakers as well as a potentially frightening identification with those caretakers. Years of therapy helped loosen that destructive negative identification. Therapy also helped her forgive herself for her imperfections and learn to nurture herself while she nurtured her growing children:

▶ The most important things I have learned from parenting have been about myself — that with parenting, the subconscious videotapes of one's childhood replay, and one has the opportunity to re-parent one's self with the help of others. In the process one becomes a more whole person, that is, in contact with much more of one's subconscious and therefore less likely to dump old family junk on the next generation.

Other meddling spirits may hover over the bassinet as well. For "a baby is such a perfect piece of projection," as Jeree Pawl of San Francisco General Hospital's Infant-Parent Program succinctly puts it. Even the tiniest baby has many characteristics on which parents can project memories from the past, images from the present, or wishes for the future. Is the baby's sex the same as the parent's or different, is it the desired choice or the opposite? Is his place in the birth order the same as one parent's but not the other's? Is she an only child where the parent was one of several? Does he look too much or not enough like ourself or our mate, Aunt Mathilda or Uncle Jerome? Is his temperament mellow or volatile? Is she easy or difficult to console? All these variables interlock with our own personality to determine how we bond with our babies from the first moments on.

Until fairly recently, child development theorists described the infant's personality as a clean slate ready to be inscribed by the environment — by the parents' style and involvement, their expectations and projections, the tone and tempo of the household and the extended family. But more recently, early childhood experts have redefined early development as a far more interactive process. Yes, the environment exerts a strong influence over the infant. But equally important, experts now believe, each infant greets the world with a complex personality. In the words of T. Berry Brazelton, renowned pediatrician and one of this country's most influential popularizers of current clinical thinking:

> How much does an environment shape a child? A great deal, but less than we used to think. In the 1950s there was still a pervading belief that the outcome of a child's personality development was entirely the responsibility of his parents. We know now that it is not that simple. . . . My own conviction is that each child is born with particular strengths and marked individuality. These individual differences influence the parents and all people around the child as much as they, in turn, will affect him or her. No parent ever feels the same about two children, for each child calls up a different set of responses.

Stella Chess and Alexander Thomas, two innovative clinician-investigators, have also advanced contemporary understanding of the complicated interweaving of environment and personality. Their provocative longitudinal research on infant temperament examines what they call "goodness of fit" between the child and his caretakers. According to Chess and Thomas, infant temperaments can be divided generally into three categories: "easy," "difficult," and "slow to warm up." For each category, the researchers consider such characteristics as activity level, predictability, adaptability, responsiveness, mood, and intensity. The easy child, for instance, will show a moderate activity level, be predictable in routines, adapt comfortably to new situations, respond quickly and warmly to caretakers, and so on. The difficult child will show a high, even hyper, activity level, be unpredictable in routines, adapt awkwardly to new situations, and respond warily or negatively to caretakers. Brought by parents to a large family gathering, for example, the easy child will be all smiles, the difficult child will throw a frenzy of protest, and the slow-to-warm-up baby will cautiously appraise the situation before being able to relax and enjoy.

But the most striking of Chess and Thomas's theories, and the most relevant to the discussion here, is their "goodness of fit" model. This conceptual framework describes the fit between the infant's personality and the parents' expectations, between infant reality and parent fantasy. The model suggests that healthy functioning and development occur when the infant's personality fits well or is compatible with the expectations of the environment, and that emotional growth is impaired when the infant is incompatible with the environment. The "goodness of fit" model shows that harmony or dissonance in child raising has everything to do with how each *particular* child interacts with each *particular* parent. An intense and very active child might be a rough match for a mild and rather passive parent but delightful company for a high-energy parent. A slow-to-warm-up child might be frustrating for the high-energy parent but an easy companion for the mild parent.

But there is always reciprocity and influence between parent and child, and that affects their fit as well. Their relationship is not a stable equation, but rather each side influences the other and both evolve together over time. A slow-to-warm-up baby whose cues are very subtle may at first perplex a parent who worries about not being "sensitive" enough. But over time the infant's signals will become stronger and more meaningful, and the parent will become more confident about interpreting them. Gradually the parent's increasing confidence may also encourage the child to respond more readily.

For my purposes, the "goodness of fit" model thickens the plot some more, since "goodness of fit," like all the other variables I am exploring, is influenced by the footprints of the past. In mutuality of fit there can be both vulnerability and opportunity. The vulnerability is that cues from either side may be missed or may end up at cross-purposes. But the opportunity is that parent and child can evolve a better and better fit over time. They can become more attuned to each other's needs from the lessons of life experience or from the outside guidance of pediatricians or therapists.

Gloria Feiner is a teacher and a mother in her early fifties whose three children are now in their twenties. But as for many mothers, her children's infancies were times of such conflict and growth that she still recalls them vividly. An inquisitive, outspoken, and psychologically minded person, she has used the perspective of the intervening years to understand what her infants brought to her — gender and temperament, demands and intensity — and what she brought to them — history and personality, her own demands and intensity. How she and each of her three children fit together psychologically was a complex and changing equation involving history, temperament, and circumstances. Their story illustrates many of the themes this chapter has introduced.

The daughter of immigrants, Gloria was the older of two sisters by three years. She married a childhood sweetheart and made a world with him defined by academics, intellectual pursuits, and self-scrutiny, but softened by dedication to each other and a shared sense of humor. Although she says she had "dreams and feelings about having a baby from the time I was tiny," at twenty-one she was not prepared for the emotional earthquake caused by having two sons only fourteen months apart. The inner rumblings started slowly because her first baby was a classically "easy" one, and mother and infant made a good fit:

▶ My first son, Adam, was passive, no, easy. I felt nurtured nurturing him. I felt very good about myself during those early months. Then, when he was five months, I had an ovary removed and got pregnant soon after. I was amazed at how out of control I was, and for a time Adam seemed to withdraw from me.

Her second son, Eric, had a different and more "difficult" temperament from the moment of birth, and this time the fit between mother and child was a rougher one:

▶ Eric was born shrieking and colicky. We discovered he had a tear in his anal region that was causing him terrible pain. I felt injured in being able to mother.

Their emotional symbiosis was such that the baby's injury made the mother feel "injured" in her mothering. Having an "easy" baby made Gloria feel like a wonderful mother; having a "difficult" one made her doubt her calling. But having two babies with such different temperaments born so close together also drew on different sides of herself and stretched her abilities:

▶ I had to pull different things out of myself. Adam needed more stimulation and playing, whereas Eric was already so stimulated internally. Good mothering has to do with responding to what each baby brings. It's a chemical thing.

Another part of the chemistry had as much to do with gender and birth order as with temperament. As the older daughter in an all-girl household, Gloria had had little experience with the high jinks of two energetic boys:

▶ It was a hard time. The physicality and competition between the two boys was an amazement to me. I didn't handle it well. I was so overwhelmed. They were a terror, but I was more of a disciplinarian than I needed to be.

After thirteen years of mothering and a part-time teaching career, Gloria still wanted to have one more baby. This time luck brought her the girl she had hoped for. Her increased experience and confidence combined with this baby's gender, birth order, and temperament to make the relationship an entirely different one. Gloria's attitude and approach as a mother had also matured with the years:

> ▶ Emily was almost nine pounds and very content. Eric had been so demanding that I tried to ward him off and not give him everything he wanted. But I decided later that that philosophy was wrong. I decided to give to Emily until the giving played itself out. If she cried, I picked her up; if she wanted food, I fed her. I never saw her as tyrannical. Now, at sixteen, she's seen as a kid with a sense of self who gets what she wants and is very centered. That could be seen as selfish, but I think it's healthy. The boys now seem more neurotic. They need to please where it's not always appropriate, especially Eric, who has turned out to be the kookiest of the three.

The echo of family resemblances across generations also played a part in Gloria's relationships with her children, both as infants and later on:

> ▶ When Adam was born, I thought he looked like my father, which was unfortunate for Adam because I have a complicated relationship with my father. But my strong love for infants helped. I see Eric and Emily as more like my husband, and that distanced and protected them a little from me. Since I see myself as like my father, I also see Adam as more like me. My father has a stubborn streak which I see in Adam and in myself, also being fearful and phobic. I know I was always more critical of Adam because I'm critical of myself. As a result, Adam is very guarded and protective from me and maybe from all women. Of course, when you see a child, you often see him with your faults, not your strengths.

Hindsight reveals how the differences in Gloria's relationships with her children resulted from the combination of their temperaments and her history, of their looks and her associations, of their needs and demands and her capabilities and responses over time.

For all parents find the different phases of their children's development more or less of a struggle, more or less of a joy, depending on their own strengths and resources. A woman who had organized my community's first newborn home-care service because she was so skilled and confident with infants complained bitterly about her relationship with her teenage daughter because she felt so stymied. Another mother rejoiced in her intimacy with *her* teenage daughter but confessed that her daughter's infancy was the hardest time of her life.

For every parent who finds infancy a bit of a psychic death ("I felt for months like I had died," mourned the mother of a ten-month-old son), there is another who finds it a time of rebirth, joy, and discovery. "I now stop and literally smell the flowers," beamed the mother of a two-year-old. "I feel a sense of rediscovery. Everything is new to a baby. There's a lot of joy in what we usually take for granted." For many parents the feeling is a delicate ambivalence that comes from having both of these responses at once. "This is the best time of my life," I remember a friend saying at our mothers' and babies' group as she jounced her six-month-old on her knee. "Why is each day so difficult?" Bouncing our own babies around the circle, we nodded as one in recognition. She spoke for all of us.

Margaret Mahler, whose landmark research surveyed mother-infant symbiosis and separation, comments on two contrasting maternal reactions to infancy:

> For some, confrontation with the infant's helplessness and total dependence . . . coupled with his often unclear signals, proves to be a frightening experience, attended by anxiety lest the fragile infant somehow be damaged. For other[s], the very lack of clearcut cues from the infant provides the opportunity to live out a fantasy of symbiotic union with him.

From infancy onward, our responses to our children's changing demands and expectations are colored by our own inner struggles and ghosts. One parent relishes the "yes" of infancy but fears the "no" of toddlerhood; another thrills to the "why?" of the middle years but shudders at the "why not?" of adolescence.

I have chosen to begin this book with a careful exploration of infancy because our children's personalities take root then, and so do our personalities as parents — ready to unfold, influence each other and evolve in mutuality over time. And the characteristics that I have discussed here — family resemblances, birth order, temperament, and fit — will continue to engage us throughout our children's childhoods.

Beginning with infancy, we also reconcile the loss of the fantasy of ourselves as perfect parents and the loss of the fantasy of having perfect children. Most of us come to parenthood with images and expectations from childhood, when we vowed to be more perfectly loving and responsive than our own parents ever were. And we also dream of having children who, naturally, will be more loving and responsive than we ever were.

Throughout the early months of my first child's life, and continuing intermittently even now, I carried on lengthy internal dialogues with a kind of fantasy "good mother." This intrapsychic creation was partly the mother I had, partly the one I dreamed of, and partly the one I thought I was striving to be. Where I unraveled at four in the afternoon, this mother maintained unflagging energy and good spirits. Where I lost my patience when my baby refused to nap even though hopelessly overtired, this mother was always patient and understanding.

She was also an exacting perfectionist and unfailingly demanding — of me. For many months I bargained with her to allow my imperfections, my self-avowed maternal failings (if she allowed me to procure two hours of afternoon baby-sitting, I would promise to cheerfully recite nursery rhymes all morning long). But gradually I began to reconcile my fantasies of perfection with the realities of spilled milk, lost sleep, short fuses, and children who willy-nilly pursue their own dreams despite our dreams for them. And a budding confidence in my own mothering skills, however imperfect or inconsistent, began to supersede the harsh edicts of my internal commands. As Bruno Bettelheim explains in *A Good Enough Parent*:

> I feel that a parent's most important task is to get a feeling for what things mean to his child. . . . The best way to get this feeling is to remember what a parallel issue meant to us when we were children, and why, and how we would have liked our parents to handle it,

us, and themselves. Thus we can put to creative use our own life events, which acquire new and deeper meaning as we recall them and work them through in the light of our own parenthood.

Here lies the potentially healing power of the "second life" our children offer us, the hidden message of the ghosts in the nursery. Here is our chance to reexperience and maybe this time master our own childhood aches and uncertainties as we help our children handle and master their own.

From the desperate howls of our infants to our toddlers' fears of the monster under the bed, from our teenagers' moody withdrawals to our grown children's push and pull toward independence — if we can dig deep enough to remember these emotionally charged events in our own lives and recall how we wished our parents had responded to us, the memories can help us figure out what will work for our children now. And even if memory is hazy and problem solving slow, simply the process of searching and the effort of empathy will bind us closer to our children. Adds Bettelheim:

> Whether or not parent and child really manage to discover the deepest sources of their interlocking anxieties, the fact that the parent delves into his past to understand his child and the child feels that his parent is doing this to help him brings the child and parent much more closely together as they wrestle with the situation. This is why I say that the child and the parent are the problem, but also the solution.

As I worked on this book and mothered my boys, I began to observe both a selfless and a self-focused quality to parental empathy. True empathy requires us to suffer and rejoice along with our children both to understand their experiences and to help give them meaning. But the most generous form of parental empathy is being willing to put ourselves in our children's shoes while continuing to stride securely forward in our own. Explains Sara Ruddick in her illuminating book *Maternal Thinking*, "The idea of empathy as it is popularly understood underestimates the importance of knowing another without finding yourself in her. A mother really looks at her child, tries to see him accurately rather than herself in him."

The self-focused part of parenting is the knowledge that doing the best we can as parents is something we are doing both for our children *and* for ourselves. As we become more attuned as parents, we deepen and enrich our own lives.

Empathy for our children's growing pains can ease both their pains and our own. Empathy helps our children thrive while we mature as parents. "Nurturing, I felt nurtured," said Gloria Feiner. I experience this connection every night as I round out the bedtime rituals with my sons. As I flip on the night light to ward off ghosts and pull the alphabet quilt up to my older son's chin, I, too, feel as safe and cozy and loved as he is. As I settle our baby in his crib, close the calico curtains, and open the window to let in the breeze, I, too, feel as settled and secure and loved as he is. For the moment all the old ghosts have been put to rest, and only the most innocent dreams float through the nursery with the boys' breathing.

Becoming a Family:
The Language of Family Systems

THAT MOMENT

It is almost too long ago to remember —
when I was a woman without children,
a person, really, like a figure standing in
   a field,
alone, dark against the pale crop.
The children were there, they were
   shadowy figures
outside the fence, indistinct as
distant blobs of faces at twilight.
I can't remember, anymore,
the moment I turned to take them,
my heel turning on the earth, grinding
   the heads of the
stalks of grain under my foot, my
body suddenly swinging around as the
flat figure on a weathervane will
swerve when the wind changes.

· · · · · · · · · · · · ·

      . . . I cannot remember that
instant when I gave my life to them
the way someone will suddenly give her
   life over to God
and I stood with them outside the
   universe
and then like a god I turned and
   brought them in.

Sharon Olds

If having our first son vaulted us into parenthood, having our second son three years later widened our field and deepened our roots by making us a family. Before Nate's birth, we were two grown-ups, intimate but still savoring a taste of independence. After his birth, we became hopelessly besotted with our child. We were two lovers standing at the shoreline watching the sunset, watching the bands of neon orange, fuchsia pink, smoky violet, silvery gray, inky blue. With our firstborn, we felt as if we were doing absolutely nothing but watching, not missing a nuance.

The two of us and Nate for those first three years came to think of ourselves as a close-knit unit of three. But expanding to embrace

Willy, our fourth, we unquestionably defined ourselves as a family, linked to the size and shape of our own childhood families.

But gone were the hours of uninterrupted gazing at the sunset from the shoreline. Getting to know Willy, drawing him into our orbit, was more like the dizzying experience of a circular, multi-screened movie. We stood in the center, and all around us roared 360 degrees of nonstop and simultaneous action and entertainment: airplanes careening over the Rockies, vast fields of waving grain, cars zooming across the Golden Gate Bridge.

The impact of all this activity was exhilarating, breathtaking, and, more often than not, exhausting. Our horizons were undeniably broadened, but, alas, we missed a lot, too. The sheepish confession of a friend with two sons summed up our predicament as well. "When our first son started teething," she confided, "I watched his gums for weeks at a time and charted the little buds reddening and the tiny teeth poking through with the concentration of a gemologist. When our second son was about nine months, I glanced in his mouth one day and, shocked, saw, my God, it was filled with teeth! I had simply been too busy to notice." Or as another friend confessed weeks after the birth of his second child, "With our first child, we were constantly worrying, Is he happy, is he learning, is he stimulated? Now the only question we have time to ask is, Is he bleeding?!"

Feeling guilty, of course, at times that we were slighting our younger — or our older — in the mad rush of increasingly complex family logistics, we could also see that our benign oversights could be a blessing in disguise. Out of the glaring spotlight, the fishbowl of parental intensity to which we subjected our firstborn, our secondborn has discovered an adaptability that will come in handy for life. And our firstborn, too, has found that sharing the stage has eased the pressures of single-minded parental scrutiny.

So we have gotten to know Willy not in the crisp-curtained atmosphere of the nursery but in the heaping stewpot of family life. No longer a doting couple with a single offspring, a discrete pair of parents with one portable babe, we are now an infinitely more complex unit of four. We are a family system with our own subsystems, satellites, and extended networks. With three family members, we were one cozy triangle and three manageable dyads;

with the addition of our fourth member, we jumped to four possible triangles and six dizzying dyads. (I find it altogether too head-spinning to contemplate the ten dyads and ten triangles that adding a third would bring.)

The increasing complexity of family relationships changed the atmosphere of family life the second time around. Where once we crooned love songs unabashedly to our older, now we crooned to our younger *sotto voce*, stealing glances over our shoulders to make sure we were not making his brother feel left out or jealous. Where once we hopped at infant Nate's first peep of protestation, now, when our newborn cried out, we paused several moments to appraise all of the elements in the bigger picture: which of us had a free hand, which of us was occupied with Nate, which of us had a last shred of energy to meet our new family's nonstop needs.

As the number and complexity of our relationships increased, so did our interdependence. In every area of family life, we began to see how each seemingly independent action affected us all. The ebb and flow of mealtimes and bath times, of attention inside the house and activities outside, was constantly influenced by the interconnected needs and demands of four individuals.

And the process of influence was not just linear but circular, loops of influence drawing all of us into the web. Even after we went to sleep, the clock of our connections refused to stop ticking. If Willy woke in the middle of the night and I was the one who got up to take care of him, I would have less energy for Nate the next day. And chances were that I would carry some resentment toward Bob for his full night of sleep, thus fraying our bond the next day. But Bob, fully rested, would have that extra charge of energy required to keep up with Nate. And Nate, rested and well cared for, would be more likely to be cooperative with his baby brother, even if I was considerably more ragged. If Bob handled Willy's nighttime waking, then the reverberations would play themselves out in a different but no less circular manner. And if Willy — miracle of miracles — slept through the night and Nate chose to wake up, then the yawns from interrupted sleep would occur in yet another circular pattern.

Virginia Satir, one of the founding mothers of family therapy, created an exercise to show family members how interconnected they are. She would ask the family to stand together holding hands. Then she would have one family member move or do something while still holding hands with the others. As the entire family was twisted into all sorts of new configurations and contortions, they were able to understand both physically and emotionally how inextricably linked they are. This pivotal insight of family systems theory — that a disturbance in one part of the system disturbs the entire system — began to be more lucid and more relevant to me as my own new family was organizing itself.

If, for example, in a family with a two- and a four-year-old, the mother gets the disturbing news that her mother is seriously ill with cancer, the repercussions will affect each member of the family according to his or her role and needs and developmental stage. The mother, distressed about her mother's illness and possible death, will be sad and distracted, less available both emotionally and physically. The father will be dismayed both at his wife's distress and at the complicated juggling of responsibilities he must now undertake. The two-year-old, who has just taken the first steps away from mother, may start to cling again. And the four-year-old, rather independent and full of bravura, may want to push against Mom in despair and anger but, feeling her too frazzled, may start wetting his pants. So the entire family feels the tremors.

A corollary insight from the family systems perspective is that a symptom showing up in one member usually suggests disharmony or dysfunction in the entire family. Typically children develop symptoms or act out when there is conflict between their parents. A child may develop sleep problems when she realizes that her parents fight after she goes to sleep. She forces herself to stay awake to keep the parents from fighting. Or a child who suddenly develops a phobia about going to school may be trying to protect a very depressed mother from having the house to herself — and having the opportunity to end her life.

Furthermore, family therapists believe that if, through time, awareness, or family therapy, the disturbance is resolved or the symptom relieved in one place or one individual, the whole system feels the change.

Family therapy had its origins in the mid-1950s when a number of clinicians working independently in different parts of the country began to treat individual problems by observing the family all together rather than by seeing its members separately. This live observation was made possible by the one-way mirror, a breakthrough one early observer called "analogous to the discovery of the telescope." When these clinicians began to compare notes, they found evolving an emphasis on family context and interconnectedness in what had long been considered only personal and intrapsychic problems.

Lynn Hoffman, who has been involved with the family therapy movement both as clinician and chronicler since the early sixties, has characterized it as a new system of communication. And that seems the appropriate metaphor for my own investigation, which began with my family's communication, with the letters and words passed from my mother to me and from me to my sons.

The theory that appealed to me as my new family began to take shape reached far beyond its origins in the hands of clinicians like Murray Bowen and theorists like Gregory Bateson. Although family therapy's vocabulary, guidelines, and techniques originated in a clinical setting, primarily as a tool for treating schizophrenia, they are useful and applicable in day-to-day family life. My intention in this chapter is to sound out the language of family systems and show its potential for raising healthy families.

One compelling idea that came home to me in the push and pull created by Willy's arrival was the family's strong tendency to cling to the status quo despite pressures from the winds of change. Unhealthy families, I learned, tend to cling to a "rigid homeostasis" — in the phrase of another family therapy pioneer, Don Jackson — holding tight to an inflexible but familiar structure. Healthy families are better able to balance stability with change and to see change as an opportunity for growth, not as a signal to fall back into old patterns.

When my husband and I wished desperately to drop everything and dash off to the movies the way we used to before we had kids, I could feel our rigid desire for the structure of the past, however outmoded and irrelevant now. When, instead, we dashed off to the video store, made a bowl of popcorn, and watched a video with our kids cuddling around us or sleeping peacefully upstairs, I could tell we were gradually learning to adapt.

Family therapists are keenly interested in what happens to families as they move through transitions and struggle to cope with change. Viewing the family as a unit, many theorists describe a predictable series of life turning points: marriage, the birth of children, child rearing, launching teenagers into the world, retirement, the arrival of grandchildren, deaths of older family members. Stress is always highest around the transition from one life phase to the next, as the family struggles to reorganize its patterns.

Families whose boundaries are most flexible and whose communication is most open adapt most successfully to these transitions. Families with more rigid patterns, boundaries that are either too rigid or too loose, and less open communication are more likely to get stuck in a phase and be unable to move on — or to develop conflicts as they try unsuccessfully to move forward.

Stress, or what theorists call "the flow of anxiety," occurs both vertically and horizontally. Vertical stresses are the ones passed down through the generations — all the family history, its attitudes and messages, expectations and taboos. Horizontal stresses are the ones the family encounters as it moves forward in time, coping with inevitable bumps and bruises, losses and gains. For example, if a young mother has a painful childhood history of unresolved issues with her parents, that is vertical anxiety. When she encounters the inevitable crises of early parenthood — horizontal anxiety — the family may have a particularly stressful time.

Family therapists working with a troubled family often keep track of these two axes of stress — the vertical or transgenerational and the horizontal or unfolding family context — by using a shorthand map called a genogram. The genogram is a symbolic representation of a family tree that charts the story of many generations. The quality of relationships is diagramed with symbols representing "normal," distant, close, conflicted, or estranged bonds. Symbols with dates represent expected events in the family life cycle — marriages, births, deaths — as well as the unexpected disruptions that often provide clues to current family troubles — miscarriage, childhood death, separation, divorce, remarriage, illness, suicide, untimely death, and so on. Genograms "let the calendar speak" by suggesting possible connections among family events.

In interpreting a genogram, a family therapist typically looks for information about family structure (are there divorces, remarriages, intact families, three-generation households?), life-cycle fit or discrepancy (marriages occurring within the usual period or very early or very late in life?), repeated or alternated patterns across generations (is there a repetition of alcoholism or suicide, or success in one generation followed by failure and then success?), clustering of life events (any grouping of stresses or anniversary reactions at particular times?), balance or imbalance between two sides of a family (is one rich and the other poor, one healthy and one ill?), and relationship patterns and alliances.

In their classic *Genograms in Family Assessment*, Monica McGoldrick and Randy Gerson show the usefulness of the genogram in illuminating family life through the generations:

> The genogram helps both the clinician and the family to see the "larger picture," both currently and historically. . . . Numerous symptomatic patterns, such as alcoholism, incest, physical symptoms, violence, and suicide, tend to be repeated in families from generation to generation. By noticing the pattern repetition, the clinician may be helped to understand the family's present adaptation to the situation and may suggest interventions to short-circuit the process.

Outside the clinical setting as well the genogram can provide a meaningful tool for family awareness. First and most basically, the process of working on a genogram can produce insights about the transgenerational context of a current family issue or the stress around a particular turning point. Sometimes seeing oneself, one's current family, and one's problems along a continuum of generations can provide understanding. Whether the issue is drinking, an attempted teenage suicide, or a floundering marriage, noting its recurrence and exploring how it was handled in the past can often generate momentum or even a strategy for change.

Then, too, observing when one is not in step with a repetitive family pattern — divorced when the other family marriages are intact, having children late when other children came early — can alert one to prepare for an additional charge of stress around these life-cycle watersheds.

Finally, the multigenerational outline of a genogram provides a comforting perspective on life's seasonal curve balls and a deeper sense of compassion for one's current family and one's predecessors. Observe Murray Bowen and Michael Kerr, "If a person can look at a four- or five-generation diagram of his own family and really see it as a living organism, a multigenerational emotional unit that changes gradually over time . . . he is beyond blaming self or others."

Viewing my new family as a system struggling to reorganize itself after a major change, becoming aware of the vertical as well as the horizontal stresses on us, and using the genogram to see my new family as one small, if vivid and important, square in the quilt of many generations — all of these insights from the language of family systems helped me place my family in a wider and deeper context. When patience frayed, tempers flared, and sibling squabbles sputtered, I found it comforting to have a frame of reference beyond the practical day-to-day wisdom of Dr. Spock.

So when I tumbled into bed each night, ravenous for my sure-to-be-interrupted sleep, I nevertheless had a feeling of well-being. It was the feeling that comes from having cleared a set of obstacles that once seemed insurmountable and reached a life goal. After the years of bone-chilling fear that I would never have children, and the months when I wagered with destiny that if I could have one child, I would never ask for another gift, I now miraculously had two healthy, beautiful children. My dream of family was complete, balanced, symmetrical: two parents, two children, one on each hand when I was on the town with them alone.

My inner blueprint for a family comes from the four-member family I grew up in. Fewer than two kids would seem lonely; more, unwieldy. Each of us creates our dream of a new family out of our response to our old one. If its small size felt cozy, we hope to repeat it; if it felt constricted, we hope to enlarge it. With a different history, another couple might feel securely entrenched with a single child; still another couple might need at least three children to feel truly like a family.

Suzanne Steinem Patch grew up lonely in a family of two and dreamed only of marrying and having a big, rollicking family, she once confided to me in an interview. She and her lawyer husband had six — happier, if not cheaper, by the half dozen. From the same family of two, her celebrated younger sister Gloria Steinem neither married nor had children. Her dream of family played itself out in the wider circles of a sisterhood beyond the nuclear family.

If as children we were lost in a sea of siblings, we may swear to have only a few children and to lavish each with unfailing attention. If we relished the high-spirited camaraderie of a large clan, we dream of bringing up a similar brood ourselves, zero population be damned. One friend who grew up in a family of six children used to applaud every young family she knew who chose to have only one child "because that leaves more for me to have." Though she has four daughters now and has turned the corner on forty, she still tweaks her husband now and again about that fifth — or sixth — without which her inner image of family is not quite complete. And she holds fast to her dream even while remembering the times when siblings were unwittingly left behind in gas stations on family car trips because her parents had simply lost track of them.

If the size of my new family dovetailed with both my history and my dreams, its composition was a departure and a challenge. Raised as one of two sisters with a bevy of girl cousins, educated at a girls' school and a girls' camp, I grew up in a world of women rarely punctuated by boys and men. During those endless childhood hours playing house, playing dolls, playing teenage sisters, I simply assumed that when I became a mother, I would have two little girls just as my mother had. They would come complete with smocked Liberty dresses, porcelain-faced Ginny dolls, and dog-eared copies of *Little Women*. If anything, writing my first book about the delicate rivalry and solidarity between sisters consolidated and enlarged upon the expertise that was my birthright and that would — I was sure — be the cornerstone of my future family life.

But fate works in mysterious ways, and both of my imagined girls turned out to be boys. The Liberty dresses have been replaced by Oshkosh overalls, the Ginny dolls by dinosaurs and Superheroes, the dog-eared copies of *Little Women* by *Stuart Little*. With the years, and with the guidance of my husband, who has two brothers, I am gradually learning a whole new language, new patterns, another tempo. Although my mother is as captivated by our boys as we are, she will sometimes remark wistfully, "I remember how you and your sister used to sit on the floor, playing quietly with puzzles by the hour." This memory is invariably prompted by the sight of my two sons zooming back and forth across the living room with the speed of pinballs, crashing their riding toys into each other, clattering their Legos, hurling tennis balls despite our umpteenth injunction not to throw balls in the house.

Still, while a moment of regret may flicker for that docile daughter I seem to have been and will probably never have, most of the time I appreciate the poetic justice of the family fate has offered me. For if the family we create helps complete the business left unfinished from the family we are born to, then surely my new family has helped me edit the limitations of my past. Raising two sons has opened me up to a side of life my own childhood closed off. Where I used to believe with Manhattan humorist Fran Leibowitz that the outdoors is what you must pass through between your apartment building and your taxicab, now I am out there with my boys rain or shine, hiking, biking, running around on the playground, on the ball field, in the back yard playing catch. And for every kite unfurled, every ball tossed back and forth till dusk ends a summer evening, I feel a knot from my past loosening and freeing up. "You're a better pitcher than I thought you'd be," my five-year-old tosses over his shoulder after a session of catch one day, and my heart swells with pride no National Book Award or Good Housekeeping Seal of Approval could ever match.

Raising sons rather than daughters has broken the mold of my past in other ways as well. Coming from a tight-knit matriarchy where overinvolvement is part of the territory, I can see now how my two sons may help me separate in a healthier way than would have been possible with daughters. The organic boundary of their opposite sex may spare us all what might have been, with daughters, a painful and difficult symbiosis. Then, too, my sons have helped me find a better separation from my own mother. They have given me the liberty and leeway to make my own way as the mother of sons. Hearing about their diaper rashes, their sibling spats, their night-owl tendencies, my mother shakes her head. "I just don't know how to advise you," she apologizes. "You both were little so long ago — and anyway, you were girls. I just don't know about boys." And though I may fake a little flattering disappointment, secretly I am relieved to be making my own way, with my own solutions and mistakes.

Still, if the differences in gender provide a buffer between my past and my present, the number of children provides a constant reminder of the past. Raised as one of two and now raising two, I see how the birth order and sibling dynamics of my new family take me back to my childhood. For our relationships with our children call up not only our deep connections with our parents but also those equally deep and complex ties to our siblings. Looking at our children, we are constantly reminded of our siblings' looks, tastes, temperaments, the way they hooked us into their games, the way they left us out. And once we become parents, the way we look at our siblings is forever altered by what our children teach us about family dynamics and about ourselves.

As the elder of two, I see and feel most clearly the perspective of my firstborn in relation to his younger brother. On the day I am leaving for the hospital to have our second baby, Nate goes out for a short walk with our baby-sitter. But they return after just a few minutes, their outing derailed by having seen an unsavory character on the street. Rather uncharacteristically, Nate has dissolved in tears. "We saw a scary stranger," he sobs, and throws himself into my arms, weeping and shuddering. He demands to be comforted with such vehemence that I know immediately who the "scary stranger" is he is shaking over — and it is not the one on the street. Thirty-odd years later, I, too, remember the grief over the "scary stranger," the fear of displacement, the anxiety over the unknown interloper. I, too, mourned losing the cozy comfort of the original triangle of mother, father, and me. And though I will try nobly, just as my mother did, to assuage this grief with promises of special time together for Nate and me and enticing gifts "from the baby," I know that these are temporary Band-Aids for a wound that will heal only in its own time.

But I also know with the perspective of the intervening years that the "scary stranger," the interloper and rival who was my sister, turned out to be my dearest friend and supporter. And as I hold three-year-old Nate in my arms and rock him, I hope that in the aftermath of his loss, he, too, will discover the gift of brotherhood.

Still, I am not surprised and mostly sympathetic when for weeks and months after Will's arrival, Nate pesters me again and again with the same question, part fear, part incantation. "When I'm five," he asks, "how old will Willy be?" "When I'm ten? When I'm thirty-six?" And in another guise, "When Willy is three, how old will I be? When Willy is ten? When he's thirty-six?" Over and over again, he poses his riddles, like a Zen master with his koans. And over and over again, I give him his answers and his reassurance. Having been there myself, desperately holding on to my five-year edge of seniority over my younger sister, I read the subtext, too. I can promise him with a confidence rare in parenthood that Willy will never catch up to Nate's years. Into the sunset, Nate will remain the older.

What I can't yet explain to Nate is what I now more clearly see on the stage of my children's lives. The seniority he so cherishes, as I did before him, comes with its own hidden agenda. Along with the privileges of being the older, those last vestiges of primogeniture, comes a set of expectations that can all too quickly become pressures. Nate, at five years to Willy's two, or ten to Willy's seven, will always seem older than Willy will at the same age. When Willy is three, I'm sure he'll still seem part tender family baby, while Nate at that age was vaulted to older brother, "big boy" status. When Willy turns five — the age Nate is now — will we be so busy expecting lofty things of Nate — a worldly eight — that we overlook Willy's slips and give him more leeway than we give Nate now?

From my new parental perch, I see the blessings and curses for both firstborn and secondborn. What is expected of the firstborn can be both impetus and burden; the indulgence of the latterborn can be both detriment and gift. As a firstborn daughter, I may have chafed against the restrictions of my role; as a parent, I struggle to balance the pluses and minuses for my sons so that each feels cherished in his own way.

On the battlefield of my sons' inevitable sibling squabbles and their jockeying for my attention, I notice my own perspective, my own allegiance and identification dramatically shifting and changing. At first, my heart goes out to Nate when I watch him watch my loving ministrations to Willy. "You like him a hundred and me, one," he mourns plaintively, and I hurry to balance my attentions.

Or when I move to protect Willy from his older brother's advances, Nate complains, "When I hit Will you like him better." And though I can still remember the snakelike sting of jealousy when my mother reprimanded me for a transgression and my little sister, unscathed, remarked gleefully, "You not yelling at me, Mama," my sympathies now must be divided. I see Willy's frustration at his smaller size, his more limited reach, his desperate running, running, running to catch up, and as a parent I have far more compassion than I did with my sister's attempts to close the gap with me. What was once a nuisance to me is now poignant, and I review and revise the script of my past in light of this new information.

With the insights gleaned from raising siblings we bring both empathy and even a chance for restitution to our present sibling relationships. Observed a mother of three — a girl, a boy, and a girl — who was herself the bossy and judgmental oldest sibling, with a younger brother and sister, "I see my son, my secondborn, like my brother, who also had a sister twenty-one months older. After my son was born, I came to understand my brother better, coping with a sister — me — who was often competitive and verbally abusive. I bring a strong sensitivity to my second child because my brother had such a hard time being second, and I was partly the cause of his pain."

Sometimes it can be hard to extend one's compassion beyond one's remembered role, and our children may pick up on the shortfall. A friend who is a firstborn married another firstborn and had two sons. When her second son feels mistreated — either by his parents or by his older brother — he retreats to his room with one damning statement: "The trouble with this family is that no one around here knows what it's like to be born second!"

The sibling issues of our childhoods are continually replayed and reworked with our own children. The memories of camaraderie and heckling, the expectations of birth order, the hierarchy of family roles — all the underpinnings of family systems continue to shape our families now. What was permitted or encouraged emotionally in our original families often limits our vision for our children now. But by carefully watching the family process unfold and staying open to possibilities for change, we can find new emotional options both for our children and for ourselves.

Sheri Glucoft Wong, a gifted family therapist in Berkeley, California, who shared her insights with me during my work on this book, describes an illustrative case where the ghosts of siblings past haunted not only current sibling relationships but also the health of the entire family:

"I once had a very poignant session with a family. Both parents were the older of two children and grew up with a troubled or incompetent sibling. As children, both parents had been unable to pursue their own needs, because they were trying to redeem their sibling and also take care of their parents.

"These two got married and now have two girls, ten and seven. The older girl was always parenting the little one, telling her what to do, how to act, how to be responsible. In some ways, she was like a little dictator. And the parents finally came to see me because they were concerned about how aggressive she could be, especially toward her younger sister."

At the end of this particular session, the time came to put away the toys. "The younger girl was cleaning up so slowly that it just wasn't getting done," Glucoft Wong continues. "At two minutes before the end of the hour, the older girl got up in a huff, wagged her finger and said, 'It's time to clean up, you nerd.' The little one stiffened and of course didn't do it."

Watching the two sisters, Glucoft Wong began to see the pieces of the intergenerational puzzle slide into place. She turned to the parents and said, "Doesn't it bother you that your daughter is handling this situation for you instead of letting you take care of it?" But the parents were at a loss and didn't respond. Then Glucoft Wong turned to the older girl and asked pointedly, "Why does it matter to you?" And the ten-year-old answered, "Because I'll be late for gymnastics if we don't leave on time."

Glucoft Wong could see how the unmet needs from the family of origin were still unanswered in this family. "Then I realized that the older daughter was trying to manage her sister and take care of things for her parents rather than directly addressing her own needs. So I asked her, 'Can you turn to your parents and say, "What about me?" ' It was a powerful moment, because the child was finally asking to be taken care of. And the parents finally realized that because of their own histories, they hadn't even thought such a competent child needed to be taken care of."

What about me? A powerful and pivotal phrase that neither parent had ever been able to say either in their childhood families or in the rest of their lives. "Now their daughter couldn't say, 'What about me?' either. And not surprisingly, her symptoms came about when the baby was born. And I think the problem was that there was never an opportunity to say, 'What about me?' There are some things parents can't teach their kids because they didn't learn them themselves."

With help, with luck, with awareness, these parents will not only start to hear their child's "What about me?" but will also be able to articulate these words in their own lives.

Without intending any harm, we may pass on our own limitations to our children, particularly when our partners' histories compound rather than undo the damage of our own. There are certainly families where limitations compound over generations, narrowing the scope of emotional health with each successive generation. But my premise in this book — and one crucial to family systems theory — is that just as insights from the past help us revitalize our current family process, so, too, insights from our current families can help us repair the damage of the past and move us forward in our adult lives. Mental illness can be intergenerational, but so can mental health.

Our alliances and identifications with our children are often shaped and circumscribed by our roles in our childhood families. Leader or follower, dependable or flighty, clown or philosopher — we often replay our original family role in the family we create. More than that, we tend to assume the same "emotional position" — in the words of family therapist Peggy Papp — that we had in our family of origin. If we felt left out by our siblings, we may also feel shut out by our children; if we felt victimized by a parent's or sibling's angry outbursts, we may again feel victimized by a child's temper tantrums and have more difficulty handling this anger than would parents with a less charged history. But again, our new arena gives us a chance to rework the old patterns, given the difference in family composition, the commingling of marriage, and the changing expectations of the times and of our new families.

What further complicates this intergenerational family process is the tendency to project our own internal dilemmas onto our children. Too often our children — particularly when there are two — provide a convenient screen on which to project our own dichotomies: competent/soft, decisive/confused, intellectual/physical. If we have not yet integrated these opposites in our own lives, we may let our children play out our conflicts for us.

Glucoft Wong cites the example of a family she worked with that had two girls, thirteen and ten. The older girl was quiet and shy, bookish and sensitive. The younger girl was vivacious and extroverted, bright and articulate, right out there, quick to respond. Other children flocked around her, and she loved to play and party.

Now in this family, the father was quiet and shy, and the mother was more outgoing. So the older daughter was more like the father and the younger one more like the mother. Over the years, the mother began to be concerned about the older girl, who seemed to prefer reading to going to a party. Although her husband always reassured her, she remained overly anxious. Finally, exploring the issue with her therapist, she revealed herself to be a "closet shy person." The fact of her older daughter's shyness was very exposing to the mother of a part of herself she was embarrassed about.

"We split off whatever we haven't integrated," Glucoft Wong explains. "Maybe having kids is like having markers identifying the areas of your life that you have to develop that are previously undeveloped. When parents tell me in therapy that their older child is like the mother and their younger child is like the father, I will work to get the mother to identify with the younger and the father to identify with the older. Usually the child whom the parent is not identified with represents parts of that parent that are less known to him, parts that are undeveloped and scary. It's easier to distance themselves from that kid than to own that quality."

Another interpretation of the family who consulted with Glucoft Wong is that when the couple threatened to become polarized around the issue of shyness, they looked for another focus for their anxiety — the shy daughter. And the shy daughter allowed herself to be pulled into the marital conflict because tension between the parents was unacceptable to the well-being of the family. By allowing herself to become a new focus for anxiety, the daughter took the heat off the marital twosome.

Family systems theory identifies triangles like this one as the predominant pattern of relationships in a family. And as family theorists, especially Murray Bowen, have observed, triangles typically appear in a family when two family members bring a third member into their relationship, usually during an intense or stressful time. Since any twosome naturally seeks to stabilize itself by adding a third point, family theorists believe, triangles are not necessarily destructive. Two people in love, for example, often want to add a baby to their twosome for the most loving reasons.

But often the third leg of a triangle becomes a kind of conduit for the anxiety between the initial twosome. Diffused among three points, the anxiety can't be coped with or corrected. So the family therapist's task is to help uncover the original anxiety and put it back where it belongs. In the family where shyness was causing anxiety, a family therapist might help the parents work out the conflict in their own marriage and then allow the "shy" daughter to find her own comfortable social niche.

Without awareness or outside intervention, the more damaging emotional consequences of family triangles may last for generations. Explain Kerr and Bowen:

> Once the emotional circuitry of a triangle is in place, it usually outlives the people who participate in it. If one member of a triangle dies, another person usually replaces him. The actors come and go, but the play lives on through the generations. Children may act out a conflict that was never resolved between their great-grandparents.

Bowen believes that family therapy can interrupt the inevitability of triangles marching through the generations. Detriangling means "achieving emotional neutrality" or the ability to see both sides of a process between two others and to have the awareness not to label it but to accept it as a manifestation of the system. As a family detriangles, its members strengthen their own separate identities, their "self-focus," often learning for the first time to ground communication in straightforward "I-messages" ("I felt angry when you broke your curfew") rather than blaming "you-messages" ("You always break your curfew"). Detriangling also means that family members learn to deepen the intimacy of their twosomes without needing to bring in other members to stabilize stressed relationships.

*   *   *

Several decades after its inception, family therapy theorists and clinicians have evolved a variety of approaches. In each of the five distinct schools of family therapy — psychodynamic, experiential, structural, strategic, and systemic — the therapist works with the family to uncover its vexing patterns of behavior in a slightly different way. In a lecture at a Harvard Medical School Continuing Education Conference, Anne Fishel, a clinical psychologist at Massachusetts General Hospital, with a family systems perspective, illuminated the differences this way:

"The psychodynamic family therapist — Murray Bowen, Norman Paul, James Framo, for example — is like an archaeologist trying to elucidate the present by digging up the legacy of the past. The goal for the family is more self-awareness, and the therapist helps each family member express secrets and repressed feelings of anger or grief. The experiential family therapist — Virginia Satir and Carl Whitaker, for example — is like a car mechanic who intervenes to repair damage without concern for why the breakdown occurred. The focus is on the here and now, affect — or feeling — is valued over awareness, and the therapist provides an experience, an opportunity for self-expression and spontaneity.

"The structural family therapist — notably Salvador Minuchin — is like a building inspector who asks how the building should be renovated, without being interested in the furnishings. The focus of change is on structure, not content or affect or insight, and change occurs when structure shifts, so the symptoms are not needed anymore. The strategic family therapist — Jay Haley, John Weakland, and Paul Watzlawick, for example — is a master strategist, a chess player or stockbroker who looks for maladaptive behavior, not structure or affect. And finally, the systemic family therapist — including Mara Selvini Palazzoli and Lynn Hoffman — is like the detective in an Agatha Christie novel whose job is to understand each family member's viewpoint, construct an intervention that takes everyone's vision into account — and then give back a slightly altered version. Change occurs not when behavior changes but when beliefs or the meaning of behavior changes."

All of these pioneers have contributed valuable ingredients to the stew we now refer to as family therapy. This book draws on a blending of these approaches, favoring strategic, structural, and systemic family therapy for their innovative techniques, experiential therapy for its emphasis on clear communication (and Virginia Satir's refreshingly clear prose style), and the psychodynamic therapy of Murray Bowen for its focus on intergenerational issues.

One technique of strategic family therapy that has been very useful in family life beyond therapy is "reframing," or relabeling a family's description of its behavior to see it in a new way and make it more open to therapeutic change. Underlining the mutuality of a family problem instead of pointing a finger of blame at one member reduces defensiveness and resistance. Turning what had been defined as a vice into a virtue gives a new, and often liberating, spin to some of the thornier issues of family life. A single-parent family, for example, comes to therapy describing its problem as an out-of-control older daughter, a mom who can't take charge, and a younger daughter trying to play parent. The family therapist reframes the behavior by describing instead a family exquisitely tuned to one another with a mom who "listens so well that she has trouble finding her own voice." Guided by the therapist to see that its structure can be enabling rather than constricting, this family begins to make its first steps toward change.

Another powerful technique of strategic family therapy whose usefulness extends to everyday life is "prescribing the symptom" or "paradoxical interventions." To counter a family's typical resistance to change, the strategic family therapist may intervene in a paradoxical rather than a direct way, often *prescribing* the very behavior the family would like to change. A couple with a lack of sexual interest might be advised not to make love, a bedwetter advised to wet his bed — but on alternate nights, perhaps. The strategic family therapist is like the wonderfully wise children's book heroine Mrs. Piggle-Wiggle, who cures the bath hater by prescribing no baths — until he begins to sprout seeds from the dirt on his body.

Strategic family therapists trust their hunch that families will tire of a behavior after taking it to its nth degree or will try to outsmart the therapist by changing the behavior in spite of themselves. Even more important, a *prescribed* behavior is robbed of its usual effect and function. A prescribed wet bed no longer means that the child is bad or defective or that the parents can't control their child. Prescribing the behavior undermines the meaning of the behavior — and allows the family to give it up.

Even my five-year-old knows the efficacy of a "paradoxical intervention." "You can't get in the bathtub with me," he tells his stubborn younger brother — and sure enough, the little recalcitrant immediately plunges right into the tub.

For the intergenerational explorations of this book, the psychodynamic perspective of Murray Bowen has been the most frequently relevant. For Bowen, especially, the two main pivots of family therapy are differentiation of self and family-of-origin work. In the early phase of his work with families of psychotics, Bowen observed an extreme blurring of psychological boundaries among family members, a "pre-existing emotional stuck-togetherness." The goal of Bowen's treatment became to help all the family members find, define, and explore their separate selves and learn to differentiate between intellect and emotions. According to Bowen, differentiated people can think independently and act on their beliefs, and in intimate relationships they do not lose their sense of self.

Most family pathology, especially chronic anxiety, is the result of poor differentiation, Bowen believes; as differentiation improves, so do the family problems. For Bowen, as for many family therapists, differentiation must be accomplished against a backdrop of mutuality. This does not mean "emotional cut-off" or estrangement but rather supporting each person's separate self as well as the interconnectedness of the entire system.

Crucial to the artful dance of differentiation is what Bowen and his followers call "family-of-origin work" — awareness of the extended family and its history. Bowen believes that all current family problems are connected directly and inextricably with past family issues. So in his current work with middle-class professional families, he counsels as a first step that his adult clients go home to their families of origin and reexamine their relationships with each of their parents. Instead of phoning home and making superficial chitchat with Mom and Dad on separate extensions, the adult child must carefully and consciously rebuild her relationships with her parents in such a way that each family member is fully revealed and defined.

"What kind of behavior in your parents are you allergic to?" is the provocative question one of Bowen's clients remembers her therapist asking. A barrage of images crowded her mind — the way her parents wouldn't let her finish her sentences, the way her father barged in on her when she was on the phone, the way her mother criticized her friends. The goal of her family-of-origin work and her visits home was "to get more objective about my parents and less emotionally reactive." She practiced seeing her parents' behavior in the context of their own unresolved family issues rather than as personal attacks against her.

Newly married and about to start a family of her own, she felt an inner mandate to work things out with her parents. "What's the point of raising children if, as adults, you can't communicate?" she asked herself and used her visits home to clear out the cobwebby channels between her parents and herself.

To illustrate the burden of poor differentiation from one generation to the next and to show how increasing differentiation can improve relationships across generations, Bowen tells the story of a family with a particularly troubled mother and teenage son. This mother felt that her own "emotional insecurity" was the result of "emotional neglect" by her mother, who was cold and aloof. She was determined to be warm and close and "emotionally available" to her son in the way that she wished her mother had been with her.

Until her son reached adolescence, this mother's efforts were successful, and their relationship was harmonious. If her son showed any signs of distress, the mother simply redoubled her efforts: spent more time with him, assuaged his worries. "His problems were her problems; his pain was her pain."

By the time the boy became a teenager, this awkward lack of differentiation, this blurring of boundaries, had taken its toll. Despite all the mother's efforts and reassurances, her son remained "aimless and insecure." Never having been allowed, and certainly not encouraged, to do the difficult work of hammering out a separate self, the boy had scanty inner resources to draw on. Now he felt —

and could finally articulate — that his mother rejected his need to be his own person. And ironically, despite his mother's herculean efforts to prove otherwise, he did not feel that she loved him enough.

In therapy, Bowen encouraged the mother to reexamine her relationship with her own mother and the intergenerational triangle that included the mother, the son, and the mother's mother. Her blaming attitude ("she should have eased my lonely feelings") had undermined her emotional separation from her mother and reverberated to the next generation, eventually undermining her separation from her son. Although this woman's parents were both dead by the time she began therapy, she made an effort to reestablish contact with other members of her family of origin. Talking with them, she began to piece together a more objective picture of her past, realizing that she, too, was responsible for creating the distance between her mother and herself. She also saw that her mother had always rushed in to "fix" her children's defects, just as she was doing with her son. This intrusiveness hadn't worked for her mother, and it certainly wasn't working for her. She began to focus more intently on her own feelings, strengthening her "self-focus" rather than overfocusing on her son.

Armed with a little more objectivity and this new self-focus and awareness, the mother relinquished some of her stringent control over her son's life. Her changed attitude and actions also helped promote a better emotional separation between her son and herself. Some of his problems began to resolve, and he began to take responsibility for the ones that remained.

But where, the curious reader might ask, is the father in Bowen's story? Bowen gives him a passing mention after pages of focus on the mother, on her contribution to her son's troubles, and on the psychic work necessary to undo this damage. When the father appears, he is quite literally in a footnote. Bowen warns the father that his wife may try to involve him in helping her get unstuck from their son. And the master therapist then suggests to the father that he would be most effective at promoting the mother-son separation if he detriangled from their relationship. Nowhere does he suggest ways that the father could increase his involvement in family life and rebalance the family system that way. Nowhere does he turn the family's attention to the pitfalls inherent in a social system in which fathers remain invisible and guiltless and mothers are held guilty and responsible for family ills.

But since the mid-1980s thoughtful feminists have begun to critique and redefine some of the long-held assumptions, theories, and methods of family therapy. They have sought to widen the social context and consciousness of their clinical practice and to add gender to the core of family systems thinking. They have challenged what they now view as family therapy's long — and largely unconscious — history of mother bashing, where mothers — in therapists' eyes — "could never get it right." Judy Myers Avis and Cathryn Haig studied one hundred cases reported in four leading family therapy journals from 1978 to 1987 and found that the mothers "were either 'overinvolved' — that is, 'nagging,' 'too permissive,' 'intrusive,' 'domineering,' 'crushingly overprotective' — or they were not involved enough — 'distancing,' 'stony-faced,' 'cold,' 'cerebral,' or 'overcontrolled.' "

And most to the point for my discussion of Bowen, feminist family therapists have made a priority of reinterpreting the "unholy triad" or "perverse triangle" that many first-generation family therapists saw at the heart of family problems: the overcontrolling mother, the distant or peripheral father, and the troubled child. This, of course, is the family Bowen trains his telescope on.

The new gender-conscious and mother-sensitive family therapists are of course still concerned with resolving family problems. But they do so "not just in any possible way" — in the words of Deborah Luepnitz, one of the movement's most articulate spokespeople — "but in ways that allow the family to be less patriarchal, less father-absent, and more connected to the community than before." They pay special attention to the rigid, inherited constraints of social roles and to the opening up of richer possibilities for both women and men in the family and in the outside world. Says Marianne Walters, one of the founders of the Women's Project in Family Therapy and director of the Family Practice Center in Washington, D.C., "Therapy can validate *his* capacity to be involved with the children, *her* capacity to be competent and independent."

This new consciousness of gender and the wider social context has helped many family therapists redefine the complex sources of family problems. As clinicians "cast their net beyond the immediate family," for example, they may

> find that a child is failing in school for reasons that have nothing to do with mother. Perhaps he is so terrified of school bullies that he can't concentrate; maybe she is constantly fighting with a rigid, overbearing teacher. Maybe the child simply doesn't like school; perhaps he lives to play the trombone, and ignores all his other subjects except band.

As I cast my net beyond these clinical examples to the family stories of repetition and change that make up the rest of this book, I will draw on the language of family therapy's first generation of therapists, while staying mindful of the expansive revisions contributed by the newest generation of feminist therapists.

3

Family Snapshots:
From Our Parents' Generation
to Our Own

THE ENVELOPE

It is true, Martin Heidegger, as you
  have written
I fear to cease, even knowing that at the
  hour
of my death my daughters will absorb
  me, even
knowing they will carry me about
  forever
inside them, an arrested fetus, even as I
  carry
the ghost of my mother under my
  navel, a nervy
little androgynous person, a miracle
folded in lotus position.

Like those old pear-shaped Russian dolls
  that open
at the middle to reveal another and
  another, down
to the peasized, irreducible minim,
may we carry our mothers forth in our
  bellies.
May we, borne onward by our
  daughters, ride
in the Envelope of Almost-Infinity,
that chain letter good for the next
  twenty-five
thousand days of their lives.

    Maxine Kumin

Thinking about what makes a family work best, I searched for
the words and images that each generation passes to the next,
like poet Maxine Kumin's "old pear-shaped Russian dolls that open
at the middle to reveal another and another." I began my search
by listening for the similarities from generation to generation —
the tender songs, the angry outbursts — but I soon turned my
attention to the differences, the ways that each new generation
takes the material it has inherited and makes of it something new,
something fitting and appropriately contemporary.

Then, comparing the liveliest and best-functioning contemporary families to some of the most troubled and stymied families of the past, I asked, what makes a family flourish best, what allows each member to be heard and encourages the family as a whole to thrive?

In interviews and discussion groups and on questionnaires, I posed the following questions:

"Imagine your childhood home with you and each member of your family of origin placed in a typical pose or activity, speaking a typical phrase or statement, either separately or together. Arrange them in your mind as if posing for a family snapshot. Look both at the surface image and the subtext beneath the surface.

"Are your family members separate or together, independent or in clusters? Who are the leaders and the followers? What are the family roles and where are alliances or triangles formed? What are the family rules and subliminal messages? What is the tone of the family and its communication style — mellow or intense, orderly or chaotic, open or reserved? Are there any family secrets, anything hidden or avoided? How does the family feel about outsiders? And most important, how do you feel in the bosom of this family — accepted or discounted, nurtured or neglected?

"Now imagine your present home with you and each member of your current family placed typically there, speaking their characteristic phrases or statements. Take another family snapshot in your mind and ask yourself the same questions. Now observe the overlaps and digressions, watch for the patterns that are similar as well as the ones that have changed. What worked well or didn't work in your original family? What works similarly or differently in your present one?"

I borrowed this approach from the technique of "family sculpting," a "therapeutic art form," in the words of family therapist Peggy Papp, "in which each family member arranges the other members in a tableau which physically symbolizes their emotional relationship with one another." Papp uses family sculpting in therapy sessions "to shift the family balance," choreographing the triangles, alliances, and conflicts in order to explore and begin to change them.

I used the family snapshots that I collected to capture and interpret some of the changes from our parents' generation to our own.

From *Christine Collins*, an only daughter and thirty-five-year-old mother of three small children, came this response:

▶ I see my mother in the kitchen, smoking and scowling and yelling. I can remember her smiling only ten times from my early childhood to my wedding. My father is sitting in the dining room, writing and being angry at me as well. But I can also remember him telling me a bedtime story while I drifted off to sleep. I see myself not in the house, but in the car. I went from sitting in the middle of the front seat to sitting in the back to disappearing altogether.

In my family now, I see all of us in the family bed. Our five-year-old son, who has been very intense since day one, is jumping up and down on the bed; our two-and-a-half-year-old daughter is piling stuff into the bed, and our baby girl wants to be held. My husband is busy doing fifteen things at once. By the time everyone else is up, he has read or written something in bed. I wake up groggy, but I don't want to miss anything. I start organizing from the minute I wake up.

From the marginality of the moving car to the centrality of the busy, warm family bed, Christine's snapshots describe a transition from a family tone that is distant and alienated to one that is intimate and involved. Once an only daughter loitering on the outskirts of her original family, then "disappearing" completely, now, as a mother, she has finally made herself visible. Plunk in the heart of her new family, she is information central, "organizing" from daybreak to day's end. Born to a father who was brooding and removed, she has chosen a husband who is pivotal — albeit still writing. Like many members of her generation, she has struggled to change her family dynamics by changing the externals of size and style first. "As a small child," she remembers, "I vowed never to have an only child. I vowed I wouldn't let my child be alone the way I was. That camaraderie was lacking."

But having changed family size, composition, and spirit, anger is still the hot intergenerational issue for her. She still hears words coming out in the heat of anger she vowed she'd never repeat. "I can frequently do what my mother did and shoot off orders." She pauses reflectively, ascertaining the subtle calibrations of generational change. "But I can also apologize."

The ability to apologize to one's children after a blowup or gaffe and the sensitivity to acknowledge one's fallibility as a parent is also the pivot of another young mother's stories of past and present. *Josie Devoto*, now thirty, is the oldest child of a turbulent working-class family in which "stresses were never shared." A runaway at fifteen, married at sixteen, a mother at eighteen, Josie has a twelve-year-old son from her first, ill-fated marriage. She also has a year-old son from her more grounded second marriage to a kind and involved man who has given her "the support I was always looking for." "I feel able to apologize to my son," she says about the emotional shift in her new family, "and that makes me less huge to my children than my parents were to me. It's important to share stresses with your kids in a way they can understand."

Grappling right now with a depression whose roots reach back to the unanswered needs of her past, Josie depicts two family snapshots that illuminate both the emotional strides she has made and the ones she still has to take:

> ▶ I see my father in his chair with his feet up in stinky wool socks or outside working on his car, lost in it and unapproachable. My mother is doing the laundry and taking care of the three younger kids. Often my parents' arguments get very heated and at times there's a lot of slapping around. My parents don't have much of a relationship; there's not much genuine loving.
>
> Against this background, I see myself taking off for the woods. I spent the early part of my youth being the "good girl" and the "smart one," and when that didn't work, I started being the bad girl and running away from home and taking to the streets.
>
> Now, in my present family, I see my older son in the TV room watching TV with headphones on. My husband and I are talking at the dining-room table with the baby in his high chair between us.

Although Josie's present family is more communicative and responsive than her original family, there are still jarring discordancies. Her trio with her new husband and baby is a cozy one, but it does not include her older son. He has isolated himself in front of the TV, all communication short-circuited by the headphones — an updated version of her own escape to the woods.

Negotiating a balance between separation and closeness, between independence and interdependence is the sticky intergenerational issue for this family. Josie, struggling to find this balance, calls her need to depend on others the common thread winding from past to present and continuing to entangle her. "I want to nurture my new child, but my own needs keep coming up," she confesses. "I feel anger and sadness that my old needs were not met. After I had my new baby, I left my full-time job, and coming home to the empty house was like coming home to an empty place in me." Trying to give her children what she missed as a child is made more difficult because the experience of giving stirs up painful memories of her own unmet needs. Despite a new family atmosphere that is more connected and communicative, the emotional residue from the past still haunts and troubles her.

For a third mother, family style, structure, and emotional content have all changed considerably from the past generation to the present, enabling her to feel at home with herself for the first time. At forty, *Elaine Hanson* has been married three times and is separated from her third husband. She has a twenty-year-old daughter from her first marriage, a sixteen-year-old — the only one still at home — from her second marriage and two stepdaughters from her third. The middle child and only girl in a family with four boys, Elaine was fifteen when her parents divorced. But in the family snapshot in her mind's eye, she is eleven; it is Easter Sunday, and the family is still more or less intact:

▶ My oldest brother, seventeen, is totally uninvolved with any family associations other than the baby's excitement at the Easter candy; his phrase is "Leave me alone!" The next brother, twelve, more of a rough, tough, angry but extremely sensitive person, wants to be outside. His phrase: "Can I go play now?" The next brother, at ten, younger than me, is the tender, loving, quiet boy, confused and wanting to be accepted by everyone. [Years later he will take his own life.] "Can I go with you?" he says. The baby, two, is the center of attention and still a totally affectionate boy. He knows he is loved by all of us and knows, too, that he can weasel his way around any "no" he might run up against. "Pick me up" is his line. In the middle of this field of boys, I am kind of the black sheep — mother's first assistant because of my sex but also desperately wanting to be "one of the boys." "Whom should I please now?" is my phrase.

My father is the one getting the yard ready for Easter eggs or fussing with the flowers in the yard or washing the car. Distanced from the confrontations of the entire group of kids, he is also the one to say, "Sure you can help me!" My mother is in a state of frantic preparation: "Go ask your father" or "Leave the baby alone" or "No! Get the dishes done."

Against this remembered maelstrom of activity and cross-purposes, Elaine's present snapshot of her single-parent family conveys a different Easter mood:

▶ Now there is only my youngest daughter left at home, and we are spending the day reading things to each other out of the newspaper or watching TV and making fun of the commercials or deciding what strange things to make for dinner or coloring four dozen Easter eggs to see who can make the most extreme. "What do you want to do now?" is my phrase.

The most striking difference in Elaine's two family snapshots is the transformation in family makeup and style: from the bustling activity and multiple alliances of a seven-member household to the quieter, more focused activity of a two-member home, from the friction and alienation of a family where individual voices were never quite heard or acknowledged to a family of relative harmony where the channels are open and the voices in sync. Beneath these external and structural changes, and perhaps made possible by them, lie the internal emotional shifts. A "black sheep" with conflicting loyalties in her original family, Elaine has found herself a new family where eccentricity is allowable, even a goal to be pursued. Deciding what strange things to make for dinner, seeing who could make the most extreme Easter eggs — instead of balking at the rather limited and male-dominated givens of her childhood, Elaine and her daughter have redefined those givens to suit their needs and fancies. Together they have turned around the previous generation's definition of "success" and expanded their self-esteem. Such is the potentially healing power of parenthood that yesterday's black sheep in her family of origin has the chance to find a new pasture in adulthood.

Poring over these two generations of family snapshots with a curiosity usually reserved for my own family archives, I began to see a composite portrait of a new generation of parents with a particular style and focus that distinguishes it from the past. The family snapshots provided clues to sociological changes as well as intrapsychic ones from our parents' generation to our own.

First and most obviously, our families are smaller in size, more varied in composition, and more innovative in structure. The snapshots of Elaine Hanson's patriarchal family of origin with five children and of her present single-parent family with four children from three different marriages bring home the changes in family size and structure much touted by the news media. For this is a time when nearly fifty percent of all marriages end in divorce, and more than twenty percent of all families are headed by single parents. For those of us weaned on the nuclear-family harmony of "Father Knows Best" and "The Donna Reed Show," the realities of present family life are better approximated by the on-again, off-again marriage of "thirtysomething" or the frazzled single mom of "Baby Boom."

No longer strictly nuclear in family format, we are also more varied and experimental in our family roles. From Josie Devoto's father sitting in his chair with his feet up while her mother does laundry and takes care of the children to her husband who feeds their baby at the dinner table, the snapshots also reveal the changing roles of mothers and fathers as wives and husbands adapt to the changing demands of our times.

Pondering the changes in her own family as well as in the hundreds of families she has counseled, Maureen Turner, director of Boston's COPE (Coping with the Overall Pregnancy and Parenting Experience), observes, "My kids have had better parenting than I had — certainly better fathering. My mother was home when I was growing up, so I had more quality time with her, but kids today — in intact families — have a lot more fathering." With tighter economic circumstances for many and with more than half of all women with children under three in the work force, the makeup of child care has also changed radically from our parents' generation to our own.

Still, while we spend fewer hours with our children, our consciousness about those hours seems to be more intense. If the classes, workshops, talk shows, and parenting books are any evidence, this generation of parents is significantly more self-conscious about bringing up children than our parents were. Because most of us have chosen parenthood rather than having parenthood choose us, we also seem to have higher expectations of ourselves as parents. Where our parents wanted to "do the right thing" by their children, we recognize a multitude of options and are often overwhelmed figuring out which one is right.

We are also child-oriented rather than parent-oriented. We focus more of our time and energy on our children than on our parents and turn to our children rather than our parents for emotional sustenance. And most important from my perspective for this book, we are more psychologically-minded, more attuned to the language of personal growth and change. Christine Collins remembers her smoking and scowling mother shooting off orders, but she acknowledges that she, too, sometimes orders her brood around — and she also knows when to apologize. We are, as a generation, more willing to admit our fallibility and more aware of how our actions affect our children's budding sense of themselves.

Maurice Vanderpol, a psychiatrist at the renowned McLean Hospital outside of Boston, a man in his sixties with children in their thirties and small grandchildren, commented on this change in orientation and awareness from older to younger generations:

> ▶ Parents today are socially and emotionally more aware of their children. I was raised in Europe so strictly that my upbringing was almost abusive. My wife and I were much less strict, and now our children are no pushovers, but they are so much more patient and aware than we were. The older generation was parent-oriented: they indulged and took care

of their parents. Our children indulge their children. My mother looked at children as having to be broken in, like horses. My wife and I did more with our children, but we were still parent-oriented. But our children are very child-oriented: their priority is by far their children. In my time, children were taken for granted. They were expected to hop to, shape up, be seen but not heard. Before the age of four, children were thought to be morons who just walked and talked. Now, there's a lot more focus from parents on children's intellectual development, and parents allow more emotional leeway.

Allowing more emotional leeway means, for many of us, creating a whole new emotional vocabulary, one that acknowledges the dark side as well as the bright, ambivalence instead of absolute certainty of the one right way. This vocabulary has inspired us to reach for a new "emotional literacy," in the provocative phrase of therapist Deborah Luepnitz, a willingness to "express, discriminate and identify a range of feelings in their nuances — shame, envy, chagrin, tenderness, despair, regret."

There is also a new willingness to face conflict openly rather than to deny it or sweep it under the rug. And with this comes a greater awareness about problem solving and more ingenuity in generating a host of solutions to puzzling family issues. Comparing the emotional vocabulary of the past and present, one mother in her late twenties sketches the differences this way:

> ▶ In my family of origin, one was to talk about the good things only. Pain, disappointment, fear, and anxiety were all dismissed, so I learned not to mention them. The same was true for my husband's family. In our present family, my husband and I have made a big point of talking with our kids about the full range of emotions.

Along with acceptance of "the full range of emotions" and encouragement to express sorrow and pity as well as joy comes a new emphasis on supporting our children's self-esteem. As one mother in her late thirties puts it, "Self-esteem just wasn't in the parental vocabulary when we were growing up." But she describes her own efforts to nurture her children's sense of self-worth despite their bouts of maddening behavior:

> ▶ Our parents wanted for us what they didn't have — as every generation does — and that was material comfort. Now I want my kids to have healthy self-esteem. I let them know they are good, good, good. Their behavior may be bad or inappropriate, but they are good, and I love them clean, dirty, whining, sad, happy, angry, loving, hating, etc.

Greater emotional leeway, a more extensive, inclusive emotional vocabulary with room for the down side as well as the up, more willingness to face conflict, greater ingenuity about problem solving, more focus on nurturing self-esteem rather than on proper behavior — all these differences add up to an enlightened contemporary perspective that sees both childhood *and* parenthood as an unfolding developmental process, with room for change, growth — and fallibility — on both sides.

I began this book by listening to the language passed from generation to generation in my own family — the letters that my mother drew on my arms and that I, in turn, drew on my son's — and in my interviews I continued probing for the language of the emotions passed from one generation to the next. How we name and define feelings to build an emotional vocabulary, what we hide and what we reveal to create emotional authenticity or a mask, how, indeed, we live with — or try to change — our family's communication style to clear the air and open up channels between ourselves and our children — this is my focus in the rest of this chapter.

From my many interviews, I have chosen three families whose challenges and solutions best illustrate the changes from our parents' generation to our own in the search for greater emotional literacy. These families are by no means trouble-free, but they have learned to use their troubles to generate solutions. They are by no means consistently open, but they have made clearer, more honest communication a family goal. They are certainly not perfect families, but are consciously striving toward a healthy balance with high self-esteem and room for individuality as well as togetherness.

Each of these three families lived for a long time with a secret inherited from the generation before, whose repercussions distorted communication and disturbed the peace of family life. For the Winiks, the secret was the anguish of family members whose lives were threatened and almost lost in the Holocaust, and the guilty relief of those who survived. For the Davises, it was alcoholism and drugs and the pain, shame, and wild unpredictability that went with years of abuse. For the Weltners, it was a more quiet desperation, the memory of parents so erratic and undependable and a childhood house so messy that guests were never invited over.

For years each of these families tried desperately to cover up their secret. They built walls of obliqueness and denial to protect themselves from outsiders, and even from each other. "There's nothing wrong here *and* don't talk about it" was the crippling double message. Family members hid behind masks, afraid to show their authentic selves. Without nurturance, self-esteem wilted like an unwatered plant.

Finally, when secrecy became insufferable, when the center no longer held and the children began to act out the family pain, each family in its own way began to take the first steps toward breaking the cycle that had deadlocked them for generations. Each family, with a helping outside hand from support groups or therapy, began to grope for a new family language based on emotional literacy rather than secrecy, talking to each other more openly, without blame or denial, and being willing to face the truth, however painful and difficult it might be. In the process, the dynamics of family life were forever changed, and a breath of fresh air and fun blew through each household.

Marta Fuchs Winik escaped from Hungary with her parents in 1956 when she was six years old and came to the United States. Besides the dislocation and alienation of being immigrant Jews in America, the family also had to live with the bitter memory of their Holocaust past. Marta's mother had spent a year and a half in Auschwitz and managed to survive with two of her sisters; both of her parents were killed. Marta's father had spent five years in Russian labor camps; the rest of his family was wiped out.

"Only in the last few years have I really felt my family's loss," realizes Marta Winik. At forty she is a family therapist, married, the mother of a four-year-old boy and weeks away from having a second child. With a wide, earthy face framed by thick, dark hair, she concentrates intently as we talk. Stretched out on the couch, her belly huge, she shifts her weight this way and that as if trying to accommodate both the weight of the future and the burden of the past. "Only in the last few years have I really gotten connected with the whole Holocaust past. As a typical child of survivors, I always sensed my parents' pain and loss and tried to make up for it. Like many families, mine didn't really talk about the Holocaust, but I always knew about it. I think both generations tried to protect each other by not talking about it. But the pain does not go away by not talking about it. *How* you talk about it is crucial."

Marta's involvement in a group of children of survivors, called Generation to Generation, has given her a valuable source of support and more confidence in opening up the painful and long-taboo subject with her parents. Despite her relief at discharging some of the power of the secret, she acknowledges that her parents' denial had its place as a coping strategy. "In some ways I was more fortunate than many of the people I know in the group, because I was raised in a family where there wasn't a lot of gloom and doom. My family was one of the ones that really 'made it,' and my parents translated their experience in positive terms. They were overly optimistic, perhaps. There was a real denial or minimization of anything sad or difficult, which is understandable. They had suffered so much and wanted to protect my brother and me. They wanted so much for us to be happy."

Still, she feels "more fortunate than some of the folks I know who came from families where the Holocaust was talked about all the time and they lived and breathed it. Some of these families were very distrustful, very fearful of the outside world, particularly of non-Jews. The feeling that it could always happen again was sort of the backdrop of their life. And that wasn't the case for me. My parents somehow transformed their experience and trusted people, and I didn't grow up with the fear of the outside world. I think therefore I was able to form healthy, long-term relationships with people." She smiles and tells me that the day we talk is her thirteenth wedding anniversary. This long-term relationships is unusual in her group of children of survivors, where few are married and even fewer have children.

But her parents' coping style — their secrecy and denial — unquestionably had a damaging side as well. As the years went on, Marta became more and more the family's repository for pain. "I carried the family's shadow side and felt deeply what wasn't expressed," she realizes now. When she finally began to give voice to her pain, the impact was wrenching but proved to be healing.

At times she felt that she was speaking an entirely different language from her parents. It was not just the English she learned at school while her parents spoke Hungarian at home, but also a very personal language of feeling instead of intellect. Once she told her parents that she was feeling anxious, and they looked at her, puzzled. "Anxiety — what's that?" they asked, and hurried to look it up in the Hungarian dictionary. "You think too much," her father countered, a view that had clearly gotten him through five years of Russian labor camps. "You have to create, be productive. You only have a problem if you make one."

Emotional shifts dogged Marta through adolescence and college, but it was a severe upheaval during graduate school that changed the course of her life. While she was studying to be a librarian, she felt her world turn around. When she was able to put her life back together, she felt "a real calling to be a therapist." She also felt a deep desire to have a family and made a commitment to evolving a new family language that validated and gave voice to the inner life, incorporating all the emotional subtleties she had had to hide as a child.

When her first child, Jacob, was born four years ago, she and her husband made every effort to reverse the emotional habits of her childhood family, while understanding that her parents' attitudes were a natural outcome of their survivor past. "I don't think this was at all intentional or malicious on my parents' part," she says now, "but I did grow up feeling like my own experience, the vicissitudes of being a child, those little upsetting day-to-day things were really invalidated by my parents. 'Why worry about that?' they would say. 'You worry about bigger things.' "

This is an attitude she has "really tried to turn around" with her son — and "in some ways have gone overboard with." "I think my husband and I probably overvalidate," she admits now. "We respond to every little nuance of feeling that our son has. And we wonder, 'Was he a sensitive child to begin with or did we sort of encourage that kind of sensitivity?' He's able to move through feelings very rapidly, but he feels them intensely."

To illustrate the changing response from her parents' household to her own, Marta tells a story about a little boy in the neighborhood inviting Jacob on a walk. "I'm going to hold Mark's hand," Jacob beamed. But when the time came for the walk, Mark didn't feel like holding Jacob's hand, and the younger boy burst into tears. Even though Marta ached for him, even though she feels she "can deal with anger more easily than hurt feelings, having grown up trying to protect my parents from more hurt," she did not try to "talk him out of his feelings," as her parents would have done. "I didn't say what my parents would have said, which is 'No big deal.' Because the interpretation he would have added later would be that his feelings didn't count. And at the same time my parents would have tried to divert his attention and change the subject. Often, just letting a child have his feelings and not trying to 'fix' or 'rescue' him is the help he needs."

What Marta did instead of diverting her son's attention was to "let him have his feelings" so he could "move through them much more quickly." She said a few words, not a weighty explanation, about Mark not liking to hold anyone's hand but still wanting to be with Jacob. Then Mark went home for a break, and Marta let Jacob mope and grumble and "hang out with his feelings for a while." When Mark's mother appeared later and suggested another walk — this time in Superman outfits — Jacob was more than ready to fly forward. "I think he had sort of worked through his hurt feelings," Marta realizes. "That's something I feel really good about. It's often hard to let your children feel their pain and not try to fix or change them or feel inadequate because they are hurting."

Poised on the brink of having her second child, Marta looks back at the choices she has made with Jacob and ahead to the changes she will make with the new baby. "As parents to Jacob, my husband and I both overidentified with his woundedness and overvalidated his feelings," she realizes now. She looks pensive, imagining the future. "It scares us that we won't have that luxury with the second one. And yet now I'm thinking perhaps it's not all healthy what we've been doing with Jacob. It's been real hard for us just to say 'Knock it off!' We feel that that's rude, I mean that's like the closest we come to yelling at him sometimes."

Now both she and her husband are beginning to express direct anger at Jacob from time to time, and she believes that that angry exchange can be helpful. "How is our child going to learn otherwise to negotiate angry feelings and deal with his responses and develop emotionally, if we're constantly trying to be perfectly available all the time? He doesn't then have the opportunity to work things out for himself."

By the last time I speak with Marta, Jacob is six and the new baby, Sophie, is two. As their family and their experience have grown, the Winiks have kept "emotional literacy" an important family priority. But they have also learned to strike more of a balance between validating their children's feelings and interfering with the natural trial and error of childhood. "Our daughter is also very intense, but in a different way. And perhaps she responds differently because we're responding a bit differently to her," Marta says now. "With Jacob we were being overly 'reasonable,' and often tried to prevent him from experiencing frustration. It's so much cleaner now and less emotionally entangling for all of us."

The nightmare of alcoholism and drug abuse was the shameful secret hidden by the Davis family. *Karen* and *Juan Davis* spent almost twenty years of marriage locked into a deadly cycle of abusing alcohol and drugs and denying it, a pattern inherited from both sides of their family, which only severe trauma forced them to confront and change. Although the Davises' story is more extreme than most in this book, their struggle nonetheless is of a piece with the others in this chapter. For what gets perpetuated in alcoholic families is not just the drinking but also the communication patterns — the secrecy and denial, the masks and shaky self-esteem. Beyond confronting and coping with their alcoholism, the Davises had to break the intergenerational web of secrecy and shame and open up avenues of honest communication. Only then could each family member's emotional needs be counted so that the family could flourish as a whole.

Juan Davis was the only child of Central American refugees. Although he wanted to believe that his childhood household was "pretty normal," now, in his early forties and more relaxed and optimistic than he's ever been, he admits that there were large chinks in the facade of family life. His parents screamed at each other; his father used fist fights to solve problems at the factory where he worked and then came home to a "shot of whiskey backed with a beer."

In Vietnam and for a while afterward, Juan did a lot of drugs and sold them as well. When he married Karen and started a small business, he laid off the drugs but started having affairs. He was also drinking enough that he always felt he had something to hide, wondering if his customers smelled the liquor on his breath or if he was "saying the right thing."

Karen grew up about a mile from Juan in a middle-class family. Her mother used pills and alcohol and abused her daughter verbally; her father abused her physically. Karen stood four foot eleven and weighed eighty pounds as a child. Today, at thirty-eight, she weighs more than twice that, as if swaddling her short frame in protective layers. But sitting beside her husband in the office where they now work together, she smiles at him often, if tentatively, like someone who is struggling to come out of her shell. More attuned to her own needs now, she is less sharp-tongued and brassy than she was as a child.

Back then she used her bravura to protect herself and to hide a bowel problem she was desperately ashamed of. Unable to move her bowels regularly "because it hurt," she would then soil her pants and be teased mercilessly by siblings and neighbors. "When I left home, the problem ceased to exist," she admits ruefully, adding, "From that experience, that's where I learned a lot of my hiding." For Karen, the language of the body spoke painfully about the hidden conflicts of her inner life.

Learning to become invisible to protect themselves from intense pain is a survival skill common to abused children. Writing about the lifelong search of these children to become visible, marriage and family counselor Eliana Gil could be describing Karen Davis:

[Survival skills] were necessary [as a child] because they kept you alive, or helped "pad" you from the pain. . . . One such skill was learning to be invisible. Many adults abused as children became experts. They learned to stand still, hold their breath, leave the room, or blend in with the furniture so as not to provoke an attack. They learned to avoid being hit, berated with words, or sexually assaulted or misused by being emotionally or physically distant or disconnected.

Of course, the problem with being emotionally disconnected and numbed, Gil points out, is that in addition to pain, positive, loving feelings are also screened out, as Karen Davis knew too well.

If Karen's childhood taught her the habit of abuse and the necessity of hiding, her own drug and alcohol habit became another way to hide, to avoid "facing my feelings and the attitudes I was raised with." "I started smoking weed at sixteen, which means I used for twenty years," she recalls. Her long history of substance abuse included selling and using marijuana, alcohol, and cocaine. "I used about half a gram of cocaine a day, as much as I could get my hands on. I spent about two thousand dollars a week on that, plus whatever I could steal or take. But cocaine was good for me, because it brought me to my knees," she adds grimly. "That's the shit that took me down."

By the time Karen's habit got this bad, the entire family was in chaos. She and Juan were barely speaking to each other. Juan closed himself off in work to avoid watching the family disintegrate. Like alcoholism, workaholism numbed him from his pain. Their daughters — then fourteen and nine — were traumatized and neglected (their older daughter was removed from their custody for almost a year). In Juan's words, "The home environment was not safe — it was a war zone." But for a long time, the hiding and denial remained as acute as the chaos. "When Karen was abusing her chemicals, it was like I really didn't take notice, because I was also doing it myself," Juan realizes now. "We were both numb and not communicating, because we were both loaded." But there came a point when Juan finally wanted to clear his own head, and he made the decision to give up booze. Soon after that, he found his way to a family treatment program, and a family friend persuaded Karen to go in for treatment as well.

Karen admits now that at first she planned to spend a month in the hospital program, then leave, take her younger daughter, divorce her husband, "take him for every penny he was worth and go get stoned." But a week or two into the program and "clean" for the first time in twenty years, she "couldn't believe how great it felt." For the first time in two decades she "accepted that I was an addict and began my recovery."

There was a bit of black humor going around the treatment program that year, and it hit home with Karen. The patients would ask each other, "How are you?" and the answer was always "FINE." "We knew what it meant," Karen grins now. "We defined it as fucked, insecure, neurotic, and emotional! And I can see why, because that's what I would do, I'd say I was fine when I really wasn't fine."

Beginning in that treatment program and later on in individual and family therapy, Karen and her family have begun to learn an entirely new language, a language where fine really means fine and lousy is allowed to mean lousy. After almost forty years of hiding, Karen has begun to learn to face her complex web of feelings, teasing apart frustration from sadness, boredom from dissatisfaction. She is finding more constructive alternatives to the crippling "learned behavior" of her past. She and Juan and their daughters are starting to talk — and really listen — to each other for the first time. Each is getting the space and the help to cope with individual emotional business as well as to enjoy the company of the whole family.

Only a year into recovery, Karen is still surprised at how slowly change occurs. She feels the relief of honesty blowing through the family like a fresh and cleansing breeze, but she dreams of feeling more joyous, more confident. There still are moments when she is afraid to answer the phone or hides in her room from an unexpected visitor.

Perhaps her greatest reassurance that change is being made, that the stranglehold of abuse is being broken, comes as she watches her younger daughter. Once a week she drives her daughter to an Alatot meeting, a support group for children whose parents are struggling with alcohol and drugs. "And while we're driving home," Karen reports with a smile that makes her face glow, "this kid who never used to talk is running off at the mouth nonstop about her feelings. So I can see that this is the avenue to talk. And she'll say, 'You know, Mommy, you do this, and this is how it makes me feel.' And that's where I see a lot of my hope. I don't have a lot of confidence in myself yet. I don't like myself a lot, and that's going to take a lot of work. But I can't wait for me to get better for my kids. And the same thing for the work my husband is doing on himself. We have all got to work our own programs and make our own decisions. Our daughters don't have to be like their mother or their father. They can be themselves."

"One of my mother's favorite sayings was, 'You have to take me the way I am,' " remembers Linda Weltner. "Neither she nor the women of her generation believed that personal growth continued through adulthood. That attitude was difficult to deal with growing up, because it meant that criticism was damning. And our parents were hypersensitive to criticism, because how they behaved was what they were, and if we complained about how they behaved, we were really questioning them."

For Linda and Jack Weltner the past held uncomfortable memories of a sort different from the anguish of the Holocaust or of abuse. For the Weltners the legacy of pain was lodged in Linda's parents' marriage and a childhood life so unpredictable and erratic that it could not be repeated, yet provided no clues or permission to change. The Weltners' challenge, like the Winiks' and the Davises' was to clear out the cobwebs of denial around the past, acknowledge the goblins that still haunted the present, and build from scratch a language of the emotions based on authentic exchanges and a belief in the possibility of change.

On a clear summer afternoon, *Boston Globe* columnist Linda Weltner reflects on the vast changes in attitudes about parenting from her parents' generation to her own and examines her own momentum toward change. At forty-nine, she has daughters twenty-four and twenty-one, one recently married, the other just graduated from college and about to make an experimental move back home. Relaxing outside her rambling house near the ocean in Marblehead, Massachusetts, Linda is slim and fit and full of a contagious zest for life's possibilities, a zest that has drawn both friends and readers since she began writing her column about the victories and crises of family life, "Ever So Humble," in the early eighties.

"The belief in personal growth makes an enormous difference," Linda observes. She muses about her own "sort of New Age Philosophy" born out of "eight years of psychoanalysis, three bouts of marriage therapy, and two full months of living at the Option Institute, a residential growth center in western Massachusetts," where she took workshops with her older daughter. "Unlike my parents," she continues, "I have encouraged my children to tell me if they don't like something I'm doing, because I perceive that I can change if I want to or that the circumstance can be altered.

"Along with that, my husband and I have always encouraged our children — and the truth isn't always easy to hear — to say how they're really feeling, to be authentic with us. Sometimes I envy people who don't know what their kids are going through. Because it's not that easy to know that your kids smoke grass or are in a car with somebody drinking and driving. You have to be able to hear whatever your children have to tell you, and not punish them and not try to control them and not panic and get upset yourself, but see yourself as a reservoir of helpfulness."

Today Linda sees an enormous split between the disengaged, dysfunctional family she grew up in and the high-energy, forthright, and intimate family she and her psychiatrist husband Jack have created. "There's a very great discontinuity in my life," she explains. "All the therapy really changed my underlying beliefs about the way the world works, so that in some ways I really am not my parents' child in the way that I was when I was twenty. Back then there were a lot of ideas like 'There isn't enough to go around.' My cousin Margery was the beautiful one, and everyone said I was homely. I was the smart one, so Margery was dumb. It was like there was a scarcity, and the sisters — our mothers — competed by labeling their children. I mean, just having let go of that one has transformed my world."

As we're talking, Jack Weltner stops by on a break from seeing his patients. Jaunty and energetic in his fifties, he shares his wife's sense of humor and her psychological-mindedness. Listening to our conversation about generational differences, he adds, "Our parents all believed there was such a thing as one right way. And they thought that the grown-ups' job was to tell the children that, and none of us believes that anymore."

"Right," agrees his wife, picking up the thread. "And therefore, they never assumed responsibility for their own wishes. They'd say, 'You have to do this because of "the society." ' Then, if you didn't do it, you had offended the whole universe."

Finishes Jack: "And they cared about what the universe thought a great deal."

The oldest of three — her sister and brother are eight and twelve years younger — Linda sees the chief strain in her family of origin as the disturbing reality that her parents did not get along. "They were unable to cooperate, period. As a result they lived apart for long periods of time, and they lived in separate worlds. When I was a teenager and his mother was still alive, my father slept at home two or three nights a week, and the rest of the time, he slept at his mother's apartment. So I had no model at all of people compromising and cooperating."

Inevitably, her father was also absent from daily child rearing. "And not only was he absent, his contribution was in great part viewed by my mother and by us as negative. To this day, my most traumatic experiences have been trying to get my father to do something with me. It has been hard to accept that he's a loner. He didn't want to take his kids with him when he played tennis. And of his three children, I was the one who was the least able to accept that."

So Linda took great care to choose a life mate who was involved and caring. "One of my primary reasons for choosing Jack was that I felt he would be a good father," she says proudly, "and it means a great deal to me to have a husband who is very involved in the welfare of his children. He used to get up with them at night when they were babies. And to this day, he and I send our daughters two birthday cards, two presents. Jack calls them separately; he has lunch with them alone when they come home. We have a strong paired relationship with each of them."

As she shows me around the house, the signs of Jack's involvement are everywhere, allying him with the attitude of a younger generation of fathers. There are the pots of pink and white impatiens marching up the front steps, which Jack grew from cuttings for daughter Laura's recent wedding; the euphoric photo of Jack and Linda after the shared effort of Laura's wedding, with Linda's head thrown back in laughing jubilance ("That's how happy we were!" she says); and the second-story shop where Jack works on carpentry projects right down the hall from Linda's study. And when she guides me through Jack's serene meditation room with its low cushions and muted yellow walls, it is clear she has found a soul mate.

Though Linda is the first to admit that midlife has been a time of great satisfaction in marriage, family life, and work, she can also admit with characteristic candor that she has not always felt this kind of fulfillment.

"My children's infancies — and up to the time they were five — was my most hopeless and emotion-wracked period. Between what I thought I should be and what I actually could be there was a huge gap, and into that gap fell loneliness, feelings of inadequacy, and anger."

Like many mothers, she traces her difficulties with early mothering to her relationship with her own mother. "My mother was pretty neglectful," she remembers. "Once we were old enough to be on our own, she was away a lot. So as a child, I spent a lot of frantic time alone, not knowing where she was."

Now Linda has worked out a truce with both parents. She forgives them their trespasses and admires their virtues and the positive traits they've passed on to her: her father's unconventionality and pleasure in shocking people, her mother's sociability. ("She never entered an elevator without leaving with three best friends, and I have that same ability to talk to strangers.")

But when her children were small and Jack would leave for work, Linda's childhood feelings of abandonment resurfaced. "I would forget that I was the mother and feel as if I were the kid who had been abandoned.

"I started serious therapy when the kids were small because I wanted to be the mother I hadn't had. Yet I was lacking so much nurturance myself, I couldn't be home alone and be comfortable taking care of my two daughters without anybody taking care of me."

Alienated from her husband and small children and cut off from a network of friends as an army wife during this period, loneliness closed around her, insidious and almost palpable, like fog. "But I worked it through," she recalls dryly, "I wrote a play called *As Lonely as American Pie*. It was so upsetting that it was only produced once. When the audience left, they said, 'Don't let anyone see this play.' But to have everyone acting out my worst moments really helped. After that, I started writing comedies."

Besides working through her loneliness by writing and talking through her feelings of inadequacy in therapy, when their younger daughter was eight months old, she and Jack decided to settle in Marblehead, and they bought the house that both grounded and energized them, as it continues to do today. The Weltners' relative affluence and the luxury of time may have afforded Linda opportunities for nesting and self-exploration that many younger, two-career couples do not have these days. But both materially and spiritually, Linda made the most of the opportunities her good fortune provided.

If a house can be said to be a symbol of the self, this one embodies Linda Weltner's spirit: warm and welcoming, full of the memorabilia of family life (her son-in-law's beer bottle collection, a nephew's tiny crib), with room enough for the four family members to be separate individuals as well as a whole greater than the sum of its parts. Originally built as a summer place, the house is full of nooks and crannies, places to cozy up for a good read, a good chat, a good cry, a cup of tea. The living room, never insulated, is now kept empty of most furniture except for a giant pinball machine and a huge mirrored ball that hangs from the ceiling and flashes to the music at summer parties. This is a family that relishes the excitement of social life as much as it pays attention to the needs of the inner life.

In this house, on the living-room dance floor, in the family room, in the privacy of her upstairs study, Linda began to chase away the ghosts of her past and create the kind of home and life she had dreamed of. Linda's appreciation of her house and devotion to her home helped, in her words, "transform me from a troubled young girl into a woman capable of taking responsibility for her life." Her house made tangible the healthy, open, joyful family she and her husband were striving to create.

Linda's attitude about making her house a home stands in stark contrast to her mother's attitude. "My parents never entertained. They never had anyone except family over to eat. My mother was messy and she was very ashamed that the house was messy, so naturally her children were, too. Whereas our house now is a social center, constantly filled with people sleeping over, eating over, dropping by.

"Another difference is that our house is just as much our children's as ours. In my parents' day, it was their house, and if you didn't like it, you could leave — or do it differently when you were on your own. Also, in this house we really haven't any formal area where the kids are not allowed. Whereas in my childhood home, I don't think I sat in my own living room a dozen times."

As Linda shows me around the upstairs rooms, the family's inner sanctum, I see how her good spirits about motherhood, her sense of whimsy and fun and openness to change have drawn her daughters to her at a stage when many grown children are fleeing their childhood home and all its associations. There is the room set aside for her older daughter, Laura, and her new husband, with its welcoming double bed, now piled high with wedding presents and several golf balls for her son-in-law's collection. The room for her younger daughter, Julie, is newly redecorated and painted by Linda herself, with a dozen new hooks and storage places to encourage a sense of order that was lacking in the past. Linda has faith that the sloppy, rebellious teenager has metamorphosed into a competent young adult, and she is vowing to "truly see my daughter, and not just my prejudices and the past."

And then there is Linda's study, with its piles of photocopies of her columns ready to be mailed off to devoted admirers, needy readers. And on the bulletin board, an eye-catching poster-size portrait by Cambridge photographer Elsa Dorfman shows Linda on her forty-fifth birthday, standing next to her best friend, Lynn. They are both wearing bikinis, holding inner tubes, looking zestful, in great shape and at the peak of life. Everywhere are signs both of this mother's strong sense of herself and of a deeply felt and nurtured sense of relatedness, interwoven threads that keep her full of joie de vivre and her family full of vitality.

"At fifty, my mother thought her life was almost over," muses Linda. "She didn't sit on the floor, she didn't wear jeans, she didn't play sports, she didn't make dirty jokes, she didn't dance. She had decided that youth was not for her. Well, for me, forty-nine is not so different from twenty-three in terms of the kinds of things I do or am interested in. So I don't feel old yet. And Jack and I are really happy. I can't believe that after all these years, he'll even say, 'You have such a gorgeous body.' "

With her dog, Buckwheat, lying in the grass and licking her toes, she smiles contentedly. This is a watershed time for Linda Weltner, in both her family and her professional life. *No Place Like Home*, her first book of columns, has recently been published, and her local reputation is creating nationwide ripples. Neither anxious nor overwhelmed by these changes, she greets them with a confidence born of a family life devoted to facing and working with change.

Looking at these three families — the Winiks, the Davises, and the Weltners — struggling to replace secrecy with openness, denial with communication, and fear with intimacy, and thinking about my dreams for my family, I began to sketch a working blueprint for what makes a family become healthy and thrive. Watching how these families were changing deadlocked family patterns into new and inventive ones, I observed five outstanding differences between the most dysfunctional families of the past and the healthiest families of today.

First, the family structure has changed from a closed system to an open one, from rigidity to flexibility, from passive to active, from withdrawn from the outside world to engaged with it. Linda Weltner's changing attitude toward her home, for example, parallels the changing attitude toward parenthood from her parents' generation to her own. Where once the boundaries were firmly drawn — the door to her childhood living room kept tightly closed — now they are more flexible. Where once the limits were severely set — no guests over except family — now life flows in and out more freely, and permission for various escapades is granted more liberally.

An open family structure is not built overnight; it may take several generations to establish. "My family of origin was secretive," observed one mother I interviewed. "My husband's family was denying, and our family is reserved." This "reserved" family is nonetheless significantly more open than their families were in the past, and their children's families may be more open, flexible, and direct by yet another leap.

Second, there is a comfortable balance between separateness and togetherness, between autonomy and mutuality. There is also a workable hierarchical structure in which parents are in charge and children are allowed to be children. "The healthy family maintains a separation of the generations," explains family therapist Carl Whitaker. "Mother and father are not children and children are not parents."

Marta Winik, who has worked as a therapist with children of Holocaust survivors and children of alcoholics, sees how both are tempted to become their parents' "emotional caretakers," until, as adults, "they often don't know what their needs are or what they're feeling. They may not even feel they have a right to their own feelings and needs." So she and her husband have been especially conscious of sparing their children this emotional burden. As she points out, "What I hope not to transmit is needing our children to make us feel better. And I think my husband and I have been very successful. We get very clear on what's appropriate, what needs are more appropriately met elsewhere." To illustrate, she tells this story:

"I remember when our son first didn't want to be kissed anymore. I mean, he was so cute, and those cheeks — you'd just get this urge to kiss him!" She grins at the memory. "I would see others just smother him, as often happened to me as a child, and I really respected that he wanted that separation. And he started this rule that you can only kiss me when you go to work or a meeting or when you say good-bye! And I got a real kick out of that. That he knew what he wanted, felt he had a right to get it, and could even express it! I, in turn, felt good that I could respect his limit and could also see what an incredible urge kissing him was — and not feel rejected! Not need him to make me feel better."

Third, these vital families have progressed from clogged and indirect to open and direct communication. They are willing to face problems and come up with solutions, using ingenuity and creativity rather than avoidance. Healthy families make it "safe and acceptable to talk about feelings," in the words of the Timberlawn

Psychiatric Research Foundation, whose well-known study, *No Single Thread*, evaluated a broad range of families to discover what characterized the healthiest ones. "Facing conflict openly, having high levels of empathy, and tenderness," the researchers added, "were family characteristics which may best prepare individuals for human intimacy beyond the family of origin."

Each of the families I portrayed have found a unique way to improve family communication, to hear and acknowledge each individual's feelings. The Winiks have emphasized validating their children's feelings, allowing their children to express anger freely, while helping them channel it ("I try to tell my children that I don't like certain words or name calling," says Marta Winik, "but it's okay for them to be mad at me"). Juan and Karen Davis have concentrated on improving communication between the two of them. Karen's therapist gave them an assignment that they have practiced each week; for thirty uninterrupted minutes Karen talks to Juan about herself and he just listens, giving no comments or advice, and then the roles are reversed, with Juan talking and Karen listening. This one weekly hour of talking and listening has strengthened their marriage and, in turn, the quality of the whole family's life.

And the Weltners have sustained themselves and cleared the family air with the ritual of family meetings. Whenever the family atmosphere got too tense, whenever somebody was unhappy, hurt, or angry, rather than giving up in frustration or despair, the four would gather for a family meeting. Attendance was compulsory; everyone could speak without interruption; each tried to focus on feelings instead of blaming others; no one could leave unless all were satisfied with the resolution. Although Linda admits that she often "wept at these meetings because I wasn't perfect," the meetings proved helpful and healing in the end.

Fourth, there is a change, partly as a result of improved family communication, from unsatisfying and deadlocked marriages to healthy and satisfying ones that meet both partners' needs. Family roles and sex roles are defined with greater flexibility and freedom of choice for everyone. For Karen Davis the greatest change in day-to-day family living is the new group spirit about taking care of the house, with everyone pitching in and doing a share. "We have worked out a schedule where everyone helps me — it's all written down on the calendar. So Juan cooks three days, I cook three days, I do dishes two days, and the girls divide up doing the dishes the other days. People pick up their things and help out more. So I'm accomplishing more at home while working full-time than I did being home full-time!"

She beams as she continues, shocked but delighted at the impact of each practical change on family life. "And Juan is helping out. And if you would have told me — this man never washed one plate in nineteen years. Not one plate. And now he does dishes and sweeps the floor and takes out the garbage and cooks three nights. So to me, those are things that I'm not solely accomplishing but they're happening because we're all working together."

Because we're all working together — this is the clue to the fifth change I observed in all three families, the change from a family atmosphere scarred by pain and hostility to one of harmony, high self-esteem, and fun. What breathes liveliness into every corner of these families like helium into a bouquet of balloons is their good times. "Another difference between the generations," offers Linda Weltner, "is that high on my list of adult priorities is having fun. I don't think our mothers viewed raising children as a way to have a good time. And the fact that we see being with our children as fun means they see being with their parents as fun. The fact that we enjoy each other means there's no need for them to be dutiful. And I don't see that changing as I grow old."

Whether having fun means going to a family cabin without plumbing or electricity and reading *Watership Down* by candlelight, as the Weltners did for many years when their daughters were young; or walking down the street in a Superman outfit, as the Winiks' son did with them; or biking or bowling or roller skating together (instead of hiding and isolating behind drugs or work), as the Davises now do — this is the final secret of family life that the liveliest and most vital families share. "Being a family shouldn't hurt" read a billboard for a health clinic I saw while I was writing this chapter. Being a family should mean having a safe and secure space to speak, to be heard, to share, and to thrive.

— 4 —

Cycles of Pain, Strategies for Change: Undoing the Sins of the Parents

THIS BE THE VERSE

They fuck you up, your mum and dad.
They may not mean to, but they do.
They fill you with the faults they had
And add some extra, just for you.

But they were fucked up in their turn
By fools in old-style hats and coats,

Who half the time were soppy-stern
And half at one another's throats.

Man hands on misery to man.
It deepens like a coastal shelf.
Get out as early as you can,
And don't have any kids yourself.

Philip Larkin

Many of us remember a heated moment from childhood when we vowed never to torment our future children the way our parents tormented us. Maybe the vow came after an unfair accusation ("See what you made me do"), a humiliating punishment ("I'll give you something to cry about"), or an impatient insult ("Can't you do anything right?"). Most of us also remember the more mellow childhood moments when we promised ourselves as well to carry on the loving kindness shown to us — the soothing comforts ("Let Mommy kiss it and make it better"), the bedtime lullabies ("Go tell Aunt Rhodie, the old gray goose is dead"), the joyful celebrations ("Dreydel, dreydel, dreydel"). Now when I hear my own voice comforting my small sons or raised in anger at them, I hear echoes of my parents and wonder what parts of my own childhood I will carry on, sidestep, or change.

In the parenting group I taped and observed, led by Leah Potts

Fisher and Helen Neville, a single mother working to make a good life for herself and her "extremely sensitive and vulnerable" young daughter spoke hauntingly of the pain inadvertently and unconsciously passed from generation to generation in her family:

> ▶ I wonder if life has to be so hard for my daughter, and I want to protect her from that. I feel absolutely certain that my parents certainly would never have intended to put pain on me. And there's no real craziness in the family I can point to. There's no loss, nothing except people working too hard and caring too much and being of a different generation. And yet it's there: the hurt and the fear and the lack of self-esteem and the fear you're going to lose it all and you shouldn't have it all and the anger.

This single mother poignantly describes family conditions familiar to many of us, no matter what our family background. And these conditions become the breeding ground for the next generation's disappointment — "the hurt, the fear, the lack of self-esteem, the fear you're going to lose it all, you shouldn't have it all, the anger." This chapter explores the ways that family pain is passed from generation to generation — even in families without "real craziness" — and considers some strategies for breaking the repetitive cycle.

The prominent Swiss psychoanalyst Alice Miller, whose books on childhood have all been best sellers in Europe, builds an eloquent case for the inevitability of intergenerational constraints — and for the possibility of undoing them. In *The Drama of the Gifted Child* (originally, and more aptly for this discussion, called *Prisoners of Childhood*), she argues that parents unintentionally and unconsciously limit the possibilities for their children because they have neither examined nor mastered their own conflicts and projections. She illuminates the child's inner drama and the drama between the generations this way:

> Probably everybody has a more or less concealed inner chamber that he hides even from himself and in which the props of his childhood

drama are to be found. These props may be his secret delusion, a secret perversion, or quite simply the unmastered aspects of his childhood suffering. The only ones who will certainly gain entrance to this hidden chamber are his children. With them new life comes into it, and the drama is continued.

Just as the child is innocent of the intensity of the drama he has inadvertently stumbled into, so, too, was the parent innocent in his own childhood. The parent never had a chance to play freely with the props of his inner drama and was frightened of them, as his child is now:

> Understandably, [the parent] could not connect [these props] with the familiar figures of father or mother, for, after all, they represented the split-off, unintegrated parts of the parents. But the child cannot experience this contradiction consciously; he simply accepts every-thing and, at the most, develops symptoms. Then, in analysis, the feelings emerge: feelings of terror, of despair and rebellion, of mis-trust but — if it is possible to reconstruct the parents' vicissitudes — also of compassion and reconciliation.

"You can drive the devil out of your garden," Miller sums up, quoting Heinrich Pestalozzi, "but you will find him again in the garden of your son." In psychoanalytic terms, she explains that the split-off and unintegrated parts of his parents have been incorpo-rated emotionally by the child.

When parents listen to these complex and constricting voices and learn to uncover the negative internal images, they can provide an opportunity for integration, reconciliation, and change in the next generation.

Whether the parents of the new generation repeat the patterns of the past by choice or compulsion, by conscious decision or un-conscious oversight, depends in large part on whether, and how well, the new parents have separated from their family of origin and worked out a new self-definition. Where psychoanalysts like Alice Miller see patterns of repetition primarily as an intrapsychic drama — one that takes place in each individual's psyche — family therapists see the repetitions as involving all of the members in a family system.

Sheri Glucoft Wong connects these intergenerational repetitions to individuation: "I think the underlying issue is how individuated the new parents are from their parents. If they're truly individuated from their parents, then they can sort and sift through what happened in childhood and save what is useful and discard what seemed not to work or what doesn't feel right to them. However, it's an unusual person who is that highly conscious."

Few of us have lessons in parenting before we become parents, and our new babies don't come with manuals. We learn our first, most profound, and far-reaching lessons from our parents. These lessons are passed down to us through "emotional genes" — to use the term of Boston family therapist Betty Paul — just as inevitably as our red hair, color blindness, or perfect pitch comes through our biological genes. Especially at times of stress, major or minor — from spilled milk to sibling spats, from broken windows to broken promises — we revert to the responses of our own parents. We use the same shriek or slap or tears or icy turn of cheek whether or not we meant to, whether or not the response worked long ago and often — even more unfathomable — whether or not it feels right now.

Glucoft Wong recalls an amusing and illustrative moment from the sitcom "My Two Dads." The plot concerns two bachelors who each had an affair with the same woman and are now, after the woman's death, charged by the court to raise the daughter each may or may not have fathered. Five minutes after one of the brand new "dads" meets his new charge, he becomes angered. Suddenly he finds himself shaking his finger just the way his father shook a finger at him. "I've been a father for five minutes," he sighs in mock exasperation, "and already I have my dad's finger."

"That is exactly what happens," Glucoft Wong explains. "And what also happens is that the ways we haven't individuated begin to show. For example, we use the affectionate terms our mothers used. We're back in symbiosis again, and it triggers the unconscious and internal symbiosis we had with our parents. If we imitate our parents, we feel tied in to them. If we are determined to do things differently just to be distinct from our parents, then our attachment is still demonstrated by the need to rebel. These rebels think they have individuated, but it is a false individuation. Truly being free means being able to be like our parents in some ways and still know we are our own distinct selves."

Just as we tend to parent as our parents did, we often find ourselves repeating our childhood roles or emotional positions in our
new families. Our place in the family hierarchy may have shifted,
but our role remains the same. Victim or martyr, clown or placater,
we often end up in the same niche that we carved out in our original
family.

Glucoft Wong describes a young mother in therapy who complained that her fifteen-month-old baby bit her. The baby didn't
try this behavior with other caretakers, just with her own mother.
"What would your mother have done to you if you bit her?" Glucoft
Wong asked one day. "I wouldn't have *dared*," the young mother
responded. "So, as much as you're upset," Glucoft Wong offered,
"you must be relieved that your baby is not terrified of you the
way you were terrified of your mother." The therapist's interpretation: this mother is doing the opposite from what her mother did,
but nevertheless she's stuck in the same role. Now she's terrified
of her child rather than of her parent.

We seem especially inclined to treat a child the way we treated
the parent of the same sex. We become intimidated by a daughter
the way we were intimidated by a mother or indulgent of a son
the way we were indulgent of a father. Leah Potts Fisher cites the
example of a single mother who was constantly anxious for her
daughter's well-being. This mother would defer to her daughter's
feelings the same way she had deferred to her mother's. But Fisher
points out, "She also felt rage toward her daughter which she never
allowed herself to feel toward her mother. Now she's setting limits
with her child the way she never dared to with her mother." In
this way our children themselves can guide us to make conscious —
and eventually change — the patterns from the past we unconsciously find ourselves repeating. And as Glucoft Wong puts it,
"Children will push and push and push to free their parents from
their parents' parents."

Why do we repeat with our children the things we vowed to avoid?
Why do we hear ourselves saying to our children the words we
swore we'd never use?

We repeat because we're unconscious. We repeat out of instinct,
out of memory, hazy or painful, encouraging or disabling, out of
a knee-jerk response to the past.

We repeat because we had no other lessons than the ones we learned at our parents' knees. We had no other teachers, we see no other options.

We repeat in an unconscious effort at mastery and control. We repeat the painful episodes of our childhoods in the hope of making sense of them now. We are in a sense doing research into our own pasts. With our repetitions we are asking questions that may remain cruelly unheard for another generation. But our questioning may also lead us to new and healing answers and interventions from a sensitive partner or therapist — or even from a courageous child whose response shows us a new direction.

We also repeat to make the passive active, to *do* instead of *be done to*. We repeat in order not to feel out of control. This time we hope we'll magically create the happy ending we so yearned for as a child.

By repeating what hurt in the past, we are trying to understand the past, ourselves, and our parents. Particularly when there is a history of abuse, suggests family counselor Eliana Gil in *Outgrowing the Pain*, we may try on the role of the abuser, unconsciously trying to understand why the earlier abuse occurred: "I love my wife and I hit her — maybe my dad loved my mom and hit her," we whisper to ourselves, trying to persuade ourselves to believe the false logic.

And if there was terror, neglect, or pathological behavior in our infancy, we may repeat because we now identify with our aggressors, even with the aggression itself. Anna Freud named and illuminated this identification as a defense that forms in childhood. She described how the infant takes in the caretaker's attitude and makes it part of the developing self. The infant tends to resonate with the mood of the caretaker, whether positive or negative, then buries this resonance deep in the unconscious; decades later, when the individual becomes the parent of a new infant, the identification resurfaces. When the caretaker's mood is positive, the identification is a benevolent one. But when the mood is negative, the young child still identifies and makes an unconscious alliance with the very figure who should have protected him but instead did him harm.

We repeat even before we have the words to describe what we are doing. Even in the ways we touch and feed and hold our babies, we repeat the way we felt, the way we were fed and held. An unusual longitudinal study demonstrated the striking correspondence between how an infant is handled and how as a mother she later handles her own infants. For thirty years researchers monitored Monica, observing infant feedings, doll play, adolescent babysitting, and the mothering of her four daughters. Because of a congenital defect in her esophagus, Monica was fed through a tube directly into her stomach from infancy until the defect was repaired at the age of two. For those two years she was fed by her mother and by various hospital personnel during several hospitalizations. Because the tubing was so precarious, she was never held in the intimate face-to-face position most mothers use with healthy infants. And for long periods during her hospital stays, she was rarely held at all.

Strikingly, she handled all four of her own babies (as well as her childhood dolls) the same way. She never held them facing her, but mostly fed them alone with the bottle propped. The intimacy she hadn't known she could not recreate for her own children.

We repeat because we are loyal to our parents with that early, passionate, put-the-parent-on-a-pedestal admiration that all small children feel. "If you like me, then be like me," we think we hear our parents saying. And from childhood forward we will make a huge effort to prove our parents right, even if it means making ourselves wrong. If our parents get irate or drunk or abusive and call us names or hit us or neglect us, we eventually accept that we are lousy good-for-nothings if that will guarantee that our parents still hold the authority, will still magically protect our safety.

When we have children, we may maintain our childhood loyalty to our parents by continuing the name calling or abuse or neglect, ensuring that we will not outdo our parents as parents. We will do anything possible to "preserve the parent" — in Maurice Vanderpol's phrase — even if that means undermining our own self-interest or the interests of our children. Family therapists Ivan Boszormenyi-Nagy and Geraldine Spark call these transgenerational underpinnings "invisible loyalties" and caution families to tally and resolve the "unpaid emotional debts" that may otherwise haunt them for generations.

Over the years, we may find that loyalty to our parents conflicts with loyalty to our children. If we remain loyal to our parents, instinctively repeating their harsh or damaging words and attitudes, we may suddenly see our children groaning under the accrued weight of past generations. Sometimes years, even decades, into being a parent, our compassion for our children (and for the children we once were) catches up with us. Reliving our own childhood hurts through our children's poignant eyes, we may at last experience our painful and long-forgotten reactions that we were unable, in some deep sense, to experience at the time. Perhaps an all-too-familiar flinch after a punishment or a frightening withdrawal suddenly reminds us of the promises we made as children to treat our own children more kindly. That may be the occasion when we realize at last the necessity for change, both for our children's sake and for our own. That may be the time when we are first able to use our adult wisdom to help the inner child of our past and the children we are raising today.

Then how do we take the first steps toward change? How do we review and reevaluate our own childhoods once we become parents? How can we carry on what we enjoyed, alter what hurt, improve what was flawed, discard or disregard what no longer applies? How do we begin to make the unconscious conscious and turn stumbling blocks into stepping stones to more effective parenting? How can we let the very words we swore we'd never repeat become cues to what we most hope to change? These are the questions that underlie the rest of this book.

First and most powerfully, we change when we remember what it *felt* like to be a child, when we reexperience the feelings long buried under the glossy veneer of memory. This means recalling not just the cold fact of neglect but the feelings of terror and anxiety that went with it; not just the harsh reality of punishment undeserved but the feelings of shame or worthlessness or rage that were there — and buried — too. From her extensive and groundbreaking clinical work with severely pathological families, child psychotherapist Selma Fraiberg has observed, "We can report that memory for the events of childhood abuse, tyranny, and desertion was available in explicit and chilling detail. *What was not remembered was the associative affective experience.*" For most of Fraiberg's seriously troubled families, the wrenching feelings beneath the memories were not available.

But in the safety of the therapeutic relationship, Fraiberg's patients were able to recover those long-hidden feelings of anxiety, grief, shame, and self-abasement. By working through this painful childhood legacy, Fraiberg's patients were spared the need to inflict their own childhood pain upon their children. "With the reexperiencing of childhood suffering, along with the memories," Fraiberg concluded, "each of these young mothers was able to say, 'I would never want that to happen to my child.' "

Remembering these early childhood feelings, Fraiberg and many other clinicians believe, allows parents to break the cycle. And Fraiberg singles out the many parents who "have themselves lived tormented childhoods [but] who do not inflict their pain upon their children": "These are the parents who say explicitly, or in effect, 'I remember what it was like. . . . I remember how afraid I was when my father exploded. . . . I remember how I cried when they took me and my sister away to live in that home. . . . I would never let my child go through what I went through."

Many of us can begin to retrieve these early feelings and change the scripts for our new families without the rigors of therapy. We can recreate the inner drama of the past by incorporating a variety of memory jogs into our everyday lives. We can use photographs, family stories and memorabilia, tools borrowed from family therapy, and a variety of imaginative imagery to get in touch with our own childhoods, sorting back through memory for the positive pictures we hope to repeat and the negative images we hope to discard.

We can look at childhood photographs and try to recreate the scenes and moods that surrounded them. Was that a genuine smile at our costume birthday party, or was it just plastered on our face to please the camera? Were we exhilarated on our first pair of skis — or were we scared to death that we couldn't keep up with the rest of the family?

We can interview family members, asking them crucial questions about their journey and our own. We can compare notes — and realities — with siblings and cousins, enlarging our perceptions of past events in light of new information. We can trace the patterns from one generation to the next by creating the genograms described in Chapter 2, easing blame as we see events in the larger context of many generations. We can follow the shifts in family dynamics from our childhood homes to our present ones by assembling the family snapshots described in Chapter 3.

Instead of just recording the first step, first word, first lock of hair snipped off in a standard-issue baby book, we can weave in our own recollections with our impressions of our children. How do our feelings about our baby's milestones recall our feelings about our own first day of school, first trips to the doctor or on an airplane? And what do we remember of our parents' responses to these turning points and how their reactions made us feel?

We can try an imaginary journey back to our original family home, as Fran Litman does with parents in her workshops at the Wheelock Center for Parenting Studies in Boston. Was it a big house or small, tidy or messy, serene or chaotic? What do we remember of our room and how we felt there? Or we can draw portraits of our families then and now, as Maurice Vanderpol does with his students, then pick five words that characterize each family group. What are the resonances from then to now? How do our images — faces, expressions, body language, and groupings — change from portrait to portrait, and how do they remain the same?

In a mothers' group I joined when Nate was small, all ten of us were at first overwhelmed by the pressures of new motherhood and then increasingly struck by the memories that flooded us as we began to define ourselves as mothers both linked to and different from our own. As the months went on and the first postpartum fog lifted, many of us sought ways to make sense of this shower of memories. By tuning in to the feelings behind the memories, we also hoped to make them more accessible to interpretation or change. Several of us began to keep motherhood journals, tracing both the details of our babies' development and the details of our development as mothers. Rereading this journal, I mark how many entries end in midthought and midsentence, as my contemplative time was interrupted by my baby waking from a nap. But for many of us the emotional rawness of this early period was conducive to making some leaps between our responses to our babies and our memories of our mothers' responses to us.

One mother in the group dug even deeper and went back to an "emotional autobiography" she had written as part of a group therapy program years before. The autobiography consisted of a long string of vignettes from her childhood, each documenting a particular emotion and the scene that engendered it. "At four, I felt very left out and overlooked when my brother was born and all attention turned to him," she wrote. "At eight, I felt very confused and lonely when my grandfather got seriously ill and no one took the time to explain to me what was going on." This mother had long since processed these memories and the slights and angers that surrounded them. But rereading this autobiography at a time when her own child's childhood opened innocently ahead of her re-evoked the old feelings and put her in touch with scenes she hoped to recreate and those she hoped to change.

By experimenting with a variety of autobiographical imagery and writing, we can slowly uncover the landscapes of our past, bringing to light what was hidden and therefore restricting. Certainly joyful memories may emerge (our excitement at the Macy's Thanksgiving Day parade, our thrill at a sweet-sixteen surprise party), but so, too, may the painful ones, long repressed or denied.

Don Elium, family counselor and lecturer at John F. Kennedy University in Orinda, California, explains in his workshops, which he calls "Healing the Wounded Parent and the Wounded Child": "The basic reason we recreate negative patterns is that we're denying. And generational cycles are passed on because the pain hurts so bad, it has to be repressed and denied. Then our denial creates blind spots. 'I'll never control my kids the way my parents controlled me' we may promise, but then we do, anyway, by wanting them to be happy. When we deny that we'll become our parents, we do anyway — in spades."

As his students in parenting workshops struggle to make the unconscious conscious, Elium recommends having compassion for the past and begins to prescribe new behavior. In an exercise he calls "Cocktail Party," Elium asks workshop participants to attend a pretend party, acting as if they were their own parents. As they field cocktail party questions and initiate chitchat with strangers, they get an immediate gut sense of their parents' personality quirks, assets, and foibles. They begin to experience *from the inside* the things their parents couldn't control, the things they could or couldn't give.

From that exercise, Elium shifts the perspective to a process he calls "Naming the Wound." "What was the wound inflicted or crime perpetrated by your parents on you?" he asks workshop participants. "What was your response or reactive behavior? And what is the new behavior you need that you can now prescribe for yourself?" Drawing on his own family history, Elium names his wound as "being cut to the bone with criticism"; his response was "hiding — but in a flamboyant way"; and his new behavior with his children is "straightforwardness — saying what I see." In this way, Elium believes, parents can turn past wounds into healing steps for their new families.

Sandra Oriel, a Chicago therapist, also counsels the parents she works with that healing begins with acknowledging the wounded child in our own psyche. "Until we can feel compassion for ourselves," she observes, "we can't give our own children that unconditional love that allows imperfections." An exercise she created for her clients begins with inviting the childhood self into the room and describing who they see. "Often when young John appears, adult John finds he doesn't like him too well. He finds him too shy and tongue-tied. We seem to identify with the adults in our past and reflect their feelings toward us as children." The next step involves having a dialogue with this inner child and beginning to make a positive connection with him. Finally, Oriel asks her clients to fantasize that they are the Good Parents they wished they had. She suggests they talk to their inner child in a series of positive affirmations — all the words they longed for but never heard as children. "You are wonderful just the way you are." "You can make lots of mistakes." "You're a beautiful, competent, loving child."

"Gradually we have to build a model of a good parent," Oriel explains. "Sometimes I'll role-play both the bad and the good parent. We'll imagine that little Jane spilled something. First I'll play the stern parent and tell her, 'You're clumsy. Watch what you're doing.' Then I'll play the nurturing parent and say, 'It's okay to make mistakes. I'll help you clean it up.' The first way makes the child feel bad about herself; the other way helps her blossom."

By reclaiming the inner emotional life of our childhood, we are able to allow our children a happier childhood as well. When I asked on the questionnaire, "What are the most important things you learned from becoming a parent?" one mother answered, first, "I learned that children are not miniature adults and need to be able to act like children," and second, "Not to worry about every little thing. I've become a more relaxed and spontaneous person." By coming to terms with the limitations of our own childhood, we gain more freedom both for ourselves and for our children.

Then, without becoming envious or competitive, we can allow our children to experience things we missed out on or feelings we couldn't express as children. If, for example, we have confronted our disappointment that our birthdays were never lavishly celebrated, we'll be more comfortable planning a grand birthday bash for our son. Or the next time our daughter demands applause for her cartwheels up and down the kitchen floor, we'll be quicker to clap if we have recognized our dismay that our childhood antics were dismissed as "showing off." And without so many ancient strings attached, our joy at our children's happy times may make up for some of the joy we missed the first time around. Growing up again with our own children, we may find that it's never too late to have a happy childhood.

Although the route to change largely involves coming to terms with the past, fine tuning can be done in the present. If our present family style is not working, we can change it by recognizing that there are other options. We can tune in to the wisdom of other parents either informally, in casual playground or dinner party conversations, or more formally, in parenting groups or workshops. Hearing that another parent is struggling with a similar problem — a child who has nightmares or is afraid of school — and has come up with a workable solution often is the impetus we need to implement that solution or come up with one more tailored to our own family's needs.

And many times just brainstorming with our mate will generate a new and helpful perspective on family issues. Since every marriage merges two family styles and histories, a husband may uncover a memory or maneuver from his own family that will be just the trick needed to get the family unstuck from a destructive pattern. Maybe our highly involved mothering style, adapted from our own mother, has turned from nurturing to stifling. Sometimes a mate with a more laissez-faire style and history may provide the lightening up that the family needs.

Since it is impossible, and surely exhausting, to change every corner of family life at once, we can make our efforts count the most if we focus our intentions, shape our goals, and set priorities. We can't fight every battle on every front at once — not with our children, our parents, or the ghosts of our past. So each of us needs to choose the issues that are the most crucial, the ones we most want to change — and least want to pass along to our grandchildren. Are we struggling to undo the conspiracy of silence that surrounded a parent who drank too much? Do we want to find a style of authority based on limits set lovingly rather than with verbal or physical abuse? Do we want to give our children a sense of pride in themselves, even if we still feel insecure and self-doubting — and raise our own self-esteem in the process?

Three chapters of this book explore the intergenerational parenting issues that I, and many parents I spoke with, found most complex and pressing: separation and closeness (finding comfortable intimacy with our children and comfortable separation from them), anger (setting firm but loving limits), and self-esteem and success (nurturing self-esteem and supporting achievement without getting hooked into it). But all parents must set goals based on the needs of their families and their own histories.

Once we've set the agenda and singled out the issues we'd most like to influence, we can begin to change by replaying and editing the internal tapes of our past. For the mother who, like her parents, uses punishment more than she wants to or the father who, like his father, finds himself being too remote, carefully listening to the tapes of present and past can provide important clues to change and hints to instilling new habits.

William Womack, a child psychiatrist in Seattle and associate professor at the University of Washington School of Medicine, has worked extensively with internal visual imagery and suggests two effective monitoring techniques. In the first, he suggests that a parent play back in his mind a troubling interaction with a child.

If he hears himself saying or doing something his parents said or did which he swore he'd never repeat, simply understanding the connections with the past and remembering how he felt as a child can help a lot. Often a parent can then monitor himself and correct what he is doing as it happens. Usually after a dozen or more of these self-corrections, the parent can change his unwanted automatic reactions and replace them with more consciously chosen responses.

Another of Womack's suggestions, to a parent who finds herself overwhelmed and very angry at a child, for example, is to ask herself if anything similar happened in her own childhood and then to make an internal picture of how she felt. "It's like having a painting where all the colors are dark and disorganized and all run together," the mother might respond. "I get sad because nothing is right." After visualizing the picture from her past, the mother is then asked to change it so that it feels "right." The new picture might have brighter colors and more structure and organization. As she is reshaping the picture in her mind, Womack asks her to observe if her attitude about the past is shifting as well, if she is feeling a greater sense of empowerment and possibility. Then he asks her to rate her feeling of change on a scale of one to ten, so that even the smallest increments of change can be recorded and appreciated. For most of us, changes in family life do occur in small jumps of daily improvement rather than in grand, all-inclusive leaps.

Although the examination of our childhood involves exposing negative patterns, we must also study and integrate what was positive, helpful, and nurturing. Without this pivotal healing step, we do a great disservice to our children, our parents, and ourselves. Some parents find it easy to recognize and embrace the loving legacy they wish to carry on. Others may want to shift their perspective on the past to redefine the meaning of past events and make them more accessible to change. "My mother did a lot better than I thought she did," a young mother might admit, reframing her appraisal of the past after a few years of struggling to raise her own children. Or "My father loved us deeply, even if he couldn't always put his feelings into words," a father might realize after making his own hesitant attempts to show affection.

Other families may need to look beneath surface behaviors at the well-meant motives that at times are obscured. The mother who raged at her children may have done so only because she loved them so fiercely and connected with them so intimately. The father who removed himself in long hours and late nights of work may have believed that being the good provider was the surest way to prove his love.

In an interview about the intergenerational concerns of this book, pediatrician T. Berry Brazelton sounds a caution to look beneath the surface of family behaviors and to balance the negative with the positive.

"Get rid of the deficit model. We can all remember the failures and the times we were miserable, but then we don't go on to see the mechanisms that led to those occasions and may become ours, too." Brazelton remembers chiding Selma Fraiberg, who stresses the importance of airing out old childhood ghosts in order to be freer, more flexible, and loving with one's own children. " 'Everyone remembers the ghosts,' " he recalls saying to Fraiberg, " 'but do they remember what the ghosts were trying to achieve?' Ghosts are the symbol of an old hang-up, but what are the processes that underlie it?"

If looking at the processes that underlie our parents' behaviors is one preliminary to coming to terms with the past, then examining our adaptations and additions to these processes is a crucial way to initiate change. I give Brazelton the example of a mother whose own parent had a violent temper and who therefore fears exploding at her own child. How would he counsel this mother to cope with and modify her anger and set up different patterns of discipline with her own child?

"She might get angry at her child and sound like a fisherwoman," Brazelton answers, "but then she can make up to her child, because she knows what that would have meant to her. Each generation adds its own new layers."

How each generation adds its new layers to the past is the concern of the next chapter, in which I draw on stories from the many passionate responses to my questionnaires from around the country.

5

Four Parenting Styles of Repetition and Change: Traditionalists, Rebels, Compensators, and Synthesizers

Maybe all that my verses have expressed
is simply what was never allowed to be;
only what was hidden and suppressed
from woman to woman, from family to
    family.

They say that in my house tradition
    was
the rule by which one did things
    properly;
they say the women of my mother's
    house
were always silent — yes, it well may
    be.

Sometimes my mother felt longings to
    be free,
but then a bitter wave rose to her eyes
and in the shadows she wept.
And all this — caustic, betrayed,
    chastised —
all this that in her soul she tightly kept,
I think that, without knowing, I have
    set it free.

*Alfonsina Storni (translated from the
Spanish by Mark Smith-Soto)*

As parents, what do we hope to repeat from our own childhoods and what do we work to change? How do our childhood memories and experiences weave their spell on our hopes and dreams for our own children?

As I reviewed the responses to my questionnaire, searching for patterns of repetition and change between the generations, four distinct styles of parenting emerged: Traditionalists, Rebels, Compensators, and Synthesizers. The Traditionalists praise their parents' parenting style, admire the past, and consciously choose to repeat it. The Rebels criticize their parents' choices and swear they will do the opposite with their children — but often unconsciously repeat the past in spite of themselves. The Compensators vow to give their children what they lacked, what they wish their parents had given them. And the Synthesizers consciously choose what from the best of the past to repeat, what to modify, and what to change.

Appraising each of these styles, I asked several key questions. How well has each parent separated from his or her own parents and defined a style for the new family? And how clear are the boundaries that separate the generations? With whom does each parent identify — his parents, his child, or some combination of both? And what, psychologically speaking, are the gifts and risks, benefits and losses, for parents and children in each group? The answers suggested a continuum, with the Traditionalists the least differentiated from and most identified with their parents; the Rebels just slightly more differentiated and still very parent-identified; the Compensators significantly more differentiated and highly identified with their children; and the Synthesizers the most differentiated and the best able to incorporate their parents' perspective, their children's, and their own.

As in any framework of this sort, the categories are only guidelines and flexible ones at that. Two partners in a marriage with totally different parenting styles may work out a hybrid that's right for their own family. One parent may take a different approach to each child, given the children's particular needs, the differing chemistry between them, or the buttons each child pushes from the parent's past. And three grown children from the same family of origin may interpret their parents' behavior in totally different ways. Something a parent did years ago might be admired by one child, hated by another, ignored or denied by a third. Out of the same family three different approaches will appear in the next generation.

Or a parent may adopt different parenting styles with one child depending on the child's developmental stage, the issues — or even moods. A parent may be more conflicted about one issue — say, setting limits — and adopt a Rebel stance there, but more conscious and confident about another — say, nurturing self-esteem — and take a Synthesizer approach there. At different times in raising my own children, I have seen in myself the loyalty to my own parents of the Traditionalist, the exasperation of the Rebel, the wish fulfillment of the Compensator, and the discrimination of the Synthesizer. Seeing my own decisions along a continuum like this has both deepened my understanding of the choices I make as a parent and given me a greater sense of flexibility and inventiveness.

The Traditionalist has the strongest sense of continuity with the past. She is the serene and efficient young mother in her kilt and Fair Isle sweater, juggling home and career. Her two children are cuddling next to her, dressed in their matching tartans and shetlands. The Traditionalist father is the one who steps out of the L.L. Bean catalogue to hike up the same White Mountains trails he hiked with his own father, carrying a pocket knife of his father's and a pocket watch from his grandfather. His younger is in a backpack, and the other walks cheerfully next to him, singing Dad's old camp songs.

The Traditionalists define themselves by their deep admiration for the past and their commitment to preserving it. Many would describe themselves — as one questionnaire respondent did — as being "as American as apple pie." They carry on the customs and celebrations of their childhoods out of joy and respect for what they remember fondly and wish lovingly to recreate. The new mother bakes Christmas cookies from her own mother's recipes and roasts the Thanksgiving turkey, which her husband then carves, using the same sure strokes his own father did.

The Traditionalists' memories are usually warm and glowing, stressing the steady nurturance of their childhood homes:

> ► I remember being awakened by an earache at about age five or six. My mother spent the entire night rocking me and singing. Leaning against her, I felt warm and safe. We were all alone and it was a special evening.

> ► Birthdays in my family growing up were a big deal — breakfast in bed, whatever you want for supper, cake, candles, sometimes a party, presents. Christmas is the high point of

the year — tree, dinner, Santa Claus, presents, singing, decorating the house, church, friends, etc.

Domestic life and family spirit are as precious to the Traditionalists as their grandmother's Wedgwood or the boxes of holiday decorations saved for generations. They have a secure feeling that their parents enjoyed being parents, and they appreciate this legacy and will contentedly carry it on. Both parents in these families cherish their home life — husbands often valuing the family over professional status or achievement, wives stressing the pleasures of hearth and home whether or not they also work. Often, if these mothers can choose whether or not to work, they defer their professional plans until their children are in school:

> ▶ My mother did just what I plan to do. She was always home with us and started nursing school when I was eleven. I remember helping her study and how proud we all were when she graduated.

Thrift and religion are two cornerstones of the solid house the Traditionalists build — values shared with the parent generation:

> ▶ Our (my husband's and mine) attitudes are very similar to our parents'. Saving money for college and retirement is very important to us. We don't buy anything, except a house, on credit. I keep a good accounting of our monthly expenses and we set money aside each paycheck for savings.

And here a mother describes the overlaps in values and interests between her parents and her in-laws, and the two interlocking triangles that bind the generations together:

> ▶ My folks and my husband's folks are very close friends and would have been even if we hadn't introduced them. Both families are very loving and caring, outdoor oriented, service oriented, and both moms stayed home to raise the kids. The biggest difference is religion. While my father's religion was

a sailboat, my husband's parents, especially my mother-in-law, are deeply involved in their church.

Of the four parenting styles I examined, the Traditionalists, by their own definition, are the most closely identified with their parents — in a positive way, of course. Fathers talk about their own fathers' steadfastness, patience, willingness to take the time to bring their children into the wider world. Mothers remember their own mothers' loving nurturance, comforting caretaking, genuine interest in their children's world. A mother of two daughters, ages five and three, speaks for many Traditionalists in this paean to her parents and her commitment to carrying on their good work:

> ▶ All in all, I'd say my parents did a wonderful job. I just took it for granted that everyone had such a happy, loving childhood and a great relationship with their parents as adults, but I know that isn't so. When people comment that I'm a good mother, I always respond that I learned from one of the best — my Mom. And I think about that a lot in my relationship with my daughters, that they are learning mothering from me, and just exactly what do I want to teach them? That thought can diffuse a temper quickly or give me the patience to sit for half an hour so my youngest can "do it myself."

Respect and courtesy are buzzwords for the Traditionalists. They felt deeply the respect their parents showed them as children and now want to return that respect in kind. Our society is one of the few in which children don't invariably honor their elders, but the Traditionalists are old-fashioned in that respect for parents is a cornerstone of their relationship. But, as products of a more self-directed era, they must grapple with accommodating to the demands of both past and present. Here a mother of a young daughter tries to balance the two poles of selflessness and self-interest:

> ▶ What I most want to repeat from the past: My parents (especially my mother) respected other people, found the good in other people, trusted other people, made other people feel

good about themselves because of their genuine interest. By their behavior, my parents taught me to do the same.

What I most want to avoid: Perhaps because of the above, my parents often deferred their own desires or benefits to those of other people. I want to teach my daughter to look out for herself and stand up for her own rights and happiness when it is appropriate.

And here a mother of two young sons vows to repeat the respect she remembers from her own childhood:

> ▶ We were a happy family growing up, and I want my family to be the same way. We weren't afraid of our parents but had respect for them. Our feelings and opinions were always considered, which taught us courtesy to others. I feel very strongly that respect breeds respect.

Not surprisingly, given the mellow memories, the shared values, and the mutual respect, most Traditionalists describe their parents as friends and confidants. If anything, having children has given the Traditionalists an even keener respect for their parents and a deeper appreciation of what they went through. The mother of two sons continues:

> ▶ My parents have become more my friends. I visit because I want to, not because they're my parents and I should. They give me a lot of support and are always there with advice when I need it, yet not giving it unless I ask — like any good friend.

Beyond their avowals of respect and friendship between the generations, the Traditionalists have a tendency — not always a healthy one — to idealize and romanticize their parents and the flawless fabric of the past:

> ▶ Although she disagrees, I remember my mother always having time for us. I never remember her cleaning, but the house always seemed spotless.

Not only can putting parents on a pedestal create an unreal ideal to live up to, it can also serve to camouflage a host of behaviors, from mere human foibles to severe neglect. Sometimes admiration can mask or deny the real but untenable pain of the past. Family counselor Don Elium tells of a mother who came to one of his sessions insisting that her childhood was "great." But as her story unfolded, it became clear to the group — and eventually to her — that her world was obscured by rose-colored glasses, once necessary for survival but finally possible to remove. Says Elium, "Every Saturday night, she watched her brother being beaten by her father."

This extreme case — admiration used to cover up a reality too horrible to bear — points out the Traditionalist's shadow side. Many a confused Traditionalist has come to a therapist's office feeling depressed or suicidal and insisting that her childhood was great, her family perfect. The Traditionalists' self-definition depends in large part on identification with their parents and loyalty to them. When they were small, their very life depended on this identification and loyalty. They simply had to believe that their parents were right, were admirable, and had their best interests at heart — whether or not this was actually the case. Acknowledging the reality of parental behavior means letting go of typically child-like black-and-white thinking and replacing it with a more mature ability to distinguish the inevitable shades of gray that color the day-to-day behavior of parents — and of all of us.

This acknowledgment, in turn, requires differentiation from the parent generation — something Traditionalists often have a hard time working out. In the Traditionalists' warmly positive regard for and identification with their parents lie both the gift and the risk of their parenting style. The gift is their dedication to preserving and passing on to their children the best of the past, the rich resources from which they now take their own strength as parents. But the risk is their failure to differentiate from their parents and to avoid the thorny but necessary task of working out separate identities.

Sometimes this failure to differentiate means also that they cannot allow their own children to separate from them. And at times, in their fervor to transplant their ideal remembered childhood into their own children's garden, they run the risk of treating their children "generically." The Traditionalists may overlook their children's very real need to be treated as individuals, to be respected and admired for themselves, not for the flattering reflections they cast back to the past.

Separation tends to be a particularly charged issue for the Traditionalists, as it may have been for their parents before them. Boundaries are fuzzy and enmeshed; the generations live like "one big happy family," and the younger generation does not challenge the elders' rules. Here a mother describes her struggles around separation from her young son by remembering the discomfort of an early separation from her family and her parents' extreme reaction to it:

> ▶ I remember going away to camp, which I always enjoyed, and one year not receiving any mail. My parents thought this would keep me from getting homesick, but I felt very forgotten. I suppose that this probably has influenced me as a parent. When my four-year-old does go away with my parents now for a weekend, I try to call to say good-night and always hope he's not missing me too badly.

Another mother confesses that she hopes her daughter will grow up to reflect her image, pushing away the unwanted reality that her daughter is indeed a separate person:

> ▶ My daughter's face and legs are shaped like my mother-in-law's. That's okay, but I have fleeting fears that that means when she's an adult she'll look like my mother-in-law. I don't want that to be the case, because I want her more "in my image."

Still, for some Traditionalists, observing their children's drive for independence is a necessary and healing reminder of the inevitability of separation between the generations. Their own children may push them to a separation they could not successfully complete with their own parents:

▶ My major turning point was going to college. I went out of state specifically to get away from home and not feel like I could go home every weekend. I wanted my independence. The major turning point for my daughter and me was weaning. She did it herself, just stopped one day (at thirteen months), and I wasn't ready to stop. I guess she wanted her independence!

In their very real and pressing daily demands, children may help their parents complete and transform some unfinished business from the past. And though the resulting family life may be more offbeat than their original storybook vision, the new traditions and texture of family life may ultimately be more satisfying for all.

If the Traditionalist is the parent who repeats the past by choice, the Rebel is the one who repeats it by default. The Rebel listed in her childhood journal all the outrages her parents perpetrated — sent her to her room without supper, humiliated her in front of friends, grounded her for weeks — and accompanied each charge with a solemn promise never to do the same to her own future children. Her adolescence was often a stormy one, her young adulthood spent in far-flung places with lovers carefully chosen for their "inappropriateness." But when she marries and has children of her own, she often finds herself becoming the parent she most hoped to avoid — her own. Suddenly the style she most criticized, the discipline she most abhorred, in fact, the exact words she swore she would never utter, are creeping into her household as insidiously as the furry mold growing on the leftovers stashed away in her refrigerator.

At first glance the Rebel seems to be everything the Traditionalist is not: critical of parents rather than admiring, differentiated rather than symbiotically linked, running in the opposite direction from the parent generation rather than following in its footsteps. But the differentiation turns out to be a false one, and the bold promises, bravura. The Rebel is as deeply and unconsciously linked to the past as the Traditionalist is. The boundaries between generations are often as undefined but are guarded by accusation instead of compliance. The Rebel rarely begins a statement about the past with a grounded "I" point of view. Rather, she leaps over into her parents' space. "You never gave me ballet lessons," she might accuse, not "I never told you how much I wanted lessons."

Rebels are often blithely unaware of what to outsiders is obvious, as this mother of two girls points out about her former husband:

> ► My husband could literally interchange positions with his father in his working/parenting. Doing exactly as his father and without knowing the things he disliked in his father are exactly what he is doing.

After years of going out of her way to make choices contrary to her mother's, this mother in her late forties with three grown children acknowledges how inexorably the generations are tied together:

> ► I think that, like it or not, we become more and more like our parents. Every way from repeating their actual phrases to their global philosophies. Now that I'm the age that I remember my mother as the mother of teenage me, things become clearer. My brother, though a very different person from my dad, as I am from my mom, is looking and sounding more like our dad every day. Another rather sobering fact is that I am the only person left alive who remembers back and can see the similarities. Recently I read my maternal grandmother's diaries from her motherhood years. I hardly knew her; but there were my mother's origins. How many of my mom's words, phrases, reactions, nervous complaints had been Grandmother's? There is no way to know now; they are all dead. But the glimpse at the past that the diaries gave me confirms my definite sense of this continuum.

The Rebel typically defines the parent as a negative role model and strives to do with his own children just the opposite of what his parents did with him. If the Rebel's family of origin was churchgoing and devout, his new family will be atheistic and laissez-faire. If his family of origin was outdoorsy and macho, his new family will spend weekends at art museums or catching the latest films. But not surprisingly, this "negative identity" often backfires.

In a study by Sampson, Messinger, and Towne of schizophrenic women, some women assumed a "negative identity" as a possible alternative to becoming like their own mothers. "Such women," the study cautioned,

> attempted to perform the roles of housewives, wives and mothers in a manner opposite to that of their own mothers. However, autonomy of action was still largely lacking, since they had adapted all their decisions about house-keeping or childcare from their own mothers. All too often, negative identity fails to achieve its purpose and the woman finds herself experiencing the very crisis of identity she had hoped to avoid.

If the Traditionalist's perception of the past is often romanticized by rose-colored glasses, the Rebel's perception is often clouded by dark shades. Looking backward, the Traditionalist tends to exaggerate the best and camouflage the worst; the Rebel does just the opposite. Neither of these parenting styles is highly conscious, but the Rebel's choices especially are often obscured and limited by her own negativity.

Maurice Vanderpol describes a revealing workshop exercise in which he asks parents to draw a portrait of their childhood family and then of their present family and label each portrait with five characterizing adjectives. In one woman's family-of-origin portrait her mother and father are off to one side playing golf; she and her sister are standing by the family house. The artist draws her own head in pencil; all the rest is drawn in crayon. Her words for this scene: "separateness, responsibility, independence, self-sufficiency, peer groups." Her current portrait shows a tennis court where she and her husband play tennis on opposite sides of the net. This time her words are "learning, self-confidence, loving, caring."

But, suggests Vanderpol, despite the new labels, she has really repeated the past. There's still no real home base, still a sense of separateness and isolation. "Her father was an interior decorator who would decorate a house and then leave. She's just now awakening to the lacks of her original family. She doesn't really know what a home is." For the Rebel, lack of awareness often begins as a childhood defense against a family scene too painful to tolerate. But when this defense is continued in adulthood, the Rebel often ends up recreating the reality she is running from.

Sometimes the Rebel's oppositional stance boomerangs in the next generation. Family therapist Betty Stone describes a client whose father had no respect for college and wouldn't finance his son's education. This man, a classic Rebel, sharply resented his father, and when his own son turned eighteen, insisted that the son go to college. This father thought he had reversed his own father's position, but he was being just as controlling as his father had been with him.

Nothing describes the Rebel's boomerang more succinctly than the famous Jules Feiffer cartoon. "I hated the way I turned out," moans the intense and world-weary heroine, "so everything my mother did with me I tried to do differently with my Jennifer. Mother was possessive, so I encouraged independence. Mother was manipulative. I have been open. Mother was evasive. I have been decisive. Now my work is done. Jennifer is grown. The exact image of my mother."

In the Rebel's fervor to escape the tangling web of the previous generation, she often traps herself — and her children — all the more stickily. Explains family therapist Norman Ackerman, "An overfunctioning parent is often simply repeating the early experience of having grown up with an underfunctioning parent. The parent may rationalize this behavior by saying that it is a deliberate attempt not to make the same mistakes as the grandparent, to spare the third generation the pain of the second and to 'prevent my child from having the same hang-ups as me.' The result is that the third generation turns out to be like the first."

More than any other parent, the Rebel is still separating from her own parents. In this struggle she may be slightly more conscious than the Traditionalist who has not even considered that separation is a prerequisite for adult life. Despite their protestations to the contrary, Rebels are strongly identified with their parents. Here the mother of a new infant struggles to evaluate both a negative and a positive identification with her own mother and describes a confrontation with her mother on the battleground of separation:

▶ My mother is very nervous, a real worrywart. I claimed that I wouldn't worry, that I'd be more relaxed and mellow and yet . . . worrying just comes into you. Once you have things to worry about, you can't stop. My mother is always worrying about my baby: "Is he cold?" "Don't you think you should feed him?" "Is he getting enough milk?" Now I worry when I leave him that something terrible is going to happen. Once I told my mother to let me be a mother and learn to make the mistakes myself. It hurt her feelings, but I'm glad that I did it. Things have been better since then. But my mother is also a warm, loving person, and I try to be that way. She's very generous and willing to help. I hope I'll be that way, too.

Rebels are also sometimes excessively tied to their children, particularly their negative attributes. Two mothers speak:

▶ My son is most like me — shy, nervous, withdrawn, unassertive and passive. I guess I'm sorry about it.

▶ My son reminds me so much of myself because he is sensitive, quiet in his nature, easy-going, but timid when it comes to asserting his own feelings.

Given this push and pull between the generations, the relationship between grandparents and grandchildren also tends to be strained in Rebel families. Here a mother of two young sons describes the complex intergenerational identifications that therapy unraveled:

▶ My mother and I didn't always have the best relationship — I'm sure it's because we're so much alike. I feel that with the help of therapy I have been able to curb some of the not-so-good aspects of parenting that were ingrained from my mother raising me and that I then continued while raising my first son. He and I have very similar personalities, so I see a lot of myself in him. Our relationship was in pretty bad shape until he started therapy. We clashed a lot! I withdrew from him quite a bit. The more I withdrew, the more he'd act up — a vicious circle. We still have our moments, but we're friends again.

And finally she acknowledges the frayed connection between her mother and her older son:

> ► My eldest son especially has been tough for my mother to build a relationship with (probably because he's so much like her) and has not been an easy child to get to know.

Intellectually, Rebels may reject their parents' style or values, but emotionally they may often find themselves still tied to both. Whether the issue is religion or social life, protectiveness or limit setting, Rebels may sing one tune to the world but hear a different one inside. Weighing the intellectual and emotional legacy from his father, the father of a grown son and still young daughter describes the balance he has struck:

> ► I'm intellectually different from my parents, but turned out emotionally like my father. I didn't escape being his son. I'm nervous, but I let my daughter do things anyway. Whereas my father wouldn't let us do things. "You'll get hurt," he'd say. I deal with my concerns on my own.

Parent educator Fran Litman, the mother of children now grown, remembers when she and her husband were trying to create rituals for their new family and struggling with the conflict between head and heart:

> ► My husband and I had decided we would not replicate our families' style of Judaism. We began an unaffiliated Sunday school and designed a new curriculum for our children. Still, when Yom Kippur came around, I wanted everyone to come together just as we had in my childhood. Emotionally, I still really wanted what I remembered from my own childhood, even though intellectually I had rejected it. I realized when I started to cry how important it was to me. Now I realize that

you live what you learn — though not always on a cognitive level.

If separation is the most highly charged issue for the Traditionalists, anger and limit setting are the most explosive issues for the Rebels. Often raised in homes where anger was uncontrolled and punishment excessive, Rebels remember their own fury at the injustices they felt but could not correct. Many of them struggle to find a way of setting limits and establishing family harmony without resorting to the outrages of the past. A mother remembers the vicious cycle of punishment and resistance from her own childhood:

▶ I experienced a lot of anger at the authority forced on me as a child. I never liked feeling as if I were under someone else's control and found that if I were demanded to do something "or else," it was always found to be deficient and more force was used. I would get even angrier at whoever was using the force — and at myself for not doing what *they* expected. It took a long time, and after some self-imposed painful experiences, I accepted that I was allowing my anger to blind me. When I stopped being angry at myself for being a failure, I also stopped allowing anyone to have authority over *my* determination of success or failure.

Another mother remembers a similar cycle of authority and resistance to it — and a moment of teenage rebellion that had far-reaching repercussions:

▶ My father told me once out of the clear blue sky I couldn't see the boy I was seeing anymore, a boy I later married at eighteen. I told my father he couldn't tell me who to see and who not to see. He was drunk, so he let it slide and never said another word. I almost wish he had.

Later, after divorcing this youthful partner and marrying again, she was determined to break the angry cycle of her past. Like many Rebels, she took seriously the challenge of trying to find a new approach to anger and limit setting in her new family, one that would allow everyone to express a full range of feelings and be accepted:

> ▶ What I want to avoid is not allowing my children to feel free in their own home to show their emotions, whether it's happiness or anger. I can remember always having to hold anger inside because we were not allowed to express our angry emotions in my childhood home. Now it's very important to me to be able to let my children express their anger; it's a natural emotion that everyone feels at times, including parents. We have tried very hard to allow our children this freedom and to teach them constructive ways of showing anger.

Other Rebel parents speak of similar efforts to hammer out a new family style around questions of discipline. Some have worked out solutions with the help of mates or friends; others seek the deeper perspective of therapy to uproot long-entrenched and restricting habits. The first mother here has two sons, nine and seven, and a daughter, three; the second mother has two boys, six and two:

> ▶ My husband and I listen. If the children disagree or fight we try to help them solve it. In my home it was "I don't want to hear a word about it! Go to your rooms." Nothing was ever resolved. The guilty never paid for it. My mother still thinks it was brilliant!

> ▶ My family used a lot of physical punishment — spankings, face-slapping, wash our mouths out with soap. My mother had an explosive anger and would come at us with her hands, fly swatters, wooden spoons, whatever was available and then would finish it all up by saying, "Wait till your father comes home."
> We use time-out (one minute per year for the age of the child), family conferences, incentive charts. Physical punishment (spanking only) is very rarely used for either child. We've found through our therapy and experience that the physical stuff doesn't work nearly as well as the positive reinforcement,

nonviolent discipline. There were times before therapy when I felt out of control. My eldest son really knew what buttons to push, and I didn't always handle my emotions well. "Time-out" has been the best discovery for both of us as it separates us and gives us time to calm down and then approach the problem rationally.

Sometimes the Rebels' tendency to go to extremes will eventually and almost in spite of themselves lead to awareness and change. Sometimes in the process of taking an old pattern to the *n*th degree, a healing alternative will emerge. And sometimes a crisis, a fluke, even a *deus ex machina* will jolt a Rebel parent out of unconscious repetition and toward a new choice. When a Rebel mother of two school-age daughters discovered that she had a serious illness, possibly incurable, her world was turned upside down. She found herself reexamining her priorities, not the least her decisions about parenting. Suddenly she saw clearly what mattered the most and what needed changing. "I had a stern upbringing and followed that lead in spite of myself," she realized. "Now I'm starting to say 'Yes' instead of 'No.' When my daughter says, 'Can I wear my bathing-suit?' on a coolish day or 'Can I eat breakfast outside?' I say 'yes, yes, yes,' instead of 'no, no, no.' " Replacing the old noes with new yeses is a first step toward change for many Rebel parents. "Maybe" or "sometimes" may come later.

The process of change often involves finding a middle ground between the extremes of repetition and rebellion. This mother of two daughters, eleven and seven, describes her struggles to be a "powerful parent without being authoritarian." Her discussion underlines the fear of being too authoritarian *and* the fear of not being authoritarian enough:

▶ My perception of my father was that he was so authoritarian — "You do it because I say so." I err most in trying so hard *not* to be authoritarian that I'm not authoritarian *enough*. With a sometimes feisty older daughter who pushes against me all the time, it's hard to be authoritarian. It's easy around safety issues like plugs or crossing the street. But it's hard around value judgments like telling her when she's had enough candy. I still have a general feeling of powerlessness from childhood: that I wasn't listened to. That catapults to my parenting: I'm so afraid of being powerful as a parent.

This mother's struggles with authority and her lingering sense of powerlessness suggest both the gifts and the risks implicit in the Rebel's style of parenting. On the one hand, the Rebel uses her soul-searching about the past and brainstorming for ways to spare her children the abuses of authority, both verbal and physical, she so hated as a child. This thoughtfulness and concern are the gifts she gives her child. But because her solutions often come from an unresolved place, she sometimes replaces the hated abuse with alternatives that may be preferable but are not altogether workable — neglect, uncertainty, or even a reluctance to set limits with a child who really needs them. Such oversights are the risks of being a Rebel. The good news is that the energy Rebels use to try to filter out negative experiences for their children is healing. But the bad news is that sometimes in trying to reinvent the past, they throw the good out with the bad.

The Compensator is especially easy to pick out at the holiday season. She is the mother burning the candle at both ends to give her children the magical, glittering holiday she always dreamed of but never had. The night before Christmas she is up till all hours embroidering the last child's name on a stocking and winding the popcorn chains around the tree. Then she lovingly puts together the handmade dollhouse she would have swooned to find under her own childhood tree, where instead she found mittens or a flannel nightgown. He is the father practicing the Hannukah blessings and songs under his breath the week before the holiday so he can teach his children the soulful cadences he yearned for but never knew as a child. He is the parent putting together the electric train he wished for every year as a child but never got, whistling to himself as he imagines his children's faces lighting up at the dazzling surprise.

Like the Rebel, the Compensator hopes to be as different as possible from his own parent. But where the Rebel runs with conviction in an opposite direction, the Compensator uses imagination and fantasy to envision altogether new ground. The Rebel is still tangled up in his unresolved relationship with his parents; resistance is the emotional motor that drives him. The Compensator, more successfully differentiated from his parents, instead identifies with his children; restitution is the impetus that motivates him. There is overlap between the Rebels and the Compensators in that both want to avoid the perceived negatives of their pasts. Sheri Glucoft Wong explains the difference between the two groups this way: "The Rebels might say, 'If my mom was very controlling with me, I could refuse to set limits with my own children.' The Compensators would say, 'If my mom was controlling, I could not set limits with my kids. Or I could set the limits and apologize twelve times. Or I could set the limits and feel guilty about it.' " Rebels see the world in black and white. Compensators realize there are shades of gray — even mauve and lilac — but are ambivalent about how to handle them.

Compensators have separated from their parents but are still struggling with how to do things differently. Their uncertainty comes partly from their inability to identify with parental figures and partly from their tendency to identify with their own children, especially in the heat of confrontation. Where the Rebel leaps over her boundary into her parent's space, the Compensator invades her children's space, projecting her own feelings and attitudes onto her children. "You are me, and you'd better not have ideas of your own," is her implicit message to her children. Often the overly close identification with her children prevents her from assuming parental responsibilities.

Glucoft Wong tells of a friend whose mother brought her up with a strict sense about the appropriate clothing to wear in each season. The mother saw to it that her daughter didn't wear cottons in winter or wools in summer. Now the daughter, who felt so controlled by her mother and swore that she would be easy-going about clothes with her children, finds herself fighting with her three-year-old daughter about "inappropriate" clothes. And every time she starts an argument with her preschooler, she soon finds herself on her daughter's side. Still caught in the bind between the generations, she has not yet figured out how to offer the control her child needs without feeling guilty about it.

In contrast to the Rebels, whose responses are dominated by

anger about the past, the Compensators are suffused by sadness. Describing their families of origin, Compensators mention disappointment, neglect, and loss as the thorny plantings on their childhood landscapes. Compensators are more likely than Rebels to express sympathy for their parents, but they still feel a deep personal grief that they are trying nobly to repair with the next generation. This mother of a two-year-old daughter, who was herself the middle child of five, recalls in a kind of stream of consciousness a series of memories whose subtext is characteristic of many of the Compensators — lack of attention, criticism, and oversights:

> ▶ I remember a general lack of affection in our family. No one ever hugged or kissed each other or anybody. I remember my first communion. I had a gorgeous dress and everyone made a fuss over me. For my confirmation, no one from my family could come. I had to hitch a ride with a neighbor. Everyone else's families were there except mine. I remember being very shy all through my years well into adolescence and being made fun of and misunderstood because of it. I remember having to wear hand-me-downs while my younger sisters got new clothes because the old clothes were too big. I became a clothes fanatic in later years because of this and to this day, I still am. Now I am a clothes fanatic for my baby.

Here again this mother speaks for many Compensators in her hopes and dreams for her new family, stitched firmly and lovingly together like the motto on a sampler:

> ▶ I want my daughter to grow up feeling good about herself. Proud that she's who she is and with support and encouragement from us to do what she wants to. I want to keep the pointless criticism at a minimum. It breaks down the spirit and makes one feel useless. I want her to have the opportunitites to do things I never did because of lack of interest or money on my parents' part. Like dancing or piano lessons or girl scouts or summer camp. I want her to grow up knowing her parents. Both of them. And knowing that we are here for her if she needs us and not to feel afraid to come to us if she's

in trouble or needs advice. I want open communication in this family about everything. If we can't communicate, then that's where the trouble begins. Our family at home was a family of secrets. Make believe it didn't happen or what will the neighbors think.

Despite the memories of oversights and disappointment, she ends on a note of appreciation:

▶ I want to bring her up knowing her background and the traditional things that were so important to us growing up. I will always be grateful to my parents for the wonderful times we had.

She now has the distance and compassion to put herself in her parents' shoes:

▶ I know my mother would have been happier without as many children as she had — five — because she felt she couldn't pay the needed attention to all of them. Being a middle child I think I felt that lack of attention more than anyone. The baby was the baby; the oldest was beyond needing so much; and the middle sort of muddled along.

In another mood, she speculates on the differences between her family of origin and her present family:

▶ I don't know how my parents did it. Financially, emotionally or any other way. We find it difficult with one child to do everything for her, and my parents had five. At times, I guess they *didn't* do it. I understand more now than I did before. My relationship with my mother is better. She's a lot more loving and kind a person than she was. She was never very easy to get next to. Never had the time.

The Compensators struggled more keenly than others with their burgeoning sense of identity in their childhoods, and as parents they still struggle with uncertainty about their choices. The Tra-

ditionalists grow up confident in the security of their parents' traditional values; the Rebels create an identity, albeit a negative one,
out of opposition to their parents' world. But after the perceived
vacuum of their childhood homes, the Compensators often flounder
to get their bearings in the world. The questionnaire responses of
the Compensators are laced with a sense of differentness, apartness,
aloneness. For some, like the mother quoted above, this aloneness occurred in the bustle of a family where there was simply
not enough time and energy to meet the needs of a lonely middle
child.

In other families, children were left frustrated and adrift when
family life was too different from the mainstream and parents were
unable to cope in the hoped-for and expectable ways. Here the
daughter of a Chinese immigrant describes how her mother's alienation cut the rest of the family off from social life as well. Now
she puts into perspective the gaps in her own childhood she is trying
to fill for her two daughters. She speaks with the understanding
born of being a mother herself:

> ▶ My major problem in my family of origin was my mother's
> never being able to adjust to life in the U.S. She immigrated
> from China as a teenager after World War Two, and to this
> day contemporary American culture is still an enigma to her.
> Since becoming a parent I have gained insight into the diffi-
> culties my own parents had while raising a family under less
> than ideal circumstances. My mother didn't drive and that left
> us stranded in a suburb. We did not participate in any orga-
> nized recreational activities or classes like other kids. I still
> feel short-changed but am now able to discuss with my father
> why I provide my children with the opportunities I did not
> have. My mother and I have not become any closer, but I
> have always had a good relationship with my father, and be-
> coming a parent has given us more to reminisce about.

For another mother, this one with a nine- and a six-year-old, the
sense of childhood differentness came from having parents who
were blind:

▶ We had a somewhat different childhood in that both of my parents are blind and have been since early childhood. It didn't occur to me that we were different from other families until I was in junior high school. Sensitive issues in our family have been my sister's "illness" (diagnosed as schizophrenia); my brother's rebellion and open disdain for my father (he was angry because my Dad didn't fulfill his need to have a "normal" father); and frustration because my parents' handicap made doing simple things so hard. For example, we always had to walk to the grocery store or go with someone who could drive there. Not having transportation made us dependent upon buses, taxis, and friends, and we all hated that.

And for still another mother, this one with two boys, an early sense of alienation came from the most profound loss of all:

▶ My mother died when I was nine. I feel she was never comfortable with me as a young child, because unlike other children I was often a loner, though I actually preferred to spend my time with the adults. My mother's death left a void in our lives undoubtedly. I feel that my siblings and I all suffer insecurity to some degree, because the absence of a mother made us different from other children and we felt it. To this day I long for a solid relationship (warm, caring, giving) with another woman, yet it eludes me as it has since my childhood. I suffer from low self-esteem, because I never felt "right" in my mother's presence and then I lost her.

Out of her wrenching early loss came a special sensitivity and a Compensator's typical commitment to giving her own children what she ached for as a child:

▶ I work very hard at loving my sons openly and giving lots of praise. I want very much for them to feel good about themselves. I have learned that in spite of everything else my children bring me happiness. They give me strength and also self-confidence. I feel I am a good mother though I had so many doubts beforehand.

For this woman, being a good mother began to compensate for the mothering she so desperately wanted as a child.

Maurice Vanderpol tells the story of a woman who had first sought treatment in her early twenties and then came back to see him in her fifties, still bitter and angry. She had always demanded that her mother tell her she loved her; if the mother refused, the daughter would become enraged. Now in her fifties, she was depressed, because her elderly mother still wouldn't come through with the love she craved. Meanwhile she had repeated with her daughter exactly what her mother had done with her. She was distant and withholding, and the young daughter had become very depressed and was hospitalized. The mother simply didn't want to grow up and take responsibility for her new family until her own mother could say "I love you." She was, in a sense, on a parenting strike — not going to give love to her daughter until her own mother gave love to her.

"I explained that what this mother didn't get from her own mother, she could still *give* to her daughter," reports Vanderpol about his intervention, which encouraged more of a Compensator approach for this mother. "Then, by identifying with her daughter, she could also receive the love from her daughter that she missed from her mother." Now, after learning to express her love to her daughter, the mother is indeed more content and on a more even keel; her daughter, in turn, is also much better and is out of the hospital. Such is the healing power of parenting that parents can compensate for their own losses by making up for them in the next generation.

From the younger generation's perspective, the most welcome giving comes from a parent who is giving out of choice and desire, not out of an image of self-sacrifice or martyrdom. The most conscious Compensators are able to give generously both for their children's sakes and for their own needs and growth as parents. If too many strings are attached to the gifts, children feel burdened and beholden. According to Ivan Boszormenyi-Nagy and Geraldine Spark, whose book explores the unpaid emotional debts that accrue between generations, there are serious pitfalls to parental selflessness:

[Parents] may minimize or deny their own feelings of deprivation and make efforts to give their "all" to their offspring. What happens though to their own unmet hungers? They may overtly become the all-giving, sacrificing, martyr-like parent. This not only inevitably produces guilt feelings in the receiving child who feels that he must overpay for what is given in such a selfless manner, but more importantly, the child feels forever bound to live up to the parent's expectations.

If separation is the most highly charged issue for the Traditionalists and anger for the Rebels, then intimacy and affection are the most troubling areas of family life for the Compensators. Many Compensators describe their original homes as having little affection and intimacy. Often this lack of affection seemed to originate in the parents' marriage, and the strained emotional tone trickled down through the family. Inevitably, the Compensators hope to repair this gap in their new families. They are more finely tuned than most to the calibrations of family intimacy and committed to securing it both as partners and as parents. A mother of a three-year-old boy describes the emotional tone of her new family against the background of her old:

> ▶ My parents were never openly affectionate. The most was a kiss between my mom and dad when he got home from work. There weren't very many hugs and kisses from parent to child in my family. They expressed their love verbally and with cards and gifts. Although there was no physical or sexual abuse, I might say that my parents' rigidity and lack of dialogue-type communication and lack of affection was emotionally abusive.
>
> My partner and I are more openly intimate than either of our families. We have longer hugs and kisses between the three of us, and they are more frequent throughout the day.

Here a mother with two young girls describes her efforts to reverse the habits of her childhood home and give her daughters the affection she craved as a child:

> ▶ There was very little affection or intimacy in my family of origin. My parents rarely showed affection for each other in the presence of their children. As we grew up, there were infrequent physical expressions of affection from our parents.

The personalities of my children have determined how we express affection. My older daughter doesn't like to be touched or cuddled as much as her sister. She does, however, reach for my hand sometimes when we are in public places. My younger daughter is more apt to hug and kiss, so naturally we do this more often with her. I craved affection while growing up, so I do not want to perpetuate these feelings in my own family.

Along with repairing the lack of family closeness, Compensators often are concerned with trying to foster for their children the self-esteem they felt they lacked. A mother of three teenage boys and a new baby remembers:

> ▶ My parents didn't encourage me to feel good about myself. I encourage my children to feel good about themselves by telling them that I love them, giving hugs and expressing my pride in them on their accomplishments.

Given the Compensators' special sensitivity about affection and self-esteem, about how much — even whether — they were cherished and valued as children, birthdays, holidays, and family rituals have extra symbolic meaning. For it is often with the loving attentions of birthday celebrations that a child comes to feel he is uniquely special. And with the magic festivities of holidays a child feels profoundly connected to his own family and protected by the whole clan. Bruno Bettelheim points out how holidays' "symbolic meanings are built permanently into our unconscious experience of the world":

The "gathering of the clan" reassures the child that for his security against desertion he need not rely solely on his parents, that there are many other relatives who would be available in a crisis and would protect him against desertion. . . . Family holidays are, both as a conscious experience and on an unconscious level, one of the most reassuring experiences the child can have in regard to his most fervent anxieties. They are among the most constructive experiences we can provide for him to buttress his security. The wonderful thing about the positive magic of holiday happiness is that it can provide security all during the year when it is most needed, even under life's worst circumstances.

Having often missed out on this special holiday magic, both real and symbolic, the Compensators are determined to shine it on for their own children. Rituals are lovingly thought out and planned — a wish fulfillment from the parents' own past. A mother of two young girls describes how she has enlarged on the scanty celebrations of her childhood:

> ► Birthdays and holidays were celebrated with very little fanfare in my family of origin. In our family now, we have our own private celebration of birthdays that fall on weekdays, while the extended family gets together on weekends. I also allow my children to invite a limited number of friends for a kids' party, something which my mother never did for her children.

The mother whose parents were blind reports proudly every detail of the attentive birthday celebrations she plans for her two daughters:

> ► In my family growing up, birthdays were usually quiet. We never really had parties. I didn't have many friends (there were no kids in my neighborhood), and it never even occurred to me to have a party. My mom usually ordered a cake from a bakery.
>
> I have always had parties for my kids, ever since my older daughter was one. Since they've been five, they've been allowed to choose what kind of birthday party they wanted. Sometimes it has been games at home; other times at a gymnastics school or ice-skating rink. The night of their birthday, they're allowed to choose the restaurant or plan the dinner menu.

At Christmas, she again savors every fine point of festivity:

> ► Christmas we usually spend at home. The kids help to decorate the tree and house. I love to drive around and see

the lights. I also like to go to community events, and every year I take my older daughter to see "The Nutcracker."

For this mother there is an extra poignancy to the savoring of the Christmas lights, the sharing of the magical "Nutcracker," all visual pyrotechnics. Here she acknowledges the connections:

> ▶ As I write this, it's very clear that I've tried to provide everything for my kids that I never got as a child. I like to do it for them, yet I know that I'm really doing it for myself — a chance to redo my childhood.

Doing it for them yet really doing it for myself — this is the Compensator's double-edged sword. What these parents give their children is the love and attention, the nurturing of self-esteem, the magical celebrations they didn't themselves get. In return they get a feeling of well-being. But their risk is that in the intensity of the desire to compensate for their childhood lacks, they miss seeing their own children's specific needs and desires.

Family therapist Virginia Satir gives a vivid example of the unconscious traps waiting for parents who struggle to give their own children what they did not get. Not surprisingly, it was just after Christmas when a young mother whom she calls Elaine came to see her. Elaine was in a rage because she had given her six-year-old daughter a costly and fancy doll for Christmas, and her daughter had reacted with indifference. Gradually, Satir helped her realize that this doll was what she had yearned for as a girl and had never gotten:

> She was giving her daughter what was really her own unfulfilled dream doll. She expected Pam to react as she, Elaine, would have reacted when she was six. She had overlooked that her daughter already had several dolls. Pam would much rather have had a sled so she could go sliding with her brothers.

Unraveling the strands of the past, Satir helped this young mother identify her own needs as distinct from her daughter's so that she could begin to take steps to fulfill her own needs and become more available to her daughter:

The doll was really Elaine's. I suggested that she claim her own doll and experience her own fulfillment, which she did. This particular yearning from her childhood was satisfied directly, and she did not have to do it through her child. Instead, she bought Pam a sled.

Observes Satir:

Is there any good reason why adults cannot openly fulfill, in adulthood, some of the unfulfilled yearnings of their childhood? Oftentimes, if they don't, they pass off these old needs on their kids. Children rarely appreciate passed-off satisfaction (unless they have learned how to act like yes-persons). Nor do they like parental strings on their gifts. I am thinking of fathers who buy trains for sons or daughters and then play with the toys all the time, setting out strict conditions under which the children can use their own trains. How much more honest it would be for the father to buy the train for himself. It would be his train, and he then might or might not allow his children to play with it.

Disentangling the needs of the past from the demands of the present is a crucial challenge for the Compensators. And though they often struggle desperately to provide glittering and golden where they knew only tarnished and broken, sometimes when they pause long enough to look beneath the cracked surface of the past, they may also see there a source of their own strength. Often in their herculean efforts to intercept their children's disappointments — or even to distract them from awareness of their parents' humanness — these parents are robbing their children of opportunities to experience some of the more difficult parts of life. These are the very opportunities that may help prepare these children for becoming adults. Buffering their children against all hardships may not be the pure gift that the Compensators intend, just as experiencing hardships was not the pure drawback that they feared in their own pasts.

The Synthesizer is the highly conscious parent who has achieved both distance from his past and his parents and compassion for them. He is able to take from the past what works best, alter what hasn't worked, and set aside what has become irrelevant or outmoded. The resulting style is a synthesis of the best of the past and present with a sprinkling of dreams for the future. The Synthesizer has a finely honed sense of mission, purpose, and intentionality about being a parent. But she also has a joyful, playful attitude. And the energy released after the hard work of separation from her own legacy gives her freedom to have fun with her kids, to be fully with them in the present. The Synthesizer both does and doesn't take her job lightly. She may often be the parent others consider a "natural," the one who goes with her instincts no matter the pull of the crowd.

The Synthesizer is likely to have a stack of books by her bed on families and child raising. After the last child has been tucked in, she will settle down and savor the stories of family life, noting different families' choices and approaches the way other people might relish the quirks of character in a good novel. She reads not for answers or directions but for the pleasure of sharing kinship with fellow travelers on the parenting journey. She knows she will always follow her own heart, her own instincts in raising her children, but she likes the company of other parents along the way.

The Synthesizer makes an art of parenting and brings to it a creative, almost spiritual zest. He strives to see meaning and pattern beneath life's daily demands. Sometimes this occurs willy-nilly in the whirlwind of family life when he shares a special confidence with a needful child or a private joke — or giant belly laugh — with an exuberant one. Sometimes he has to find the time to create space to connect with a child. And sometimes he needs his own breathing space — or a quiet time with a partner — to take the longer view and appraise the leaps of development that every family experiences.

For writer Jack Kornfield, an American Zen Buddhist, parenting is "one of the most rewarding and demanding practices that one will undertake in this life. It makes a very demanding guru seem like a piece of cake." For Kornfield, a highly conscious Synthesizer himself, it is the focused attention — or mindfulness — on daily domestic demands that makes parenting a kind of meditation, a highly focused contemplation:

> Not only do you learn the [skill] of being very present with your attention, but you also learn the other special practice called in

Sanskrit sampajanna, which means to be able to do many things mindfully at once: like change a diaper, hold the child still and get some other clothes or take care of two or three children, one who's pouring things on the floor, and one who's running around, and the other who needs to be fed and all at the same time, while you're also trying to answer the phone that's ringing. For me it's been a very different kind of meditation, that of walk when you walk, eat when you eat. Kids know how to do that. Eat when you eat and play with your cheerios when you play with your cheerios.

For Kornfield, and for many Synthesizers, the real challenge of parenthood is how to stay mindful and attuned to several things at once:

> Being a parent is more like the Korean Zen Master Seung Sahn, who was sitting at the table at the Zen Center one morning eating his breakfast and reading the morning paper. A student came up to him very upset and said, "How can you do this, Roshi. Here you teach us to just eat when you eat, walk when you walk and sit when you sit and now you're eating and also reading. What kind of example is that?" He looked up and laughed, "When you eat and read, just eat and read." Keep it simple.

The Synthesizer sees parenting as a central life work, despite other commitments. Both mothers and fathers strive to balance the necessities and demands of their work lives with devotion to their home lives and to their communities. They often put family before professional advancement and achievement. Synthesizers may seem better than most at juggling a variety of commitments. Partly that emotional sleight of hand comes from a bedrock of values emphasizing family and service to others and partly from a psychological astuteness that emphasizes the importance of listening to inner needs. The Synthesizer is not the perfect parent but is attuned to parenting as a process, truly believing that it is the journey, not the arrival, that matters. Being a Synthesizer is an ideal many of us strive for, even if we reach it only intermittently.

Synthesizers may move through other phases before achieving this kind of perspective about parenting. They may have the Traditionalists' strong sense of values and admiration for "how their parents did it" combined with the Rebels' sharply discerning or even critical eye and the Compensators' vision and imagination.

But where Traditionalists identify positively and Rebels negatively with their parents, and Compensators identify with their children, Synthesizers have the mature ability to see all sides of an issue — their parents', their children's, and their own — and to have compassion for all three generations. In the Synthesizer's family, boundaries between generations are clear and well defined. The Synthesizer is able to tell the difference between his own issues and his parents', between his children's problems and his own. If his parent or his child is in pain, for instance, he can comfort and help look for solutions while striving not to absorb the pain himself.

Synthesizers' descriptions of their changing relationships with their parents show both their differentiation and their compassion. Their attitude embraces both an emotional autonomy that allows for differences of opinion and direction as well as an admiration for the best of what their parents did for them. Here a mother in her early forties who has an eight-year-old daughter carefully discriminates between her parents' values and her own, like a quilter choosing which colored squares to keep and which to eliminate for the balance and beauty of the design:

> ▶ I think we share a lot of our parents' values in terms of valuing education, verbal skill, kindness, generosity, integrity, honesty. Our parents tended to think we ought to strive to be something special, like a teacher, engineer. We feel we want our kids to feel free to explore themselves in terms of varied interests, but we want them to be honest, kind, generous.

For a mother of a young daughter and son, the differentiation shows itself in a newfound ability to be assertive with her parents — for the sake of her new family. But her assertiveness is tempered by a loving appreciation of all her parents accomplished:

> ▶ I am in awe of my mother for having raised four children. I don't know how she did it, especially without much help from my father. I think I am more understanding now of their shortcomings, the mistakes they made. I am also more willing to stand up to my parents and assert myself if it involves the well-being of my family.

The Synthesizer uses both head and heart, balancing a keen analytical approach to parenting with emotional sensitivity. Three different mothers — the first with a young daughter, the second with teenagers, and the third with grown children — describe what they want to repeat and what they want to change of their parents' approaches:

> ► I try to analyze what I feel my parents did right and wrong and what effects their actions had on me. I like parts of myself and don't like other parts. I hope to learn from my experiences and treat my daughter accordingly.

> ► I loved the warmth and affection; didn't need so many judgments. My parents knew all the answers; I don't. I think we've conveyed to our kids that it's okay to disagree.

> ► I would like to repeat the way my family loved me unconditionally, showed pride in me and would do almost anything for me. I truly believed I was the most important person in their lives. I do not want to manipulate my children into conforming by lying to them (I didn't realize the extent to which my mother did this until recent years), and I want them to have more freedom in their choices provided they don't reject the values with which they were raised.

And a grandmother in her sixties with three grown children and two small grandchildren looks back over a lifetime to chart the crossroads between the generations and the new ground broken as well:

> ► I promised I would never say to my kids what my mother said to me: "She's a good girl when she sleeps," and I made my kids promise never to say that. I know that I'm similar to my mother in being — what's the word? — orderly? inflexible? setting the table in the same way, everyone sitting in the same seat. I'm unlike her in that I long ago decided if my kitchen floor isn't swept every day, so what? I'm not nearly as meticulous. But I'm like her in that my kids are very im-

portant to me. When I see my daughters as mothers, I see a lot of similarities with me. But my youngest is less inclined to pay as much attention to her daughter as I did to her. I was shocked to see her reading a newspaper at the breakfast table with her daughter toddling around her. Still both my daughters talk to their kids a lot just like I talked to them.

Elaborating on all the ways he wants to follow in his parents' footsteps as well as diverge from them, this father of two young girls shows how the Synthesizer draws on both intellect and emotions in his decisions. Indeed, his list could be a kind of Synthesizer manifesto:

▶ I want to repeat:
1. Providing a reasonably stable, predictable home in which there is plenty of nurturance but also structure and limits.
2. Encouraging and respecting my kids pursuing areas of talent/ability without pressure to pursue just *parents'* agendas.
3. Training my kids to be polite.
4. Modeling and encouraging humanistic values — respect for democracy, consideration of others' feelings, etc.
5. Modeling a sense of humor.
6. Modeling critical thinking and intellectual curiosity.
7. Giving my children some training in music and/or other arts.

▶ I want to do differently:
1. As a father, I want to spend a lot of time with my children.
2. I want my marriage to be more mutually satisfying than my parents' was when I was growing up.
3. More acceptance and appreciation of simple pleasures. My parents were achievement oriented and were very judgmental about what leisure pursuits are "good" or "bad."
4. I want for neither of us ever to hit our children.
5. I want to model an ethical attitude that is pragmatic and positive, emotionally based versus guilt or shame based.
6. I would like to include my children's opinions a little more in family decisions than my folks did.

More than any of the other groups, the Synthesizers see themselves as the architects of a new philosophy of parenting. The new model they are fashioning reflects changes both social and emotional, both widespread and personal. This new model stresses democracy over authoritarianism; balance and well-roundedness over achievement for its own sake; a psychological approach over judgmentalism; and the father's involvement in family over absorption in work. Above all, the new model described by the Synthesizers emphasizes the pleasures of being a parent — the humor, fun, and occasional absurdity of it — over the duties. Four parents reflect on the changes in values from their parents' generation to their own:

▶ My parents valued intelligence; I value being well-adjusted.

▶ I enjoy my relationship with my son — playing with him, watching him grow and learn new things. . . . I find the drudgery and predictability of being on a schedule for his benefit to be the least enjoyable part. I would guess that my parents didn't expect parenting to be enjoyable and that whether it was or not didn't mean anything to them.

▶ I do a lot more of the immediate care than my father did — diapering, being the one our son comes crying to. My father was a pretty good father, though he had a lot of competing interests. He always liked to do things with his kids, especially outdoors. I would criticize him most for his focus on athletics. I undoubtedly would want our son to do athletics, but I've been more interested in verbal skills, too. One crucial difference is that I'm a good deal older and have only one child, whereas my father had four. Another big difference is in what my wife expects from me and what my mother expected from my father.

▶ I want to raise my children to be "risk-takers" which is how I see my parents raised me. They really encouraged me to go after my goals and not be discouraged by obstacles. I think they also taught me about responsibility to myself and others.

I would like to avoid pushing my children too hard towards achievement and do a better job of balancing my needs and desires for them with their needs and desires for themselves. I would like to be more sensitive than my parents were.

When Synthesizers speak about their choices as parents, their tone is considered and psychologically astute. Synthesizers emphasize compassion over judgment, acknowledgment over denial. Two mothers share stories about the new ways they are learning to resolve family discomfort:

> ▶ Our family recently went on a vacation to the mountains. We were coming home on a beautiful windy road in the snow. My son said, "I'm sad to leave here." My mother would have responded to that: "You had a good time. Don't complain. Enough is enough." But I said, "I can really understand how you feel. I remember feeling that way. We'll try to come back sometime." Saying that was such a gift for him. I felt good. I didn't come to this on my own. I got a lot of guidance. Mirroring and echoing is what I'm striving to do with my kids. Even as an adult, you need to be acknowledged.

> ▶ One thing I know I do very differently is this: when I was growing up, whenever I fell, my parents used denial — "It didn't really hurt" — and distraction — "Look at the birdy" (but there was no birdy). But I feel that children treated that way cry longer. When my children hurt themselves, the very first thing I say is "I'm sorry you fell down; that really took you by surprise." The minute I say that, they run back to play and are fine. The fear for my parents was that if they acknowledged the hurt, they'd make it more painful. But the opposite is true.

For Synthesizers, every important area of family life is open to observation, critique, and change according to their families' changing needs as well as the changing demands of the times. In such matters as limit setting and self-esteem, working, sexuality, and religion, among many others, Synthesizers use their abilities to see all sides of an issue to come up with new parenting strategies and solutions. Their attitude toward discipline and limit setting, for example, is considerably less authoritarian and dogmatic than their parents', more open to having discussions and allowing children to "save face." Anger by both parents *and* children is considered a natural and inevitable part of family life, but its expression is channeled and focused in a constructive way.

Three other parents compare the differences between their parents' style of disciplining and their own:

> ▶ Discipline in my original family: LOUD. My father was a bellower; my mother, a good screamer. No discussion. No reasoning. No options! No hitting. No chance to be heard.
>
> We're discussers. All four of us share an aversion to criticism. From the earliest times (two-year tantrums), I remember how important it was for the kids to save face. Now we talk. Our kids are great negotiators.

> ▶ There were times my father would get irrationally angry, with me as the focus. But I knew I wasn't really the focus: he was just frustrated, because he had been ill for so long. I felt that anger was something I wouldn't do to my kids: I didn't want to experience it nor transmit it. I've achieved that more often than not. I can get my anger out and it's not devastating.

> ▶ Both my husband and I grew up in Catholic families with an authoritarian father who spanked us! My Dad got tired of it after the first five kids (there were ten in all) and pretty much quit. Anger, as parents and Church taught, was "bad" and certainly not something children should ever express towards adults. In our family now, there are definite limits, clearly stated, but we are far less dogmatic in our authority. For example we don't force the kids to eat things they dislike (whereas we had to sit there until we finished those peas!) We don't hit them; they have time-out. They very openly express anger and so do we, but violence is not allowed. We also state what we are angry about, i.e., "I don't like it when . . ." instead of "You're a bad girl for doing . . ."

Sex and religion are two other issues where Synthesizers are able to acknowledge their parents' values and choices yet come up with a less traditional approach, one that is more attuned to their families' unfolding needs. Synthesizer parents often value and want to repeat the warmth and affection of their childhood homes, but also want to integrate a more open and comfortable attitude toward sexuality. Two mothers in their forties, the first with three grown children, the second with two young ones, reflect on their more liberal sexual attitudes:

> ▶ I am more comfortable with my sexuality than my mother was and is with hers. I'm able to talk more freely about the subject to friends and my children. I was less threatened by my children's developing sexuality than my parents were about mine. However, we both don't condone sex outside of marriage.

> ▶ What I most want to repeat: the openness in communication that went on in our house. We were welcome and encouraged to discuss anything and often did at our suppertime forum. What I most want to avoid: the over-modest behavior of my parents around sexuality and reproduction. We got "the lecture" one time and it just wasn't discussed after that. We certainly never read any book together about babies and so forth, which I make an effort to do now with my young daughters.

Many Synthesizer parents, especially those with young children, are actively engaged in exploring their family's religious and spiritual needs. Often they have recognized their departure from the organized religion in which they were raised but are still thinking about alternatives:

> ▶ Religion is one area where there is a large difference between the way we were raised and the way we're raising our kids. Both my husband and I went to Sunday school and church weekly and were brought up with religion. His family is still very involved with the church, and it's the major focus of their

lives. My husband and I have drifted away from organized religion, although not to atheism.

▶ The family in which I grew up emphasized the religious (Christian) meaning of certain holidays equally with the secular celebration. At this point, my husband and I are just beginning to create our own family celebrations and "traditions." During the most recent Christmas, we discussed our different opinions and views of the role of religion, but we came to no conclusion. A big obstacle for me is my own reluctance to be involved in a church and my uncertainty about creating spiritual meaning with no reference point. To be continued.

To be continued — that sense of ongoing process and discovery is a hallmark of the Synthesizers' style. And nowhere is this open-ended search more passionately explored than in the area of work, self-esteem, and finding the balance between focus inside and outside the home. The shifts in generational attitudes about women and work are highlighted by the Synthesizers' descriptions of work histories from their parents' generation to their own. The mothers of many Synthesizer mothers did not themselves work but passed on to their daughters a strong impetus toward achievement. Often they overtly pressured their daughters to fulfill their own dreams, which had been put aside for full-time mothering:

▶ My mother wanted to be a nurse but didn't have the money for school. She has always been sorry and has somewhat pressured my sisters and me to have a "career" rather than a job.

▶ I feel it is absolutely vital to the children's well-being to be here at home for comfort, encouragement, discipline and whatever else arises. My mother didn't have the choice, and though I know she's proud of my mothering abilities, she's also disappointed that I haven't chosen a paying career and pursued it.

But for many of these Synthesizer daughters, the quest for professional achievement for its own sake seems less important than the quest to find a comfortable and satisfying balance between accomplishment outside the home and satisfaction within. Two mothers whose own mothers did work, but unhappily, compare their attitudes to their mothers':

> ▶ My mother felt conflicted between working and mothering, which she constantly struggled with, especially when we kids expressed our needs. I feel I can be an effective and attentive mom and work, too.

> ▶ My mom went back to work when I was twelve. I loved it! All the kids came to my house after school! My mother bitched and complained about work, but I love it. It's better for me and my kids. But I don't believe in working full-time until they are school age.

For Synthesizer mothers in the new generation, the decision to combine work with parenting is also eased by the changed social and economic climate and by the support of their new families. For many, their mothers' backing is a crucial support and incentive. The new mother of a sixteen-month-old and the single mother of a two-year-old describe their indebtedness to their mothers:

> ▶ I like combining work and motherhood, and my mother supports me on this all the way. She also helps care for my son at least one day a week, which gives her a role in his development and probably fulfills her more than she realizes.

> ▶ I really don't think I could be as effective a single parent if I didn't have the model of my mother. She loved her work. She also loved family living. She also taught me how to manage time and make money go the farthest. I really enjoy the balance in my life.

If the parents of Synthesizers underlined the message of achievement outside the home, the Synthesizers themselves are underlining a message of balance and well-roundedness. Synthesizer parents may work full-time, part-time, or not at all — the key is their sense of balance between life at home and in the outside world.

"My parents valued intelligence; I value being well-adjusted" — that mother's observation could be the byword of many Synthesizers. In their stated ideals and life plans, Synthesizers are modeling for their children the satisfactions of a life balanced between work inside and outside the home, commitment to family and commitment to a wider community. This, indeed, is the greatest gift the Synthesizers pass along to their children: their sense of balance and equanimity, their judiciousness and insight, their ability to see all sides of a question. In word and deed they convey a compassion for the past, a zest for the present, and an optimism about the future, a sense that whatever comes up can be well attended to. Their gift is one of consciousness and awareness, a compassionate sensitivity to their children, their parents, and themselves.

Of the four styles explored, clearly the Synthesizers' is the most flexible option. Yet it is also not without risks. Being a Synthesizer is tough and challenging work. All choices are up for grabs; no decisions about parenting are taken for granted. All the other parenting styles have a certainty — even an intransigence — about their beliefs and their positions. For Synthesizers, multiple options constantly shift before them like a tossed handful of colored pick-up sticks. They are certain only about uncertainty. Alongside the opportunity to exercise the most judicious option is the chance that they will make a wrong or hurtful decision — or flounder in confusion or self-doubt.

For the Synthesizers, consciousness and conscientiousness can be double-sided. The positive side is the awareness and sensitivity they bring to the most mundane tasks of parenting as well as to its most complex challenges. But the down side is too much self-consciousness, the risk of overparenting rather than allowing family life to unfold in its own course and time, letting what happens happen.

— 6 —

Separation and Closeness

SCENARIO

My parents stand by my bed.
They look down, talking
about how I am growing before their
    eyes.

They watch as my hair
darkens and curls, as my milk teeth
fall out and new ones appear.

They barely blink when the rings
of my nipples rise like blown bubbles
and soft hair tops the vee of my legs.

They step back when a boy
joins me in bed and we kiss,
touching with tentative fingers.

They stand in the doorway
as the boy grows into a man and we kiss
harder, our bodies twisting into a braid.

They stare from the hallway
as my belly swells like a blister.
They fade back when I start labor.

I stand by her bed
seeing her grow before my eyes.
I step back.

Barbara Eve

As a child I never had an easy time with separations. When I first went to nursery school at three, I clung to my mother's skirts when all the other children had long since waved bye-bye. The others busied themselves with block towers and doll baby tea parties. They crisscrossed the play yard on scooters, savoring the thrill of mastery and independence. I still desperately spun in my mother's orbit. The room was called the "green room" — green for the first young shoots, green for the tender blades of grass, and, for me, too often in those early days, green around the gills.

Once school began in earnest, I fell in step with my peers, eyes wide to the world opening up around me. But at night the bogeyman would haunt me. For years I agonized when my parents went out in the evenings, leaving me in what felt like the dubious care of baby-sitters. I would riffle through my mother's datebook, making mental notes of the dinners out and theater dates on her calendar. On those late nights I would wait for my parents to return home, eyes alert and body taut in bed, braced against the undefined and unmentionable dangers lurking in the closets and behind the curtains. My parents did their best to reassure me and, failing that, tried to lure me to maturity with the promise of a glamorous red tea cart and a shiny white-and-gold tea set from F.A.O. Schwartz if I promised not to cry when they left. But long after the mask of maturity was in place and the tea cart was mine, the tears still trickled in private. Even at seven, at eight, at nine, I longed with an infant's longing to be protected, to be at the center of their world, still, perhaps, to merge.

Slowly I grew into myself, into friendships, passions, and confidence. My world widened, and my ability to separate grew with it. There were sleep-overs and summer camps, trips across the country and to Europe on my own, finally the long-awaited leave-taking for college. But on the eve of my twenty-first birthday, three years into college life, I found myself reeling from a romance that had derailed. Facing another leap to maturity that felt suddenly like a pratfall, I saw myself slipping back into a place I thought I had left behind. Some wordless and primitive instinct propelled me home to Mom to pick up the pieces. On what could have been a wild and woolly day of independence, I needed to celebrate surrounded by the comforts of family and home. I can still see myself weeping in the taxi on the way home from the airport, wondering if I would ever be a grown-up, be separate, stand on my own feet, be free.

In the dozen years that followed, I moved across the country, became a writer, got married, bought a house, made a life of my own. But not until I had my own children did I truly begin to think of myself as adult. Even now, despite all appearances of competence — the Volvo for carpools, the children's lunch boxes packed and school clothes laid out the night before — still the old sensitivities about separation come back to haunt me. Though my place on the generational ladder has shifted, I am not much nimbler at climbing it than I ever was. In fact, I often find I have a harder time separating from my children than they do from me. My first, especially, rushes to meet life in a headlong way that often leaves me in the dust, gasping for breath. A new baby-sitter, an evening at home while my husband and I go out, the first day of nursery school — he greets each transition as a new adventure, not without the leavening of caution, but fully confident he can handle all eventualities, all comers.

Meanwhile, I take gingerly baby steps away from my boys, always looking back over my shoulder and around all corners to make sure they are still standing without me there to prop them up. Especially when they were infants, I felt an almost physical need to have them with me. For the first six months of my older son's infancy, I barely left him at all. And even many months later, when a friend with a baby the same age confided that after four hours apart from her son, she really started to miss him, I realized that I had rarely been four hours apart from mine. After two hours my heart would grow heavy and my breasts would start to leak milk.

With the path already cleared by my first son, the separations from my second have not been quite so piercing. And then, too, when I leave my second, he is often in the company of his older brother and so absorbed and entertained he barely knows that I am gone. Yet even now, with a five-year-old at school and a two-and-a-half-year-old at a neighborhood playgroup a few mornings a week, if I am home alone working and the phone rings, I startle a moment, and my stomach lurches. In the house all still and empty of children, that shadow of doubt suddenly flickers — something has happened to them because they're not with me.

Having children has profoundly shifted my perspective on separation and closeness. Loving them wildly while watching their growth unfold — and unfold away from me — I face every day the inevitability of separation. Watching my two-year-old struggle into his clothes by himself (two feet into one pant leg, jacket inside out), watching my five-year-old write his wonderful invented spelling on our computer (I am wrkg on th kinpyootr, he writes), I can see the handwriting on the wall. My children will push me to separate even if I am not ready for it. So I must spend a great part of my life as a parent learning how to be ready, and in doing so, I may also loosen the tight grip of my past.

How can I gauge the right amount of closeness, the right amount of distance at each age and stage? How can I love my children without smothering them and go on loving them even as each separation draws us a little farther apart, redefining our connectedness against the backdrop of their increasing maturity? How can I leave them without their feeling deserted, secure in the knowledge that I will always come back and will always continue loving them despite the changes in our relationship? These are some of the questions that frame this chapter.

Following my children's lead, I am learning some crucial lessons about separation, and the first is that the process is always reciprocal. I must struggle to separate from my children just as intensively as they struggle to separate from me. Watching her eighteen-month-old son Ben experiencing some separation anxiety at day care, writer Roberta Israeloff confides to her therapist in *In Confidence,* "I know he has to undergo this phase, but it's so hard on me." To which the wise lady replies, "It should be. You have to separate from him as much as he does from you."

When my son Willy, at two, goes through a similar bout of protest at being left at playgroup, I agonize over whether he's ready for this step. But looking under the skin of my own response, and disengaging Willy's separation from the miserable ones in my memory, I notice a curious thing. As I come to terms with my need to leave him for a few hours, knowing that he is in loving hands and among pals, I am able to take some steps to make the separation more harmonious. I find a photo of the family together, a backpack, and some favorite things, tokens of home to take with him. And the change in my attitude seems to beget a change in his. My mood and intentions toward this separation affect him just as surely as his mood affects me. And soon the cycle is energized in the other direction. His increasing comfort at playgroup and his excitement about being with his friends teach me that it is indeed okay, even a blessing, to let go for awhile.

As I learn to see these transitions as two-sided, I also increasingly realize that separation is actually an all-family affair. Although much of the psychological literature on separation — and much of my own material for this chapter — focuses on the original mother-infant bond and its gradual loosening and restructuring, father and siblings also play a pivotal role in the earliest separations as well as all others that follow. In our family, my husband is always the one who pushes us on to the next developmental step — the one to suggest that it's time to move the newborn's bassinet out of our bedroom, time to introduce formula, time to loft the babe-in-arms into the upright purview of the backpack, time to start toilet training, and so on. Sometimes I wonder, if it weren't for their father, would our two-year-old still be sleeping next to our bed and our five-year-old still be in diapers?

As our boys grow from infancy through toddlerhood and preschool and on to the expanding canvas of school, the dynamics of the entire family changes. From the symbiotic but sometimes insular mother-infant pair to the toddler and preschooler who tag along after Dad with great exuberance (Nate swinging a bat, Willy strapping plastic tools on his tool belt), at each new stage of our children's lives the whole family must reorganize. Each time a child takes a step away from the family and toward the outside world, not only do our internal boundaries shift, as schedules, logistics, and family groupings change, but our external boundaries shift as well. New ideas, new capabilities, new friends are introduced from the outside, and the whole family must respond and accommodate to them.

My sons have also shown me that attitudes toward separation have deep roots in the past. Indeed, of all the intergenerational themes I explored, separation stands out as the one most often preoccupying families for generations. Each time I agonize over a separation from my children, I feel my mother behind my shoulder agonizing over a separation from me, and the ghost of her mother behind her, not really wanting to let her go even from beyond the grave. The process is not linear or time-limited but, rather, circular, reciprocal, and ongoing. Every separation I negotiate with my children in turn affects my relationship with my parents, and the changes in my relationships with my parents surely have an impact on my relationships with my boys.

In their study of four Catholic, predominantly Italian families across three generations, titled *Mothers, Grandmothers, and Daughters*, Bertram Cohler and Henry Grunebaum sum up the intergenerational cross-references concerning separation this way:

In each of the four families, the relationship between the mother and her own mother influenced the manner in which issues of separation and autonomy were handled with the third generation. In the two families in which the mother's attitudes toward the issue of appropriate closeness and separation are less adaptive, conflict regarding this issue is already developing between the mother and her own children; this important psychological issue within the family is being communicated to the third generation.

Family therapist Murray Bowen believes that the new generation's ability to separate from the previous generation is circumscribed by that generation's ability to separate from the one before:

> Parents function in ways that result in their children achieving *about* the same degree of emotional separation from them that they achieved from their parents. However, not all children of one set of parents separate emotionally to the same degree. This is because the characteristics of the parents' relationship with each child are not the same. Their relationship with one child may foster more separation than their relationship with another. So it is possible for one child to achieve a little more emotional separation from his parents than the parents achieved from their parents, and another child to achieve a little less separation from his parents than they achieved from theirs.

Each generation adds its layers to the separation struggle and alters the way this struggle is handled. Often triangling in a new family member with a different history and attitude will markedly affect the way the new generation handles the challenge. Typically it is the husband who changes the chemistry between his wife and her parents and later between his wife and their children. Roberta Israeloff is a mother like myself whose struggles to separate from her own children date back to her childhood difficulty separating from her parents. She credits her husband, David, with masterminding a ritual of Saturday night dates without their baby. But she also tells how this ritual is subject to the critical voices of the past:

> Did my parents resent the fact that the same child who made it so hard for them to leave could now leave her child so easily? Did they know that I never left easily, that my only advantage was in having

David, who believed in saying good-bye and shutting the door? His ear couldn't discern the inaudible plea wafting across the generations in my family, the message that came to me from my parents, who'd heard it from theirs, the message I was trying so desperately to keep from Ben: "Never leave," they chorused, "please never leave."

In another family, with daughters five and two, the mother's history of anxiety with separations is also ameliorated by her husband's steadier keel. Here the mother describes her own complex history and the tangled intergenerational web of triangles involving her parents and siblings and *their* parents and siblings:

> ▶ Separation from my family was difficult for me. I was very homesick at summer camp at ages eight, ten, and twelve. When I went to college, I became very depressed. In retrospect, it's clear to me that I was homesick. After much therapy and self-reflection, I've realized that my problems with separation were intergenerational. Even as an adult, my mother was very dependent on her mother. Unfortunately, I think this adult dependence was denigrated in her family. Her mother saw her as loyal but somehow less good than her idealized younger sister. I believe I carried out the same role in my family. While my mother played some part in perpetuating my problem with separation, she unconsciously saw me as less capable than my sister, who separated easily, was competent and self-sufficient, like my mother's brother. I recapitulated her feelings of inferiority to her sister.

Now with two young daughters, this mother is understandably concerned about transmitting her history of uncertainty to the next generation:

> ▶ I am terrified that I will replay this scenario with my own children. I feel that awareness and insight about these patterns can play a part in changing them, but I'm not sure that awareness alone can eradicate them. My oldest has had a difficult adjustment to nursery school (she still sometimes screams "I don't want to go to school"), and I can't help but wonder if I'm transmitting my anxieties about separation. I'm also aware

that I've sometimes hated the process of falling asleep — it's a kind of separation — and wonder if my children's sleep problems are also related to my own anxieties. In writing this, I also became aware that to a certain extent, I see my younger daughter as self-sufficient like my sister, and my older daughter as less able to separate, like me.

But fortunately for this family, the father had had an easier time with childhood separations, and his confidence helped the whole family handle the transitions more evenly. Here he describes his own history and attitudes:

▶ I'm sure for me there were numerous turning points when I was young — nursery school, kindergarten, junior high (starting seventh grade). But certainly from my current point of view, leaving home to go to college was the major separation. I'd never gone to camp. It was surprisingly easy, given my enmeshment in the family. I guess my parents' resourcefulness and general emotional strength helped. I also had an eight-year younger sister to pick up the baton. (She has separated successfully too, since.) With our children, the two big steps so far for me have been the initial day care, about six months, and for our older girl, the transition to preschool at two and a half. Each step is hard for me — a kid's separation anxiety pulls on my heart-strings and stirs up my own anxiety about separation. But ultimately these separations have been gratifying to watch.

Pulls on my heart-strings, yet *gratifying to watch* — this double thread of anxiety and joy, gain and loss is yet another lesson my children have taught me about separation. Each step my children take away from me turns out to be a gain and a loss for them and a loss and a gain for me. Loving nursing them and dreading weaning — and postponing it as long as possible — I finally followed the lead of each baby and moved from the breast to a bottle with relative equanimity. Toddling around the house with his "baba," each boy was giddy with his own self-reliance. Yet when bedtime came, they still wanted to cuddle next to me and fall asleep on our bed. They didn't want to be reminded of the new stage of separation, until they woke up the next morning in their own cribs.

And from my side, I miss the closeness of the nursing embrace and the gentle harmony it brought to our days — naptime and bedtime an effortless cuddle and drifting off in my arms. Yet I was revitalized by the surge of energy that weaning brings, and I relished the extra edge of freedom. The indispensability of being a nursing mother is an opportunity I am grateful to have savored, yet a responsibility I am not entirely sorry to give up.

So it goes throughout their childhood, throughout my motherhood — anxiety and joy, loss and gain, opportunity and burden. The elation when they are finally out of diapers mixed with the hassle of rushing them to public bathrooms at the most inopportune times; the excitement of the first days of nursery school when the empty house seems serenely quiet mixed with the days when the empty house seems stifling and tomblike without the pitter-patter of little feet.

A friend with two school-age children tells me that when her children's demands and needs and jockeying for attention crowd in on her, she mutters a quiet mantra to herself, "One day the children will be gone, and then I'll have all the quiet I want." And that thought is so sobering that she returns to the buzz of family life with renewed zeal. I, too, can easily project to the time when my toddlers will be teenagers and then gone, and I can imagine the thrill of that freedom ("We can have pizza any night we want without worrying about nutrition for the kids," says a friend whose last just left the nest). And I can also imagine the chasm left by the kids' leaving and the gnawing silence of the house.

So perhaps it is just as well that I now understand that separation is a cyclical process — and unending. For every move away from me that my children make, there is an inevitable return, however brief, before the next foray, a regression before a progression. A few weeks of my younger's giddy glee at playgroup is followed by a tearful period of skirt-clinging and then a steadier balance of zest and independence; for my older, a honeymoon period of excitement about going to school is followed by a flap of resistance, then a surer confidence about his new direction. Sometimes a developmental leap is preceded (perhaps energized?) by a period of uncertainty or crankiness. Parents of infants talk of night-waking starting up again before a new milestone is about to be reached — crawling or walking for the first time. When the milestone is achieved, sleep again becomes peaceful, a relief on all sides. Parents of teenagers talk as well about the extra orneriness that often precedes the departure for college, so that that parting is finally met with relief as well as regret. Each action with a reaction, each forward momentum with a fallback, so that the process of separation is accomplished with the motion of a spiral rather than with the straight and uncompromising forward sweep of the arrow.

For a mother in her early forties with daughters eight and five, the cyclical nature of separation was a hard-won lesson. Several traumatic separations when she was in her early twenties had forced her to mature earlier than most, and perhaps because those separations came as such a shock, she was determined to provide her daughters with a series of gentler, age-appropriate separations from her:

> ▶ The major turning point in my separation from my parents came when I married at age twenty and moved out of the home. A further "separation" occurred when my first husband abandoned me when I was five months pregnant. Subsequently I had to give my son up for adoption. It was an awakening to realization for me, and also a realization that I could survive such a deep, grievous trauma. I experienced separation from my parents as a maturing process of myself. I have encouraged my children to be separate from me by providing them alternate adults to be with. They go camping with Aunt Mary. They spend overnights at friends' homes and have since they were babies. I feel every little step toward independence is a part of the natural process of separation — also activities they do without me, such as swim lessons, horse camp, art school, etc.

Now, with the sweetened perspective of the years, she has come to accept the cyclical nature of separations:

▶ I wonder if my children will learn earlier (it took me to age forty to understand) that life is a series of cycles: connections, separations, losses, reconnections, and that the really important thing is loving and caring for people, your family and friends, and enjoying the small pleasures of life.

One crucial part of the lifelong process of separation that I, like this mother, have learned from my children, is the continual gauging of the comfortable amount of closeness and distance. One week my crawling baby won't move out of my eye range; the next week he suddenly scoots from room to room oblivious of my presence. One week my schoolboy swears he'll never board the schoolbus; a few weeks later he's begging to ride it with his friends. So I must gauge their readiness — and my own — for the next step, the next phase. I must not push them before they're ready, or my crawling baby, my tender schoolboy will dissolve in tears. Nor must I hold them back after they're ready, or my schoolboy will feel smothered, my baby inhibited from making the next plunge. I must steer a course between closeness and distance, neither too enmeshed nor too disengaged, in Salvador Minuchin's terms.

To navigate this challenging course takes patience, awareness, and a good degree of separation from the parent generation. For parents who have not effectively separated from their own parents, there are two major booby traps waiting to snag them. Explains family therapist Sheri Glucoft Wong, "Either these parents pull their kids in too tightly and get a symbiosis going with their kids, or they don't get close to the kids to start with, in order to avoid the separation problem. It's interesting that I often find that people who have the most abandonment issues in their childhood worry the most about abandonment and can't leave their kids again. 'If I just say good-bye and hug them and walk away and leave them in child care,' these parents say to themselves, 'who knows what might happen?' They project their childhood pain onto their kids."

At both ends of the separation continuum — the enmeshed and the disengaged — problems crop up. The overinvolved parent cramps his children's growing room and disregards their need to learn from their own mistakes. The Traditionalist parent who has not successfully separated from his own parents often finds himself on this end of the continuum. Loyal to his own parents, sometimes to a fault, the overinvolved Traditionalist can make children feel that any step toward separation is an act of betrayal. Robbing his children of privacy and autonomy, this parent limits the full flowering of personality, the blossoming of self-respect and self-esteem. Comments Bruno Bettelheim:

> So much of what goes wrong between parents and children . . . stems from [the parents'] conscious decision to be close to their child, and their unconscious feeling that he can only be really *theirs* if he has no secrets from them. . . . They are ready to acknowledge the fact that their child has an unconscious, but while it is all right for that unconscious to be hidden from everyone else, it ought *not* to be hidden from *them*, his parents.

Closer to home, I think of the weekly letter to parents from my five-year-old's kindergarten teacher after the first week or two of school. In a gentle way, she encouraged all the parents to take a step back from their kindergarteners and respect their children's privacy while they adjust to the major transition of going to school for the first time:

> This is a transition for you, too, but when you, with the best intentions, confront a tired child with questions like "What did you do at school today???" it only increases the pressure.
>
> When children come home from school, they need time to unwind and be in a familiar and comfortable place with familiar and comfortable people who love and support them. Bite your tongue if you can, and wait for a time when you can initiate a real conversation with your child. He or she is much more likely to open up and tell you more. Your child will feel your interest and support without feeling any pressure. Lastly, your child is growing up. You will find increasingly that there are areas in his or her life from which you will be excluded. They are private areas, ones that are special to your child, not because they are bad or good, threatening or shameful, just private. We all need and value our own privacy. Let your child know that you value his or hers. This is not to say that you will never hear about school, but there may be days when your child does not feel like talking. That's okay.

If the overinvolved parent crowds in on a child and robs him of identity that way, the underinvolved parent gives a child so much psychic space that he feels uncared for and untended. The Rebel parent who has had sharp separation struggles with her parents often takes the opposite course with her children and is afraid to get too close to them. Fearing overinvolvement, she substitutes underinvolvement, and her children are left stranded in an attention vacuum.

The child of the underinvolved or disengaged parent ends up groping for identity without a frame of reference. This is the parent who never makes it to the school play, can't be bothered helping a child struggling with homework, dismisses Christmas as a commercial aberration, and sees no need to make a fuss. The child of the underinvolved parent has no one to bounce off, no one to care whether he wins or loses, no one to help him regain his balance when he falls. This child is not grounded in such a way that separation can happen in predictable — or even unpredictable — stages. He is constantly in a state of free fall.

Often one side wants more or less separation than the other does. The resulting push and pull accounts for a good deal of the pain between the generations. The Compensator parent is often caught in this push and pull with his children, striving for greater closeness if his own parents were too distant, striving for greater distance if his parents came too close. Typically, demands for closeness on one side are met with retreats on the other; increased retreats are countered with increased demands. One goal of family therapy can be to rebalance a dysfunctional system and interrupt this kind of negative cycle so that all family members give — and get — more of what they want and need.

Although much literature about families seems to mythologize the overwhelming mother and her retreating children, Cohler and Grunebaum's study came up with a different twist on the advances and retreats between generations. In the four families they studied in depth, all the married daughters sought greater closeness with their own mothers than the mothers were comfortable with. As the researchers explain:

> A complex bond was established in each of these four families between the married daughter and her own mother. In each instance, the daughter sought greater closeness and dependency than was

comfortable for her own mother. The grandmothers [that is, the mothers of the grown daughters] in these families, finally freed from the task of childcare, wanted greater autonomy than their daughters could accept. It was nice to visit with their daughters, but, even when the two generations shared a common residence, they were unwilling to make regular babysitting arrangements or to assume significant responsibilities within the daughter's household. This conflict between the daughter's dependency and her mother's wish for freedom and autonomy was clear in each of the four modified extended families and represented a major unresolved psychological issue within each of these four families.

As an adult daughter of two caring and still concerned parents, as a mother of two enterprising and still inexperienced sons, perhaps the most important lesson I am learning about separation is that its goal is not independence but interdependence. Salvador Minuchin defines the goal of the separation process as autonomy with interdependence. Boundaries in enmeshed families need to be strengthened, he counsels, to help protect each family member's individuality, and boundaries in disengaged families need to become less rigid to allow family members to support each other's needs.

Three thousand miles apart from my own parents, I see the phone lines as the sinews that bind us, the image of our interdependence. At times of trouble or jubilation, at times of loneliness or weariness, they crackle and connect us. Sometimes my father is on one extension and my mother on another at their house, and my husband and I and two sons yanking at the third phone are in place at ours. So despite our separation the generations are linked and in touch.

A friend who is near fifty, with a father of seventy-five and two sons, twenty-two and fourteen, described to me the reciprocity between the generations in her extended family:

> ▶ I'm thinking about my father and the things he did so well. He had a store, and he was always available to see or come by. I tried to do that with my own kids: they always had a phone number for me or a place they could come to when I was working. My father's philosophy was that raising children was like raising birds: you kept them in the nest, but when they were ready they could fly on their own. I thought of that

with both my sons: I wanted to give them a nice nest, but it was important for them to be independent, to learn to take care of themselves. I got strong messages growing up about being independent but always having access to my parents. I still will call my father to check in or share a problem. I ask his advice and now he calls me and asks me what to do — and I don't expect him to do what I suggest!

When my inclination to clutch at my children gets the better of me, I try to remember the wisdom of my friend's father.

At each stage of our children's development and our own, we have a chance to observe and practice separating, deepening our appreciation of this delicate dance in the process. The rest of this chapter will explore two pivotal stages — the separation and individuation of the toddler and of the adolescent — and show how, in their themes and goals, their turbulence and intensity, they are connected. As the toddler defines his own turf, his behavior foreshadows the challenges of the adolescent; the adolescent's searching breaks new ground for the family and for herself, and at the same time recalls the tasks of the toddler. And the parents of the toddler — new, inexperienced, idealistic — prefigure yet also stand apart from the parents of the adolescent, who are seasoned and experienced, but grappling with a new set of midlife priorities.

Imagine a typical toddler — mine, for example. He is somewhere between the ages of one and a half and three. Just yesterday (so it seems), he was the cuddly, nursing, wobbling, barely speaking baby. Now he is upright and in constant motion, bypassing walking for running whenever possible, so that strangers stop me in the street to remark, "You must have your hands full!" What most complicates being the mother of this toddler is that his motion, both physical and emotional, is not simply forward momentum like the jolts of his wind-up monkey, but rather backward, forward, and sideways — like bumper cars. One moment he is dashing so far ahead of me on a walk that I have to run pell-mell to keep him from careening into traffic. The next minute he is the tired traveler, holding up his pitiful arms and crying "Uppie, uppie," so I'll carry him, infantlike, down the same mean streets he just traversed by himself. One day at a party he runs off with his brother and the older kids so I'm not even aware I still have a two-year-old; the next day he stays so close to my side I can't take a bite of dinner unattended; the third day he is willing to go off on brief forays but constantly dashes back again to touch home base.

And along with the back-and-forth unfolding of motion and body confidence comes the simultaneous unfolding of language and imagination. His first words are "bye," "Nay-Nay" (for Nate, his brother), and "duck," but the word that comes soon after — the unmistakable N-word — is the one that's used most often. "No," he doesn't want toast and jam for breakfast. "No," he doesn't want cheese or cereal. "No," there is absoutely nothing he wants, except — cheese it is after all ("Changed my mind," he explained a few weeks ago).

And with the noes come other limit-testing and self-defining opinions, invariably contrary to my own, a whole range and barrage of them scattered through the house like BB's from a BB gun. "Me bad guy," he roars through the house, flailing his plastic sword against all comers. With an intensity worthy of a teenager, he makes clothes a daily battleground. Pants are too tight or too short; they need to be blue not red; socks must be pushed down not up. One day at playgroup he has a crying fit because his pants have no pockets. Another day he absolutely insists that the green light means stop and the red, go. Only on matters of life and death — or occasionally when red pants are the only clean ones in the drawer — do I disagree. When I can, I do my best to give him growing room. When I can't — and sometimes no matter what approach I take, the noes explode into a full-bodied tantrum — I must wait out the storm like a vacationer trapped by a hurricane, until the rage and winds blow over. And invariably the most bitter outbursts are followed by the most endearing efforts to be held and comforted and reassured of unflappable parental love.

But as the two-year-old approaches three, signs of mellowing are in the air, as welcome as the first tentative buds after a long winter. Separations for playgroup or an adult evening on the town are met with a cheerful "Bye, bye, Mommy" and a quick return to play. Around the house he is more and more cooperative, doing his best to accomplish tasks by himself. "Me do, me do" is his refrain. His fantasy play becomes more sophisticated — he is doctor, daddy, mommy, Superman — and I sense that he is more and more able to keep the image of his father and me in his mind when we are gone.

And it takes a month or two before my husband and I notice another change. Without our quite realizing it, the hailstorm of noes is being replaced by a jaunty sunburst of okays, heralding the pivotal transition to the amenable, yes-saying threes. Now, most of the time at least, our little "bad guy" is becoming a friendly "good guy."

The years from birth to three, but most intensively from about one to two and a half, are considered by many psychologists to be a kind of second birth. This time the birth is a psychological one in which the child finds selfhood and a separate identity. In the words of psychologist Louise Kaplan, whose lyrical and moving *Oneness and Separateness* greatly influenced my thinking for this chapter:

> Psychological birth is fundamentally different from physical birth. Whereas physical birth meant a rupturing of bonds, psychological birth strengthens the bonds of love and attachment between a child and his parents. As the child finds his optimal distance and secures his own space in the world, yes-saying and a desire to please the parents take the place of oppositional no-saying and willfulness. . . . The less the child is concerned with the issues of separateness, the more he can use his aggressive energies for acquiring the emotions, fantasies, language, memory, judgment and learning abilities that will enable him to please his parents.

It was Margaret Mahler, a world-renowned child psychoanalyst and a teacher and colleague of Louise Kaplan's, who pioneered the research on this period of second birth. Working with both normal and psychotic infants both as a pediatrician and a clinician, Mahler observed and gradually codified a series of separation-individuation phases. The infant is born to a state of symbiotic oneness, she believed, a state in which he does not experience a separate sense of self. His sense of separateness unfolds gradually through varying degrees of differentiation between himself and his mother to eventual independence, walking, talking, and being able to keep mother's image in mind even when she is gone.

According to Mahler and her followers, separation-individuation consists of two interweaving strands. In Kaplan's words, separation involves "the infant's emotional attachment to mother — approaching her, distancing, setting boundaries between them, learning conditions of loving and hating." Individuation involves "growth, sensation, muscular power, memory, sense of reality, autonomy, speech, intellectual power, sense of self." Like every stage in the story of separation between the generations, the toddler's separation-individuation is accomplished with a spiraling rather than a linear movement. Kaplan describes the second birth as a constant interplay between "clinging and pushing away, shadowing and darting away, holding on and letting go," as the toddler finds the best distance that will allow him to be part of his mother's space while keeping his own space defined.

More recently, infant researchers at Cornell University Medical Center, led by Daniel Stern, have countered Mahler's work by suggesting that the infant begins to experience a separate and emergent sense of self from the moment of birth. In *The Interpersonal World of the Infant,* Stern describes his view of the infant self continuously unfolding in different forms, as opposed to Mahler's vision of a discontinuous process in which a sense of self emerges only after a long period of undifferentiation.

These differences in interpretation, however, remain largely outside the scope of this book. My focus is on the ambivalence that is often at the heart of the toddler experience for both parents and children. This ambivalence can be most productive, as T. Berry Brazelton explains, writing about the one-year-old:

> Ambivalence is at the root of [the] choice [for independence], and the experience of it, the mastery of it, are at the base of the child's ability to become a really independent person. A mother who is not there, or one who cannot allow [the child] to struggle with this choice, undermines [the child's] future adjustment. This separation may be as difficult for the mother as it is for the child. The satisfaction of the first year's closeness is now threatened. [The mother] must allow [the child] enough time to realize she is left, to protest it, and to find her own way of coping with her feelings.

If ambivalence is often at the heart of the toddler's experience of separation-individuation — clinging and pushing away, holding on and letting go — so, too, is it often at the heart of the *parents'* experience. Moods and strategies from the past are aroused by the toddlers' intense separation process, and this web of memory and feeling inevitably colors how parents respond to this period. Although memories of their own toddler years and their own parents' response to separation are naturally obscured by the passage of time, repression, or denial, still, watching and responding to their own toddlers often stirs up strong echoes from the past.

Depending on their emotional resources and the primings of their own pasts, parents will find different aspects or phases of their toddler's separation process more or less challenging, more or less manageable. Sometimes what they lack in one area they can make up in another. One parent might overreact to a toddler's defiance and no-saying; another might take the defiance in stride but have a hard time with the clinginess or mild sadness that sometimes follows. Although the cloudburst of no-saying, willfulness, and temper tantrums makes parents call this period the "terrible twos," this very behavior helps toddlers establish their ego boundaries as separate from their parents'.

How parents respond to their toddlers' noes is crucial in setting the stage for the relationship that follows and for the toddler's feeling of efficacy in the expanding world. Too much parental resistance to the early barrage of noes, and the toddler will feel hopelessly squelched and locked in an eternal power struggle; too little resistance from parents, and the toddler will get an inflated view of his omnipotence. My own inclination is for redirection rather than resistance. I try to frame my own noes in positive terms ("Bang the hammer on the work bench" rather than "STOP BANGING ON THE FURNITURE!") and meet my children's noes with alternatives whenever possible rather than locking horns. ("Here's a juicy cantaloupe" rather than "Absolutely no more candy!") Still, I wonder if my desire to sidestep confrontation will become more costly later on with the even higher stakes of school years and adolescence.

Margaret Mahler points out that the separation process can produce diverse reactions not only in different parents but also within one parent:

For example, [a mother] may suffer feelings of loss of the previous symbiotic oneness and completeness as well as feelings of relief from the demands of the previous parasitic relationship. She may find pleasure in the new object relationship, and in the child's "choice" of relationship to his mother, while finding that his concentration upon her and unwillingness to accept substitute mothering objects are new and possibly threatening kinds of demands.

Then, too, one parent may have an entirely different experience of separation with each of her children, depending on each one's emotional needs and demands and internal resources. Sometimes a parent copes with his conflicting feelings about separation in his own childhood by unconsciously encouraging different children to play out opposite sides of his ambivalence. A mother of two children, remembering the conflicts around separation in her own childhood, describes an enmeshed family with a hovering and overprotective mother as well as two independent maiden aunts:

> ▶ My mother had a very symbiotic relationship with me. She was very nervous and high-strung, hovering around me to protect me against illness. She always wanted to keep me in view. She didn't value friends and didn't want me to nurture friendships, because those would intervene. I felt lots of responsibility — as if I was my mother's life. Meanwhile, someone dropped a seed of independence into my head. I had two maiden aunts who were role models of independence.

Overprotected by her mother but inspired to independence by her aunts, when this woman became a mother she saw in her own children from the time they were small the two coping styles of her own background. Her first son was "real independent"; at three months he started going to day care for twelve hours a week. Her second son insisted on staying right by his mother; he "cried at any separation," and as a result she did what she could to keep him home with her as long as possible. But she also began gently to give him safe, small chances to separate from her, just as she made sure to give her older boy plenty of cuddles despite his independence. Seeing the contrasting ways her children coped with separation helped her integrate her own past, and in doing so, she became more secure and confident as a mother.

Often parents of toddlers feel threatened by either too much closeness or too much distance. Margaret Mahler tells of a mother of a young son and daughter who had the most difficult time with the close symbiosis of early infancy:

> She believed that she must never tie her children, and especially her son, emotionally to herself. By nature somewhat undemonstrative, [this mother] tried deliberately from the first months not to "spoil" her children — that is, from her point of view, not to damage her infants by close bodily contact. Underlying these ideas were fantasies of the destructiveness of symbiotic closeness.

But as the early symbiosis lessened and the toddler phase began, particularly as her children began expressing themselves with words, her relationship with them improved, and she began to enjoy their company rather than feeling threatened by their closeness and nonstop needs.

Contemporary research in early infant-child attachment pioneered by the British psychoanalyst John Bowlby and by the American psychologist Mary Ainsworth, among others, seems finally to have quieted the fears of earlier generations about "spoiling." Warm, attentive care does not instill dependency, Ainsworth insisted, but the opposite; sensitive attention and immediate response to a baby's needs promotes eventual autonomy. "It's a good thing to give a baby and young child physical contact," she said, "especially when they want it and seek it. It doesn't spoil them. It doesn't make them clingy. It doesn't make them addicted to being held."

Attachment theory focuses on the security or insecurity of the attachment between mother and child. Ainsworth and her colleagues have devoted themselves to longitudinal studies of attachment during the infant's first year and beyond. Her research began with attentive home visits, observing a mother's style of responding to her infant in the crucial areas of feeding, crying, cuddling, eye contact, and smiling. Then her research followed up with an experimental observation she created called the "strange situation," in which babies were observed in a lab first with their mothers, then separated from their mothers, and then reunited.

Ainsworth discovered three major patterns of responses to separation and reunion in this procedure. The first group of infants —

those called "securely" attached — might or might not show distress when they were separated but clearly wanted contact or interaction when they were reunited and were readily comforted if distressed. The second group — "insecure/avoidant" — did not show distress on separation and seemed to ignore mother's leaving but avoided her when she returned. It may be that their insecurity about attachment was so great that they feared even to let it show. The third group — called "insecure/ambivalently" attached — tended to be clingy from the beginning and became highly distressed at separation. They were then ambivalent at mother's return, both seeking contact with her and either passively or angrily resisting contact. When Ainsworth and her colleagues compared the home situation with the strange situation, they found that the mothers of the secure infants had been more consistently sensitive, less rejecting, and less interfering in the home throughout the first year.

Follow-up studies have shown that without intervention or changes in family circumstances, attachment patterns formed in infancy tend to persist into childhood. At age two, children who were insecurely attached as infants seem to have poorer resources for problem solving than securely attached children, and by school age, they often have more problematic relationships with peers.

Mary Main, a professor at the University of California, Berkeley, and a former student of Ainsworth's, has found a relationship between parents' memories and descriptions of their own childhood experiences and their infants' patterns of attachment to them. Main and her students used a sample of mothers and fathers of six-year-olds whose attachments had been evaluated at twelve or eighteen months. She devised a lengthy and demanding interview that focused on the parents' childhood relationships with their parents. Parents of securely attached children tended to have good access to their childhood memories and were able to describe them clearly without becoming overwhelmed. Even though some of these parents had had difficult childhoods, they could report them coherently and present an integrated picture of the past.

Parents whose children had been insecure/avoidant tended to idealize their childhood experiences without having access to actual memories that would support the idealized picture. Often, when details were probed, neglect or rejection lurked behind the veneer of perfection. Just as these parents shut themselves off from the reality and replaced it with an ideal image, the children also avoided genuine contact with them. A third group of parents, of children who had been insecure/ambivalent, tended to be either passively or angrily preoccupied with their attachment relationships, often seeming still enmeshed with their own parents.

Many attachment psychologists feel that even the most insecurely attached children are amenable to change in their early years, either through intervention or through an attachment to another adult besides their parents — a teacher, friend, or caring aunt, for example. But in families where there is no help to change a habit of avoidance, children may grow up to be rigidly independent adults, emotionally "cut off," in Murray Bowen's phrase, from enduring connections with their families.

One vital characteristic shared by Ainsworth's most securely attached parents and my category of Synthesizers is their ability to keep in touch with their own childhood memories and to integrate these experiences into a coherent picture of the past. The availability of this picture, whether it was bleak or joyful, checkered or smooth, helps them to be fully present with their own children, comfortable both in forming attachments and in letting go. What marks the Synthesizers especially is their knack for finding balance between connectedness and individuation.

As they watch and respond to their toddler's cues, these Synthesizer parents are able to negotiate a balance that is neither too distant nor too smothering. Brazelton uses a vivid image — a back door left ajar by a mother so a two-year-old can go in and out at will — to describe the comfortable middle ground these parents can find to foster yet not push a child's manageable separation. The open door lets the child know that it is safe to separate and also fine to want to come back inside again.

Among the people I interviewed, a Synthesizer mother in her late twenties with a year-and-a-half-old son showed her sensitivity to both sides of the toddler's separation struggle. This mother learned to value her son's drive for independence ("There's nothing bad about having a bad temper; it's spunky"). She also became aware of his alternating cues for separation and closeness and responded accordingly:

> ▶ I want him to learn self-respect, and the only way is by doing things on his own. If I don't respect his independence, we clash. He'll climb anything — he's a monkey. Sometimes I try to protect him by holding his hand, and he'll say, "Let go." He very rarely lets me hold his hand. But he's very affectionate — he'll run his fingers through my hair. He has a wonderful personality. He's good company. He has to be — I spend all my time with him. He lives life to its fullest, and consequently I do too.

Part of what prepared this mother to respect her toddler's drive for individuation was the support and respect that was part of her childhood home. Although she does not remember the specifics of her toddlerhood, she does recall how her rights were honored as an adolescent:

> ▶ I always felt respected, and my privacy was never violated. My mother found my birth control when I was sixteen, and all she said was, "How long have you been using this?" I realized later that she was dying inside. But my mother always said she couldn't make my mistakes for me. Still, I always felt I could turn to my parents. They would always bail me out.

Besides good parental support, this young mother had the backing of her husband in gauging and balancing closeness and separation:

> ▶ I love watching my husband with our son. I took for granted that my husband would spend fifty to sixty percent of his time with him. Now we take turns being the parent of preference. If our son is tired or crabby, he often wants me, but if he wants an adventure or a shoulder ride, he turns to his dad.

Synthesizers realize that the dance of separation is not just a *pas de deux* but a family quadrille. The father's involvement and support is crucial both for his own growth and for that of the family. From the earliest months of infancy, when Dad is the one to toss the baby in the air just a little higher than Mom deems entirely safe and to tickle him just a little longer than Mom deems appropriate, Dad is the one to lure the baby out of his symbiotic orbit with mother and into a "love affair with the world," in psychoanalyst Phyllis Greenacre's evocative phrase. For both baby and mother, father provides a welcome change. For the baby and toddler, father offers a different style of play, a different tempo, a critical difference in gender, which will become increasingly important with the years and particularly when the child becomes an adolescent. For the mother, father is a partner to share both the joys and headaches of these early years and an indispensable support when the pressures become too intense.

Although family dynamics and roles have changed dramatically for many families over the last decade or two, even in the most traditional family, where mother is the main caretaker, father's presence is critical. His comings and goings deeply affect the balance of the family as a whole. A friend whose daughter is now a teenager remembered a time years ago when her daughter was not quite three and her husband went away on a business trip. Noticing her daughter's usual good spirits flagging, this mother suggested drawing a picture of what it felt like to have Daddy away. The little girl drew a big stick figure for Daddy and a little stick figure for herself and then scribbled over the whole picture and said, "I feel crossed out." "What a description!" remarked her mother. "Dad doesn't exist, so I don't exist!" So intricately linked are our children's lives and identifications with our own that any move by one family member changes the whole picture.

Now imagine a typical teenager, the one I might have been or the one I might have raised. Just yesterday (so it seems), she was the agreeable, enterprising, task-oriented, and independent child of latency, going cheerfully about her business and allowing her parents to go about theirs, or uncomplainingly joining forces for family outings or confabs. Now suddenly, along with pimples and breasts, eye makeup and torn jeans, she has become an unpredictable stranger. Overnight, it seems, she has become a creature of violent shifts in mood and attitude, in allegiances and opinions. One moment she is saying and doing the most outrageous things, anything to tweak the family's nose. The next moment she is desperately seeking unconditional acceptance and love. One moment she fairly hums with responsibility and helpfulness, masterminding a dinner for the family or a surprise song for her father's fiftieth birthday. The next moment she is more trouble than a toddler, spewing laundry all over the floor, smearing chocolate fingerprints on the sofa, missing a curfew by miles. In the same evening she will push the family away ("I'll do my homework myself") just as tearfully as she pulls them close ("Isn't anyone around here going to help me with my homework?")

And along with the back-and-forth momentum of separation and closeness, growth and dependence, come a self-absorption and an absorption with peers that seem to leave the family out in the cold. Hours are spent preoccupied with her body, her hair, her clothes. She experiments with makeup in front of the mirror, makes faces to practice finding the one with which to greet the world. She wanders aimlessly through Bloomingdale's, not buying much but endlessly checking things out, searching for a style, a look, an identity of her own. Often it seems that the real business of life is transacted on the phone. She will rush home from school and call the friends she has already talked with for hours all day. But the phone is a special kind of lifeline, linking the safe harbor of family and childhood to the alluring world beyond. She spends hours whispering into it and receiving its soothing hum, dissecting every nuance of home and school, of relationships with boys — details often more tangible and interesting in the telling and retelling than in the actual time spent together. She is always careful to lower her voice when a parent chances into the room.

When it is too late to call anyone, she lies on her bed, mooning over late-night rock radio. Surrounded by symbols of the clash of her two worlds — the childhood doll collection next to the pictures of New Kids on the Block, the locked leather journal next to stuffed bears and monkeys — she moons over boyfriends loved and lost, over friendships made and broken, over dreams caught and unfulfilled. Deep into the night, she moons with an intensity completely heartfelt, yet overcharged with an emotion not entirely identifiable.

For the teenage mooning is also a mourning for a time and a relationship that will never entirely come again. The protected harbor of childhood will soon open up into the wide seas of adulthood. And the protective relationship with parents will soon take on a new configuration for adulthood and let in new connections with lovers and others.

Where the toddlers' window-shattering noes are gradually tempered by the preschooler's more amenable and cooperative yeses, so, too, the teenager's blanket rejection of her parents is gradually replaced by more seasoned tolerance of their quirks and foibles. And with that acceptance of human imperfection, the teenager also readies herself for the deep bonds of mature love she will begin to build outside the family.

Just as the toddler hovers between infancy and childhood — one moment a needy infant, the next a swaggering child — the adolescent balances between childhood and adulthood — one moment a needy child, the next a responsible and insightful grown-up. And just as the period from birth to three is the dawning of the child's identity and separate self, so, again, is adolescence a time when the once powerless child begins to take responsibility for herself, builds mature relationships with the parent generation, and looks ahead to the time when she'll take responsibility for a new generation.

For Rousseau, the second birth of adolescence is a time when "love of oneself" is transferred into "love of the species." For Erik Erikson, it is a time of "identity versus role confusion," ideally a time when identity is consolidated and the first serious choices in love and work are made. For Louise Kaplan, it is a time of "active deconstruction, construction, reconstruction — a period in which past, present and future are rewoven and strung together on the threads of fantasies and wishes."

For Terri Apter, in her sensitive and original *Altered Loves: Mothers and Daughters During Adolescence*, the adolescent's "quest for individuation" is a search "not for separation but for a different balance with . . . parents." And as was true during the first separation-individuation crisis, the growing child balances the need to be separate with the need to belong.

During adolescence some of the early childhood issues around separation and individuation may come up again to be reworked and resolved before the new challenges of adulthood are confronted. But adolescence is, above all, a distinctive time, with its own array of needs and emotional necessities. And parents of adolescents are also in a different stage than they were as parents of toddlers. Parents of adolescents may draw on responses familiar from the toddler period but will also need to respond in entirely new and creative ways.

The most striking similarity between the separation process for toddlers and that for teenagers is that development again proceeds with a spiraling rather than a linear momentum. Staggering leaps of growth are often followed by times of poignantly needy regression. Surges of elated joy are often countered by downswings into despondency. Ambivalences and contradictions abound: self-absorbed and considerate, clingy and confident, tentative and brash. But for adolescents, as for toddlers, the regressions and contradictions operate in the service of development. As psychoanalyst Peter Blos observes, "We cannot but recognize, retrospectively, in many an adolescent's vagary, that a strategic retreat was the surest road to victory. *Reculer pour mieux sauter.*"

Peter Blos, who has surveyed the individuation of adolescence as comprehensively as Margaret Mahler has the separation/individuation of toddlers, compares the two periods this way:

> Both periods have in common a heightened vulnerability of the personality organization. Both periods have in common the urgency for changes in psychic structure in consonance with the maturational forward surge. Last but not least, both periods — should they miscarry — are followed by a specific deviant development (psychopathology) that embodies the respective failures of individuation.

Blos emphasizes the adolescents' "capacity to move between regressive and progressive consciousness with an ease that has no equal at any other period in human life." At the center of this swing of the emotional pendulum from love to hate, from activity to passivity, is an ambivalence that "remains temporarily, at least, beyond the ego's synthesizing capacity to deal with . . . constructively." Many typical teenage defenses, like negativism, opposition, or indifference, are but a manifestation of this all-pervasive ambivalence.

Rebellion, acting out, preoccupation with the body, eccentric hair styles and dressing are all ways in which the adolescent begins to define herself as separate from parents and an individual in her own right. But Terri Apter stresses that the adolescent's rebellion proceeds with one eye in the back of her head, checking out parents' responses, needing to keep the connection going even while ostensibly breaking away.

The adolescent's rebellious and oppositional behavior serves an additional purpose as well. Not only does her behavior define an identity separate from parents, but it also connects her more intimately to her peers. The rebelliousness and wild dressing may seem eccentric in the eyes of parents, but in the eyes of peers it brings, in Blos's words, "stimulation, belongingness, loyalty, devotion, empathy, and resonance." For the toddler, the mother provides the help needed to reach autonomy; for the teenager, the peer group, gang, or coterie provides this boost toward autonomy — and also helps assuage the feelings of guilt stirred up by freeing herself from childhood loyalties and dependencies.

Here lies the most dramatic difference between the toddler's and the adolescent's struggles for separation. While the toddler may strive to gauge a new distance between himself and his parent, he still remains almost entirely within the family's orbit. But for the adolescent, the central task is to loosen the bonds of attachment to parents and prepare for lifelong commitments *outside the family*. Much of the teenager's *sturm and drang* is the result of the emotional struggle to relinquish the passionate attachment to parents and reconcile himself to their imperfections — as well as to his own. This reconciliation is an important prerequisite to sexual maturity and the formation of lasting relationships beyond the family. Explains Louise Kaplan:

> Sexual maturity . . . demands some final resolution of gender identity. At stake are not only the kind of man or woman one becomes and the choice of sexual attachment but also a definitive coming to terms with . . . love for the same-sex parent — that parent begins to be seen as she or he actually is, and not as an omnipotent god who can mirror the child's wish for perfection.

On both sides of the generation gap difficult emotional work is required to move to the next stage, and at times this work is accompanied by sadness, depression, even a sense of mourning. For the child about to reach adulthood is losing the omnipotent, all-protective parents of childhood. And the parents are losing the devoted, dependent child who is part of the family at home. The parents are struggling to separate from their child and find their way in the unexplored territory of midlife and the world beyond the daily care of children.

While the parent of the toddler has only the haziest memories and hears only the murkiest echoes of her own earliest separation from her parents, the parent of the adolescent usually has much more vivid memories of her struggles to break away from her parents — and of her parents' response. These memories and impressions of course color the way she responds to her children. The more conscious she is of these memories and the more attuned to the feelings surrounding them, the more likely she is to be sensitive to her own children's process.

Here a psychologically astute Synthesizer mother in her mid-forties with a sixteen-year-old son and an eighteen-year-old daughter about to leave for college appraises her own attitudes toward her children's separation against the background of her parents' attitudes:

▶ Though I think I have "easy" kids, I find I am more confused when they enter the stages of development where I feel I got stuck — now, for instance, when they are becoming independent, private adolescents. This is the area in my own growth where my parents were unprepared and apprehensive. Too much separation from them was regarded with disfavor. I hope my children will be more resilient and less needful of other people's approval than I was, yet at the same time I want them to be considerate and kind and receptive to others.

My parents adored children but not necessarily "grown-ups." Growing up meant falling from grace. I hope my children expect us to adore them as grown-ups, too, and I trust that we will. I remember putting my daughter to bed on the eve of her sixth birthday when she asked, "Mom, will you love me as much when I'm six as you did when I'm five?" That reminds me, too, of the Beatles' song "When I'm Sixty-Four"!

For many parents of adolescents, the grown-up child's leavetaking is a time of coming to terms with the full sweep of family history and of integrating family memories into the quilt of the generations. Observes Louise Kaplan:

> [Parents] recall the day they met, their courtship and marriage — the sweet moments they had together and the bitter. They reminisce about the birth of this marvelous child, her first smile, her first words, her first steps, her first days at school, her graduations and performances, her first date. They look back with longing and regret to the "golden" days of their own infancy, to their mothers and fathers as they seemed then — so strong, so marvelous — to the schoolyard games, to the springtime of youth when the energies of growth propelled them into the future and everything still seemed possible.

Although parents begin to see that their adolescent's departure is inevitable, often their involvement in their children's lives seems to intensify just before it dramatically de-escalates. During the latency or middle school-age years parents may have become what some have called "part-time parents," coexisting comfortably with their children but not often needing to intervene. But during adolescence the emotional climate heats up, and children demand more attention. The father's involvement especially seems to increase. In an essay on the father in midlife, psychologists Calvin Colarusso and Robert Nemiroff compare the father's role during the toddler's individuation to his role during the adolescent's:

> Primarily a participant-observer in the first individuation, the father serves as a buffer for both mother and child as they struggle against the powerful regressive pull toward symbiosis. During those oedipal and latency years, father plays a role of increasing importance as a protector, provider, and example for his young children. By the onset of adolescence, his position as a parent of equal importance to the mother is established in the minds of children, spouse, and self.

Sometimes the needs of one generation are out of sync or at odds with the needs of the other, and this often contributes to the turbulence of adolescence for both parents and children. The midlife father may have grown dissatisfied with his career and turned back to the family with renewed interest and commitment — only to find that the family has passed him by. The teenage sons would rather hang out with their pals than toss a football with Dad; the teenage daughters are falling for the cute boys down the block rather than carrying on the old oedipal romance with Dad.

In other families, adult children may want to come back home and be supported again by their parents, just when parents are adjusting to their new child-free status and savoring the taste of freedom. For many years the "empty nest" was considered to be a key source of women's midlife depression; now, the "full nest syndrome" — the return home of grown children — is a potential source of angst.

In every family with adolescents, sexuality is the issue that most dramatizes the differing trajectories of the generations. Inevitably the budding of adolescent sexuality coincides with the midlife tempering of sexuality. The adolescent's energy and body presence become more powerful just when the midlife parent's energy and body show the first signs of age. In some cases a daughter's menarche may even coincide with a mother's menopause. But even without this bold physical antithesis, the adolescent's sense of limitlessly unfolding possibilities poignantly contrasts with the parent's heightened awareness of mortality and the sense of doors closing. Some parents try to stay the force of time and cope with their sadness and envy by responding either too strictly to their teenager's behavior or too seductively to their teenager's friends. Others may try to compete, denying the inevitabilities of age by last-ditch attempts at acting out — in wild dressing or parties or affairs.

The parents who experience the most meaningful, and successful, separation from their adolescents are those who don't deny but confront and accept the realities of aging and the inevitabilities of separation. They understand that both the difficult realities and the joyful ones provide opportunities for growth. These Synthesizer parents realize that they have their own psychic work to do while their children are doing theirs. That may mean searching for a new direction or passion beyond family and child raising. It may mean reexamining and revitalizing their marriage as well as forging a new and satisfying kind of relationship with adult children. And it may mean completing some of the old business of separating from their own parents while their children are struggling to separate from them.

Calvin Colarusso and Robert Nemiroff tell of a forty-year-old business tycoon who, during psychoanalysis, expressed a troubling sense of worthlessness in relation to a powerful and very successful father. Although the son's success had surpassed his father's in many ways, his achievements had little impact on his sense of self-esteem. But seeing the healthy development of his latency-aged and teenaged sons did fill him with pride and satisfaction, as Colarusso and Nemiroff explain:

> Could he really be so bad if he was man enough and father enough to produce them? As he analyzed his overidealization and fear of his own father, he was able to engage his sons in a more relaxed and positive manner. To his surprise and delight, they responded positively. "For the first time I really feel like a somebody. I'm a hell of a better father than I thought." As his children continued to develop they became living expressions of his self-worth.

The growth and development of his sons — and of his capabilities as a father — helped this man come to terms with his overidealization and fear of his own father. This awareness, in turn, helped him achieve a more comfortable separation from his father. And as he was better able to integrate childhood conflict with adult experience, he became more comfortable and effective as a father.

The first time family therapist Molly Layton confronted the double-stranded joy and grief of separation was on a long, lazy afternoon. Twenty-six and pregnant with her second child, she was taking care of her three-year-old son, David, and her sister's two-year-old son. Watching her nephew toddle away from her wearing one of her son's outgrown blue suits — one she had made for him and then passed along — she was suddenly "torn open with grief." "Watching my little nephew," she recalls now, two decades later, "I saw David there again. I hadn't even realized I had been missing my own toddler until I saw him there again."

Many years later, she wrote about this experience in "The Mother Journey," a piece that drew me to interview her because it beautifully synthesized the whole sweep of separations and attachments. She described "the bittersweet paradox at the heart of maternal thinking. The mother aches for her child's growth, but the growth is double-stranded with her joy and grief. In the baby's cup-holding, the mother thrills at his growing skills — at his intelligence, at his demonstration of his capacity to survive without her. At the same time, she must prepare to leave behind the cozy and intimate warmth of the baby at her breast. The mother's rock-bottom interest in fostering the child's growth sets her up for the continual experience of separation."

Now Molly Layton is forty-six, the acting vice-principal of a respected private school as well as "one of the field's most gifted therapists," in the words of her colleague Deborah Luepnitz, author of *The Family Interpreted.* Molly's son is twenty-three and a student at the University of Texas. The baby she was expecting on the warm summer afternoon of that far-away epiphany is Rebecca, a young woman of nineteen, taking a year off from school and living in Rome. In the intervening years there have been countless leave-takings and returns, still double-stranded with joy and grief. But Molly has learned to take the griefs with the joys, the moments her children turn away from her as well as the times they turn back. And in balancing and synthesizing these dualities, she has seen her relationship to her children bloom, her marriage strengthen, and her sense of herself grow more sure.

For Molly and her husband Charles, one of the most poignant leavetakings was saying good-bye to David when he left for college. "It was a terrible time when David packed up all his belongings and drove off in his van. 'I need something to mark this,' I thought to myself. Then, over the next few days, I had something like an out-of-body experience, because Charles and I tracked David so closely on his journey from Philadelphia to Texas. I realized then how my heart could go with him — and his stay with us. I realized how much he would take me with him."

Sometime later she had the reward of hearing her own lesson echoing back to her. As Rebecca was preparing for a trip to Cyprus, her first adventure far from family and friends, Molly heard David warn her, "When you're out on your own in a strange place, and the food is funny, and there's no bus to the next place, you may have terrible moments of depression and disillusionment. That's just part of traveling — it doesn't mean you have to go back home." She knew that Rebecca would carry his words in her heart while she journeyed far away. Just as Molly carried her children in her heart when they were gone, so, too, would her children have "pieces of people to comfort themselves."

Thinking about the lessons weaving from parent to child, from sibling to sibling, the bonds changing — sometimes easing, sometimes strengthening, but never rupturing — she reflects, "The mature family is so incredibly gratifying. No one told me about this."

For Molly, part of what has made the experience of parenting adolescents so gratifying has been her willingness to pay attention to when she needed to hold on to them and when she needed to let go. Her daughter's senior year in high school was an important time in their relationship, a time when mother and daughter consolidated their closeness but also prepared for the next transition. "This time around I knew leaving home was a particular phase," Molly remembers, "so the year Rebecca was a senior, I stayed available for her. I didn't do a lot of extra workshops or conferences. She and I did a lot of connecting up that year, and that convinced us we could be connected" — despite the major separation coming up.

Their profound mother-daughter connection, renewed in their intimacy during Rebecca's last year at home, was to provide a critical touchstone at the end of Rebecca's freshman year at college. Frazzled by boyfriend problems, financial concerns, and the pressures of final exams, Rebecca suddenly found herself spinning from anxiety. "I don't know what's happening," she cried to her mother in a frightened and frightening phone call, "I think I'm going crazy." Talking on the phone as calmly as she could, using all her resources as a mother, and a therapist, Molly quickly realized that her daughter was in the throes of a panic attack, having a rough time but not falling apart. Reassured that she was not going crazy, Rebecca was immediately relieved. Another phone call the next day helped "hold her in," remembers Molly, borrowing a phrase from Winnicott and more recently from Sara Ruddick, who calls "holding" the "fundamental attitude of protectiveness," central to mothers and therapists. Checking with a college counselor also helped Rebecca turn the tide. By the time her parents drove to see her the next week, she was "back in gear."

"Luckily, she had had enough trust in me and me in her," her mother realizes with relief. "She's gotten a good foundation. She had some issues about self-confidence, but they were not off the scale. Because we had had a strong connection, she could depend on that. I had to totally turn my attention to her, and then five days later, the problem was gone.

"This capacity to hold a child in and then let her go is a characteristic of mature families," she reflects. "It's a skill for parents and children to work on as well." It's a skill that Molly Layton has been working on for a long time. Looking back to the time when her children were toddlers, alternately sitting on her lap and then jumping off to explore the world beyond it, Molly makes a pivotal connection between raising toddlers and raising teenagers: "It's really the same thing with toddlers and adolescents — the issue of having a home base. For the toddler, it's mother's lap. For the adolescent, it's the capacity to be held within limits and understood, to be allowed to go out and still come back and be grounded in the values of the parents. There's a period of rapprochement with adolescents just as with toddlers. Every swing forward raises old regressions, primitive fears. But if the child — both toddler and adolescent — has a safe harbor, he can go back to deal with his fears."

But there are compelling differences between the two eras as well. Molly comments, "More than infancy and toddlerhood, adolescence stirs up real memories in parents about their own adolescence. It's powerful for both parents and children. There's a kind of spiraling where the same issues are played out again in a different role. Once you were the daughter wanting to date someone of questionable integrity or struggling with valuing your body. Now you're the mother of a daughter with these same struggles. This is part of being the sandwich generation caught between grown children and failing parents. The people you're intensely identified with become vehicles for your own development."

As she raised her two teenagers, she was constantly sorting out memories of her own teenage years. "I was the brainy one. I puzzled my family. Every book I read took me further away from them. It was a handy kind of rebellion, not a destructive one. But when my kids read books, it pulls them closer to us!"

Thinking about the natural ebb and flow of her teenagers' leavetakings and returns, Molly adds, "As my children start to explore the world, I did not want to lose them the way my parents lost me. I wouldn't have the dialogue between myself and my children stop. When David took a boat down the Amazon, for example, I read three books on the Amazon. If he was going to go out that far in the world, I wanted to participate with him and understand him." Her intense need to participate in her children's adventures — at least vicariously — comes, in part, from her regret that her own parents did not more aggressively try to link up with hers. "When my husband and I moved away to a different part of the country, my parents didn't come after us. This is not a criticism, just a reality that no one stopped to question. Now I believe that parents need to make an effort to connect up with their kids as well as vice versa."

For Molly, the process of encouraging and responding to her teenage children's individuation has helped further her individuation from her own mother as well as deepened her attachment to her. "Having children is so stimulating of your own emotions," she observes. "You can't be a tranquil lady anymore — if you ever were! When Rebecca became an adolescent I knew I had to become a more powerful parent. My mother is practical and indefatigable, whereas I was dreamy and socially awkward. But when I left for college, I felt myself becoming my mother — strong and energetic. To be strong with Rebecca sometimes evokes the best of my mother. But sometimes when I've struggled to be a good, strong mother I've found a kind of emptiness. You know, why couldn't someone have done this for me? The deprived kid. What's helped me a lot is supportive relationships I've had over the years — with Charles, with good friends, with good therapy. All these experiences help me put aside the old deprived child. They help me take on the caretaker role. I can be unambivalently strong.

"Now I feel more healed with my mother. And when I'm comforting Rebecca with a headache, I feel my mother's hands in mine."

In a household with adolescents, other crucial changes take place in the dynamics of the family system. This intensity is "not just the jacked-up emotionality or much-ballyhooed rebellion," Molly Layton explains, "but the intensity parents bring to the experience: the capacity to be angry, to confront sexual issues, including one's own." The intensification of sexuality, the reexamination of sex roles and parenting roles — indeed, the rebalancing of the marriage itself — is another vivid difference between parenting toddlers and parenting adolescents. Molly describes how she had to make the shift from being the "accommodating, observing mother of infants to the kind of lively, interesting, kick-ass parent that adolescents need. My marriage became lively and interesting as well," she adds. "In helping each child to resolve the ambivalence about the other parent, we were forced to settle our own massive ambivalence."

Molly explains, "When our children were young, our family was organized around me as the primary caretaker; mother loomed large. But as a mother of adolescents, that wouldn't work. During the toddler stage, at least in the days when our children were young, the father may not be that involved with the children, but ideally, the mother of the toddler is, in turn, mothered by her husband. But by adolescence, there have to be two parents. The gender issues are so strong. Charles and I had to decide who needed to fight which battles with which kid. Sometimes a same-sex fight — mother-daughter or father-son — is absolutely necessary. Our capacity to talk with each other, to get past our own problems with each other, was tested. For example, I had to get tougher with Rebecca than I ever had. I had to make a decision with Charles that he be the good guy with her. And on the other hand, it didn't work for me to fight with David.

"The things our children tested us on," she continues, "were drinking, sexuality, and performance in school. You don't stay indifferent to those things. We got good at choosing our battles. And then if we fought battles, we would take the family to a different level of trust, of talking about problems. We have to have toe-to-toe strength. That's the power we needed to have, power and love. And I couldn't have done that without Charles — it gets so demoralizing. I could then say to him, 'You've done a great job with David,' and he could say 'You've done a great job with Rebecca.' Not every family would parcel out the work this way, but it worked well for us."

She sighs like someone who has weathered a long ordeal. "It's a hard period, but then it becomes a great period when the children become civilized members of the culture. There's a real connection. In fact, when the kids revealed more and more of who they were deciding to be — making decisions about politics and clothes and friends — it dawned on me that my own children were becoming some of the most interesting people that I know."

Besides relishing the people her children have become, she appreciates the network of friends, fun, and good conversation they have woven into the life of the family, the way they have opened up the family system to the larger world. "All these other children also come into your lives, and that's also been part of the richness that's been so much fun. Adolescents are so funny, just hilarious, so in love with language.

"Cooking for them is also great. I went out and bought gigantic pots to cook for them! When I look back at our old dishes — the old skillet to cook for our family of four — they seemed so tiny. I've really enjoyed the high-powered, super-nurturant part of life with teenagers — sitting around the table and talking."

In these last years, the family has moved to yet another phase. No longer teenagers, the children have spread their wings way beyond the family home, yet they fly back to touch base and get some old-fashioned nurturing periodically. Molly has had to become dexterous at switching the pots and pans of her love and attention back and forth; sometimes the big old pots are necessary. With a few years of practice, the family "has learned to have Christmas with each other. The children come home again and the big pots come out. We don't buy expensive presents, but instead go to New York, see a play, and go to a good restaurant afterwards to talk about it together. This is the best way of 'being in the family' for us. But we reconstitute the family, and then poof, they're gone. Still, Charles and I feel we have the best of both worlds — we all have each other, but we also have room to have our own lives."

When the children are at home, the family does "the things we know to experience each other at our best." They sit around the table talking as they have for years. Sometimes they move apart in dyads. Charles and David go off to play pool; Molly and Rebecca — "we're not shoppers!" — sit on Rebecca's bed and chat. Mother and daughter used to fight bitterly over the messiness of Rebecca's room, but Molly ignores it now and Rebecca "cooperates in the public areas of the house."

After the children leave, after the good-byes have been said and the next visit arranged to look forward to, Molly has one more ritual to help her with the transition between parenthood taken up and then put aside. She goes into Rebecca's room, cursing, straightening, folding clothes. "This is how I can let go of her," she confesses. "I'm getting things cleaned up. She'll always leave me a messy room. I get the room straightened up, I put my ironing board in there, and then I go on with my life."

— 7 —

Anger and Limit Setting

MOTHER, THE SAME WITCH HAUNTS US

these dark afternoons
shrewish, I rage
between bared teeth
I careen out of control
ache to throw glass
hit the child

shaking, I see
I have your hands

after years
of looking sideways

we stare into each other
and ask

who is she
this witch
who singes our guts
who makes us sign
with blood
the pact of sisters

Judith Steinbergh

Parenthood did not become difficult for me — nor truly begin — until I first heard my voice rise in anger at my sons and felt their anger coming back at me. Somewhere between sixteen and eighteen months, the blissful harmonies of infancy were suddenly interrupted by discordant sounds — unwelcome but not entirely unfamiliar. "At eighteen months, they lose their sweet natures," an all-knowing friend with two older children had warned me during the rosy blush of early motherhood. "Hers did, but mine won't," I naturally thought to myself with that overweening pride common to most of us as we watch other people's children doing those unacceptable things we are confident ours will never do — until we notice them in our own back yard.

So when my first son started to pound his fists in rage, throw toys off the changing table, and swipe at other children in our playgroup, I felt my temperature rising. But I tried valiantly to dismiss his behaviors — and my response — as glitches, passing waves on an otherwise tranquil sea. By the time my second son hit eighteen months and began his own variation of these wild behaviors, I knew they were no accident.

Memory has frozen the exact moment when the shift occurred. My younger son is standing up on his changing table in the midst of a diaper change, poopy bottom threatening to flash all over the wall, the dangling mobile, the winsome and amusing toys. I hear my voice rise in fury at him, trying madly to control the uncontrollable. Gone in a flash is the winsome and amusing mother I know I can be. Suddenly I am manic and maniac, the witch's voice rising from within me.

By then, in the middle of working on this book, I made a mental note to mark the occasion, gathering research even while reeling from my own temper and my son's. Once again, I knew the halcyon days were passing; the true challenge of motherhood was beginning for me again. How could I allow my children's independence to thrive, set firm but loving limits — and mellow the witch's voice to express anger in a way we could all live with? How could I model a healthy and direct expression of feelings without a wild and destructive mania? And how could I interrupt what might otherwise be a negative cycle of angry behavior spinning down through the generations and give my grandchildren a saner future?

The unsheathing of our children's anger somewhere around the middle of their second year often turns out to reveal a double-edged sword. For as our children begin to flash bursts of anger at us to assert their independence and separate will, our own anger often rises to meet theirs. At times our anger restrains theirs, at times it circumvents it, at times we lock horns and clash. If our own legacy about anger is painful (if as children we were verbally or physically abused), or if our legacy is mixed or confused (perhaps our own father was vitriolic and our mother kowtowing and meek), confronting our children's anger will invariably force us to confront that legacy and sort it out.

Our children's anger becomes a mirror to our own, reflecting the past and forcing us to make internal and external confrontations with the present. Unless we have the patience of saints, our children's passion naturally provokes our own and often unleashes depths of feeling we hadn't suspected we had. And our children's anger, usually so unalloyed and uncontained, may throw our own — confused, repressed, guilt-laden — into high contrast. In a probing essay called "Mad Doesn't Mean Bad," writer Roberta Israeloff reflected on how her first son's "rage — so easily expressed, so intense, so primitive — provoked and angered me, and underscored how poorly equipped I was to cope with anger — my own or anyone else's."

If we can remember how awful and humiliated we felt when we were the target of our parents' anger, we may find clues for treating our own children more kindly. Yet, paradoxically, we often find ourselves instinctively repeating the very phrases ("Do it because I say so!"), the very demeaning punishments we loathed and swore never to repeat. "Parents tend to punish their children the same way their own parents punished them," the inimitable Dr. Spock observed in a recent article, "whether it's by spanking or scolding or reasoning or withholding privileges. In this way patterns of discipline — both good and bad — are passed from one generation to the next." If those patterns of discipline were unconstructive, humiliating, or hurtful, the new parents have to develop empathy for their children in order to begin the process of change for the next generation. As Bruno Bettelheim explained about the need for empathy:

> If we could only remember our own struggles in this area — how undisciplined we ourselves often were, and how hard a time we had as children in disciplining ourselves, how we felt put upon, if not actually abused, when our parents forced us to behave in a disciplined manner against our will — then we and our children would be much better off. . . . If we can truly remember these situations, we will also recall how deeply painful they were for us as children, how anxious and insecure we were behind our show of defiance and argumentativeness, and how we resented our parents' failure to realize all this because they were so wrapped up in their annoyance.

But much as I try mightily to empathize when my toddler begins to hurl things across the room or scream bloody murder when the only T-shirt he wants to wear is in the wash, the angry ghosts of the past often come back to haunt me. As Bettelheim also points out, it is far easier to empathize with the frustrations of an obviously helpless baby than with the temper tantrums of a seemingly more resourceful — or more manipulative? — toddler:

> It is much more difficult to empathize with our child . . . during the toddler stage, when he throws temper tantrums and screams bloody murder, instead of gurgling happily as he did when we retrieved his baby rattle for him. Then his unreasonableness, lack of control, and despair make us so distraught that we may fail to recognize that he is after essentially the same thing that he wanted when he played in the crib: to find out what he can do, and what the consequences of his actions will be. A temper tantrum is the expression of the child's despair of not having a self that works for him.

Indeed, the two-year-old's temper tantrums, no less than the teenager's moody fits, are neon signs flashing the news of the struggle to separate, the struggle to define an identity. Anger is the fuel that energizes the separation. Anger and separation are constantly interwoven themes in our lives with children, as intricately laced as the strands of a daughter's braid. How much anger or free expression of emotion a family can tolerate from a child may be directly related to the family's ability to support separation as well. In a family where children's anger is not tolerated, a child may feel that if he expresses his true and often angry feelings, he will drive his parents away.

In healthy families where children are allowed to show their authentic selves, angry outbursts are an important sign of trust: these children know they will be loved whether or not they break a lamp, sock a sibling, or talk back to a parent. And certainly many parents have observed their children be on their best behavior at day care or school and completely lose it when they return home. At least these parents know their children view home as a safe place, where emotions can be unloosed and acknowledged. In *The Drama of the Gifted Child*, Alice Miller shows how children will impose a false mask over unacceptable feelings in order to hold on to their parents' love. "Under certain circumstances," she observes, "a child may learn very early what he is not allowed to feel, lest he run the risk of losing his mother's love."

Anger and separation are poised in a delicate balance from the parents' point of view, as well. A parent without a strong sense of self or one who is too enmeshed with a child may at times feel wounded or rejected by the child's anger and by his forceful but inevitable drive to separate. This parent may feel angry and *rejecting of* a child for wanting to separate at all. He may then consciously or unconsciously punish a child for daring to express the kind of anger that he himself wanted to unfurl on his own parents but was too timid to express. Another parent might remember her own childhood timidity and covertly — or even overtly — encourage her child's free-ranging expression of anger toward her.

"Goodness of fit" between parent and child and the reciprocity of influence over time are critical. A volatile parent may overwhelm a timid child, be in constant turmoil with an argumentative one, or may eventually learn to temper his temper to adjust to a child's needs. A shy, contemplative parent may have limited resources from the past to help unlock a quiet child's feelings. A quiet parent may be terrorized by a boisterous child, or be inspired and emboldened to meet the child halfway, or invent creative ways to negotiate with or at times circumvent her.

The mother of an eighteen-month-old daughter describes how she is coping with her daughter's emerging independence and strong spirit. Within the space of just a few months this mother has learned to go along with the pull of her daughter's energy rather than constantly fight it. Yet she is also learning to balance her daughter's need for independence and assertion with her own need to accomplish some of the day's basic tasks:

> ▶ The most difficult stage with my daughter has been from eleven to fifteen months. She really started to exert her independence. She fought me when I changed her diaper or put her in the car seat. She still crawled, so we didn't have any significant outdoor playtime. She made a huge mess at mealtime. She wanted to flip through books or rip them rather than be read to from them. I expected that if I reasoned with her or spoke firmly and authoritatively, she would obey me and do what was safe and reasonable. We were always fighting.

After months of resisting her daughter's resistance, she has now learned, with the grace of a t'ai chi expert, to go along with her daughter's opposition and turn it around:

> ▶ But the easiest stage has been from sixteen to eighteen months. I have learned that I can't reason with her. When we disagree on what should be done (e.g. about diapering), I give in for a couple of minutes, allowing her to feel like the victor, then she gives in and lets me proceed. I have slowed down and altered my expectations about what I can get accomplished, so I'm more relaxed, and we enjoy each other more.

My older son has from the earliest days dared to stand up to me in a way I would never have dreamed of doing with my mother. Although I can remember my mother exclaiming after some outburst of mine that she would never have talked to *her* mother that way, she remained shocked, where I generally (if quietly) stand in awe of my son's anger. His anger has a directness, even a purity to it that I can appreciate and at times learn from, even while reeling. And the teasing acknowledgment we can make of each other's occasional explosions helps clear the air afterward. When he calls me his "bossy teddy bear," I know he recognizes that I am indisputably in charge and, though he may sometimes resent it, he loves me anyway.

Expressing anger, like negotiating separation, is a two-way street: our tempers and temperaments provoke our children's and theirs provoke ours. Similarly, venting anger and setting limits are whole-family issues. Strong emotions broadly expressed can sweep through an entire family like a raging hurricane, toppling everything in their path. Angry emotions seething beneath the surface can no less undermine the family climate, if more insidiously, like a poisoned underground stream.

Family systems theorists see the sweep of anger in terms of triangles, both interfamilial and intergenerational. Two family members locked in a dispute, for example, often try to diffuse or distract away from the angry situation between them by bringing in either a third family member or another person — or memory — from the past. Explains family therapist Harriet Goldhor Lerner in *The Dance of Anger:* "It is not simply that we displace a *feeling* from one person to another; rather, *we reduce anxiety in one relationship by focusing on a third party, who we unconsciously pull into the situation to lower the emotional intensity in the original pair.*"

Lerner's personal example of an anger triangle concerns a time she found herself unduly scolding her two sons after a trip to see her aging and ailing parents. Eventually she was able to recognize that her anxiety over her parents' failing health and ultimate mortality was being triangled into, and contaminating, her relationship with her young sons. When she acknowledged the unconscious connection and began to face directly her deep concern and love for her parents, she was able to disconnect the triangle and keep her relationships as daughter and as mother separate. As she observes:

> *All of us are vulnerable to intense, nonproductive angry reactions in our current relationships if we do not deal openly and directly with emotional issues from our first family — in particular, losses and cut-offs.* If we do not observe and understand how our triangles operate, our anger can keep us stuck in the past, rather than serving as an incentive and guide to form more productive relationship patterns for the future.

Sometimes we unleash a blast of anger at a child because we have just had an argument with a boss, a friend, or a spouse. Sometimes we explode because our child's behavior stirs up some demon from the past. At the moment of rage, the child reminded us of a difficult sibling, a bothersome great-aunt — or some unloved aspect of ourselves.

A mother in her mid-forties with a teenage son and daughter connects her painful struggles during her son's "normal two- to six-year-old physical aggressiveness" toward his younger sister with two harsh memories from her own childhood:

> ▶ My son's behavior enraged me with the memory of my brother's aggressiveness toward me (only in recent therapy have I gotten in touch with the memories of being hit by caretakers trying to get me to stop crying when my mother

was in the hospital with TB. This too underlay, I now imagine, my rage at my son).

If we can become aware of these interfering triangles both past and present — and learn to name their power to our children — we will go a long way to clearing the air and keeping our relationships grounded in the present.

Bruno Bettelheim speaks of the difference between the parent who understands his own anger and the one who blames it on his child:

> Even the kindest and best-intentioned parents will sometimes become exasperated. The difference between the good enough and the not so good parent in such situations is that the first realizes his irritation usually has more to do with himself than with whatever the child did and that giving in to it benefits no one, while the second believes his anger is due only to his child and that he therefore has every right to act on it.

As we learn, in a sense, to take our own anger more personally — that is, to understand it in terms of our own ghosts and our own personality — we also learn to take our children's anger *less* personally. Learning to use our anger as a clear communication, directly expressed, uncontaminated by the ghosts of the past, we can also use it as an opportunity to nourish family growth and understanding. Helping our children express and channel their anger, we can learn to express and channel our own.

Family therapist Sheri Glucoft Wong likes to begin her lecture on setting limits by asking how many parents in the audience successfully buckle their small children into car seats before driving off in the car. As all the parents' hands wave a proud and enthusiastic "yes," she continues by asking how many parents have equal success getting their children dressed and out the door for school or ready for bed. When only a few scattered hands wave a weary "yes" to those questions, Glucoft Wong brings home her point: when parents are unequivocal about their intentions, children almost invariably cooperate. When children spy a crack of doubt, vulnerability, or ambivalence, they madly test the limit to see if they can make their parents waffle or renege.

Still, if every issue were as clear-cut as buckling children into car seats, discipline would not be the challenge, the area of wavering doubts that it is. As Glucoft Wong and other family therapists would be the first to admit, what makes limit setting so thorny is the many levels of memory and meaning behind each of our parental noes. Each of us carries a psychic backpack of memories, models, and images that invariably are taken out when our children require discipline, limits — or just a simple "no." Glucoft Wong cites a variety of parent types who have a hard time saying "no" to their children. "One parent may have had an authoritarian parent who wasn't understanding, so now he says, 'I don't want to lay the trip on my kid that my mother and father did to me. My parents never listened to me or cared about my feelings, so I want to listen to my kid. My parents never explained things to me, so I want to explain to my kid where my rules come from. So I will explain to him why it really isn't okay to bite me, because no one really explained that to me.' "

She continues with another example. "The next is somebody who didn't have that authoritarian experience at all in her childhood and who, as a matter of fact, was indulged and cared about a lot. What happens with her is that she is ambivalent about her childhood. She is not sure she wants a child to turn out like she did, because her parents indulged her and were never straight with their anger. But this parent cannot be straight with her anger either, so she runs a similar number on her child. What she is really saying is, 'You little brat, who the hell do you think you are?' Instead she says sweetly, 'Honey, that behavior is not all right with me.' And the anger is kept covert.

"Still another example is somebody like the father in a family I'm seeing right now who was one of many children in a large family, where it was, boom! You were hit. If you didn't do something right, you were sent out of the room. There was none of that other indulgent stuff. Now this father is finally sorting through what part of his family's original style seems to be effective — and sometimes more effective than his wife's approach, because she really bends the whole other way and overindulges the children. Still, he also understands that his original family's style was abusive. So where's the line?"

From the father whose parents were too authoritarian to the mother whose parents were too indulgent, from the husband whose father was abusive and is now too firm with his own children to the wife who is not quite firm enough — each of these parents must look both at their own memories and responses and at their particular children and ask themselves, "Where's the line?" Where is the comfortable middle ground between too severe and too wishy-washy, the livable style between too authoritarian and too indulgent?

Of the four parenting styles my interviews and questionnaires explored, the Traditionalists generally have the least difficulty with the issue of anger and limit setting. Over all, they have the most positive memories of the way discipline was handled in their childhood families. For the most part, their parents were positive role models. Discipline felt fair and appropriate; children respected their parents' parenting abilities and felt comfortable with the limits that were defined. With some minor fine-tuning to adapt the disciplinary measures of the past to current customs (time-outs replacing standing in the corner, for example), the Traditionalists generally believe that the methods that were effective in their childhood homes will be useful now.

At times this admiring attitude can lead to an unwillingness to consider better solutions to new family problems. At other times an unacknowledged and buried hostility can reinforce a status quo that was of dubious value. A father who was punished physically as a child may now feel that "he deserved it" or that "it worked for him." "That's the way I was treated," such a parent might say, "and it was good enough for me, so it's good enough for my son!" Sometimes a Traditionalist adopts a dangerous defense of denial — abuse never occurred — or minimizing — "It really wasn't that bad" — to hold on to the myth of the perfect family. Then he unwittingly repeats the abuse — and the damage — with his own children.

If, by and large, the Traditionalists are the parents most approving of their original families' strategies for discipline and most comfortable at setting limits, the Rebels are the most critical of their original families' methods and have the most difficulty coping with anger in their new homes. Rebels have often grown up feeling bitterly wounded by their original families. Their parents' anger may have been wild or overblown, and discipline overly severe or inappropriate to the children's age or misdeed. And these childhood abuses, either verbal or physical, may have done even greater damage than the painful injuries of the moment. Traumatic or degrading punishment also deals a grave blow to a child's self-esteem and his sense of security in his parents' benevolence — even in their ability to care for him. In the most extreme case, these Rebel children may not even want to risk having children of their own. If the abuse in their childhood homes was severe enough, they may go to extreme lengths to avoid perpetuating it.

Such was the case with a preschool teacher in her early thirties who sent a passionate response to my questionnaire despite having no children of her own. She wrote sadly about being told she was responsible for ruining her mother's life and being threatened at knife point by her mother and chased out of the house:

> ▶ Having children of my own, I'm afraid that I will express my anger the way my mother did to me, and maybe even worse. I don't want to put a child of mine through the hurt, being afraid all the time and feeling that what happened was their fault.

When Rebels fly bravely in the face of their troubled pasts and take the risk of having children, they are nevertheless inclined to break their promises to themselves about keeping their tempers in check. A divorced mother of two school-age sons describes the tangled web involving herself, her abusive father, her passive-aggressive ex-husband, and her very bright and confrontational older boy:

> ▶ My husband's family's mode of anger was withdrawal of affection. My family was very verbal, but my father also used strong physical abuse. I swore I would never hit my kids, but I ended up paddling and spanking them too hard. I felt very guilty and got myself in therapy. My therapist said that my older son was the kind of kid who makes people angry. Geniuses are not easy to live with. He had his own way of dealing

with things like food and clothes. For instance, he wouldn't wear a shirt with buttons. Still, when my husband and I separated, I said to my friends, "The urge to kill my kids has left with my husband!"

Children who have grown up in families with abuse may have only negative models of discipline to draw on with their own children. Their repertoire of responses to conflict may be severely limited. If their partner's history is also impaired, the choices for their new family are still further circumscribed. Where therapy can be helpful is in introducing new options and more flexible responses, and in providing a new model of the kind of healing and supportive relationship unknown in their childhood.

In "Ghosts in the Nursery," Selma Fraiberg tells of a seriously troubled teenage mother from a disturbed and violently abusive family. This sixteen-year-old so feared her own destructive impulses and the repetition of her parents' violence that she refused to care for her baby at all. Although her story is clearly at the pathological end of the spectrum, it illustrates a response to conflict and stress typical of many Rebel parents. They either flee from the dangerous situation or, in spite of their own best interests, identify with their aggressor parents.

In her dramatic account of the case, Fraiberg describes how the therapist and Annie, the young mother, began by slowly peeling away the painful memories of abuse and deprivation in Annie's childhood home. After about eight meetings, a particularly emotional session occurred in which Annie spoke of her deeply buried affection for her natural father, who had left the family when she was five, and of her smoldering rage at her stepfather, who beat her. She also revealed for the first time her fear of the old woman her mother had left her with, who would periodically lock her out of the house. After this agonizing soul baring, Annie suddenly refused to come to her therapy appointments. When her therapist came to her house to see her, Annie literally locked the door against her. She was unconsciously identifying with her old aggressors, locking the door against her therapist just as it had once been locked against her. At the same time, she was taking flight from the whole unsettling process of therapy just as she may have wanted to flee from her abusive caretakers, indeed from her whole miserable childhood.

Not surprisingly, given its layers of symbolic meaning, the lockout became a turning point in the therapy. Annie's therapist used the incident as an opportunity to untangle Annie's web of associations among anger, rage, and abandonment:

> For Annie, the relationship with Mrs. Shapiro [the therapist] became a new experience, unlike anything she had known. Mrs. Shapiro began, of course, by dealing openly with the anger which Annie had felt toward her and made it safe for Annie to put anger into words. In a family pattern where anger and murderous rage were fused, Annie had only been able to deal with anger through flight or identification with the aggressor. In the family theater, anger toward the mother and desertion by the mother were interlocking themes. But Annie learned that she could feel anger and acknowledge anger toward her therapist, and her therapist would not retaliate and would not abandon her.

As this young mother began to see that it was safe to experience anger in transference to her therapist, she also allowed herself for the first time to reexperience her childhood griefs and terrors. This time she began to work them through in the safe and protected setting of therapy. "How frightening to you as a child that there was no one to care for you and protect you," Mrs. Shapiro would respond to her outpouring. "Every child has a right to be taken care of and protected."

"I was hurt . . . I was hurt," Annie would lament, knowing that she was at last being heard and understood. And then gradually she began another poignant refrain, "I don't want to hurt anybody. I don't want to hurt anybody."

Fraiberg shows how very subtly and gradually this young mother's identification with her aggressors began to shift to an identification with her tiny baby and a commitment to care for him and avoid the abuses of her past:

> Annie was no longer afraid of her destructive feelings toward the baby. The rage belonged to the past, to other figures. And the protective love toward [her baby] which now began to emerge spoke for a momentous shift in her identification with the baby. Where

before she was identified with the aggressors of her childhood, she now was the protector of her baby, giving him what had not been given, or rarely given, in her own childhood. "Nobody," said Annie one day, "is ever going to hurt my child the way I have been hurt."

Both professional and lay opinion has long held that parents who were abused as children are likely to abuse their own children unless, as in Annie's case, they get therapeutic help. But a recent study by Yale psychology professor Edward Zigler and his assistant Joan Kaufman has challenged the old assumption. Zigler and Kaufman analyzed some forty scholarly studies and papers for "proof" of the supposed connection between abused parents in one generation and abused children in the next generation. They began by discarding or discrediting a number of studies because the research methods were inadequate. A widely cited study by Steele and Pollack, for example, interviewed only abusive parents who were already being seen at a treatment center and used no control group for comparison. Other studies provided contradictory data. One by Egeland and Jacobvitz, who interviewed 160 high-risk, low-income, predominantly single mothers, found that although 30 percent of the mothers who were maltreated as children spanked their own children daily or weekly, a *larger* percentage of mothers with emotionally supportive childhoods — 39 percent — used corporal punishment regularly.

After examining and weighing the findings of all forty studies, Zigler and Kaufman concluded that about one-third of those parents who were abused as children will repeat the abuse with their own children.

To support their conclusion, the researchers subscribed to the "interactive" theory of child abuse. Abuse occurs, they and many social scientists now believe, not just as the result of a single factor like a history of childhood abuse, but as the result of an insidious combination of many factors. Among these are the absence of a supportive social network, a child with a "difficult" temperament, unemployment, low income, isolation from extended family and community, single parenthood, and an abusive or unsupportive spouse.

Certain significant factors seem to distinguish the parents who are able to break the negative cycle of abuse. Zigler and Kaufman cited a study of parents of newborns in which the researchers, Rosemary Hunter and Nancy Kilstrom, selected out a group of parents with a history of being abused as children. Then they identified the qualities that separated the parents who did not go on to abuse their babies from the ones who did. These researchers found that the parents who broke the abuse cycle had more extensive social supports, fewer ambivalent feelings about their pregnancies, and healthier babies. Significantly, they also were more conscious of their own emotional histories and more in touch with their anger about their own childhood mistreatment.

My own interviews with Rebel parents certainly corroborate these findings. Those who are not conscious of their own anger and pain at an abusive history are likely to repeat the maltreatment with their own children. The more conscious they are of their own emotional histories and the better able to admit and articulate their pain, the less likely these parents are to repeat the outrages of their pasts.

Daniel Kagan, a writer and father of a two-year-old son, Ollie, is a parent who interrupted what could have been a crippling cycle of abuse. "How did someone like me, supposedly fated to become a statistic in the abuser column, come to take the other fork in the road?" he asks in a wrenching essay called "The Sins of My Father." He documents his father's cruel and unusual punishments (being kept up half the night with a floodlight in his eyes, for example) and then his own heartfelt commitment to treating his own two-year-old kindly. His success in breaking the anguishing negative pattern rests largely in his ability to keep the memory of his childhood abuse alive, not as a fresh source of personal pain but as a healing source of empathy for his child:

> I think one explanation is that the memories of my worst childhood experiences have remained intact — vivid and excruciating, undimmed by the passage of time. The terror is still there, along with the helplessness, the noise, the rage, the pain, the panic of being cornered, the sense of utter vulnerability. The idea of inflicting physical or mental pain on Ollie is just out of the question. To inflict such suffering on him would also mean inflicting it on myself.

The Rebels' acute memories and empathy with their children's plight can be liberating influences on the family's approach to discipline. But at times the efforts to stand in their children's shoes keep them from grounding their authority. In their soul-searching struggle not to be *too* authoritarian, they may not be authoritative enough.

This is a pitfall for the Compensators as well. These parents are often so haunted by memories of how out of bounds their parents were that they find themselves unable to set boundaries with their own children, even when boundaries are seriously needed. Anger and limit setting are confused and shadowy areas for the Compensator parent. Growing up in a family where anger was outrageous, inappropriately expressed, or completely denied, this parent fears his own anger and is uncertain about setting limits with his children. Counselor and theologian John Bradshaw, whose books and public television series have brought family systems theory to millions, recalls that in his family of origin, anger — "one of the seven deadly sins" — was completely forbidden. He remembers a "well-meaning Catholic nun" passing around the classroom an x-ray of a diseased lung and telling the impressionable children that "that's what your soul looks like under mortal sin." "I vowed never to get angry again," he concluded.

Roberta Israeloff, who "grew up in a family in which angry feelings were always denied," pictures her angry responses to her children as "a sorry salad of feelings I couldn't begin to sort out." Trying to explain her confusing welter of feelings, she says, "I experience my own anger as something to be feared, an unpleasant miasma of depression, frustration, sadness."

Because such a miasma often surrounds the Compensator's feelings about expressing anger, this parent may go to great lengths to avoid conflict or confrontation. Sheri Glucoft Wong tells of a classic case of a single father whose own childhood history with anger was confused and bitter. To simplify the issue with his own three children, he held a clear-cut and often repeated policy of "no fighting" — no fighting in the house with parents or siblings and certainly no fighting outside the family. "I'll tell you the extent to which this man was into no-fighting," remembers Glucoft Wong. "During his marriage, his wife had a lover; he accepted that. His wife had another lover; he accepted that. A third lover she was in love with. She wanted the lover to move in with them, and he accepted that. Then she kicked him out of the bedroom, and he accepted that. It took a year before he moved out of the house."

Glucoft Wong continues, "He was a researcher of some sort. He was working in an academic department where there was no conflict, there was no anger, there was nothing temperamental that was a problem. It had taken quite a search to find such a conflict-free zone. And it all worked out fine until his eight-year-old son came to live with him."

When he entered school in April, the boy began to be hassled and beaten up by his classmates. Since his father had told him that he couldn't fight back, he was trying to obey, but it wasn't working. Explains Glucoft Wong, "We talked about how carefully this father had orchestrated and arranged his life in order to avoid something that's unavoidable. Now most parents don't get past the time when their children are eighteen months without conflict, and this was already way past that. So we began to discuss how there's going to be conflict; you're going to have to say no; and your children are going to be mad at you. There's a developmental stage where a child needs to go up against something, and it won't work if you're nice all the time.

"And this father had to come to terms with not being nice. So he had to let his son fight. And he really had to look at something he had sewn up so nicely that he might have gone on living entirely without facing conflict had it not been for this son."

In his effort to protect his son from conflict and from the bitter memories of his own past, this Compensator father had, in fact, overcompensated. By categorically denying that conflict is an inevitable part of growing up and of adulthood as well, he had failed to provide a model of standing up for oneself when it was necessary. When push came to shove, the father turned the other cheek; the son did not. But in forcing his father to face confrontation head on, this son gave him a necessary push to confront a part of life he had been running from. In turn, the father gave the son permission to stand up for himself and become a lot more confident.

Facing conflict, expressing anger, setting limits — in these highly charged areas our children provide us with countless opportunities for insight into our own pasts and possibilities for change. Synthesizers are the most flexible and creative about discarding what was ineffective or hurtful in their childhood homes and integrating new strategies and insights.

They might replace unilateral punishments with family discussion, bellowing with negotiation, spanking with time-outs or the withdrawal of privileges, while maintaining the bedrock of parental concern and care. The new synthesis of past and present almost always means a freer expression of anger than was allowed in their childhood home, indeed a freer unfurling of the whole range of feelings.

Synthesizers strive to be less authoritarian than their parents and more open to seeing all sides of an issue but are still committed to maintaining steady limits, clearly and lovingly expressed. The father of two young girls sums up the Synthesizer's characteristic attitude toward discipline this way: "I want our children to be able to expect continued dialogue and logical or natural consequences to their misdeeds, rather than hitting. I want to be viewed as a responsible, loving parent and not as an authoritarian."

Often parents must balance and integrate contrasting styles of discipline from their two families of origin before they can come up with a workable plan for their new families, and Synthesizers are especially adept at this. Perhaps a parent on one side was a "rage-aholic" and the other held all feelings tightly in check; perhaps one parent was physically abusive and the other made nice and denied that anything was going on. Before new parents with such contrasting histories can feel comfortable setting limits with their own children they must resolve the contradictions of their pasts.

Judith Steinbergh, the poet whose ardent "Mother, The Same Witch Haunts Us" begins this chapter, is the mother of two adopted children, now young teenagers. Separated from her husband when the children were only two and four and a half, she recalls that "there was no question that I wasn't prepared to raise babies alone." She spoke candidly in an interview about her early and ongoing struggles with the contradictions in her own history. "I always wanted to be peaceful and calm, because my mother had a terrible temper. She eventually died of colon cancer, which could be connected. My father, on the other hand, tried to hold it all in. He eventually had a triple bypass from holding it all in. I've turned out to be a parent who couldn't be more inconsistent, but I don't think that's so bad after all. I can be sweet, funny, and loving, but also after teaching hundreds of students all day, I can come home and really lose it. My mother looked as if she'd always had whatever she wanted, but she really didn't. A lot of her rage came because she didn't go to work. Still, my mother never looked at the bright side, and I do."

The challenge of Steinbergh's single motherhood — and the passionate subtext of much of her poetry — has been trying to integrate the contradictions between her mother's explosiveness and her father's containment; her mother's despair at not working with her own frazzled nerves and occasional short fuse from working too much; her own sweetness and humor as a mother with her witchlike outbursts. If the style that results often seems inconsistent, the desire to explore and try to reconcile the contradictory options rather than hiding behind either extreme is the hallmark of a Synthesizer.

Sometimes the contradictions that parents must balance come from the different perspectives and approaches of the two partners. The opposite natures that attracted two people to each other may become sources of conflict when they try to work out a unified family approach to discipline. Perhaps he was placid and she was fiery. As lovers, his placidity mellowed her and her heat excited him, but as parents, his placidity seems passive and uninvolved to her, and her fiery temper seems excessive and uncontrolled to him. Or perhaps their contradictions come out as different thresholds, different hot buttons. He hates disorder and wild behavior; she can better tolerate chaos but burns at back talk and disrespect. The differences themselves may make family life more lively, giving children a greater sense of possibilities. But what too often happens if differences are left unexamined is that the contrasting styles push the parents to extremes. Father's placidity enrages Mother all the more; Mother's flamboyant rage numbs Father to even greater passivity. Children may feel trapped and unprotected in the middle.

If their temperaments threaten to become this polarized, Synthesizer parents realize that they must find a comfortable middle ground between the opposing extremes. They rely on negotiation and open discussion both between themselves and with their children to find a livable balance, with caring and conscious limits. Synthesizers are constantly working out ways to maintain authority without being authoritarian. They realize that much as children campaign for free reign, if they get it they can become overwhelmed, even devastated. These parents understand that much of children's provocative behavior serves to test parental limits. Explains pediatrician T. Berry Brazelton:

> The child realizes that he might not be able to control [his behavior] himself, and therefore behaves so provocatively that he demands an answer from his parents. Punishment should be immediate, it should be appropriate, and it should be limited in time so that the adult and child can make up the rift. After discipline is meted out, and the episode is terminated, the adult can comfort the child and point out that someone else still has the controls which he must learn. Implicit in these controls is the promise that they can be incorporated by the child himself.

Synthesizers know that their children's security rests on the parents' ability to take charge without guilt, to control without manipulating, to set limits without unduly punishing. These parents have the savvy and sensitivity to set realistic expectations both for their children and for themselves. They realize the importance of learning about child development to identify what behavior to expect at different stages. These parents know that when a two-year-old says no all the time, a three-year-old demands a party dress for school — and a sixteen-year-old wants to stay out without a curfew — these children are not trying to drive their parents crazy but are simply acting appropriately for their age and stage. These parents learn to see children's behavior in a developmental context. By learning not to take their children's random outbursts too personally, they spare themselves a lot of unnecessary grief.

Just as Synthesizers learn to have realistic expectations of their children and to forgive them their trespasses, they learn to be realistic and forgiving with themselves. They realize that just as noes, inappropriate clothing, and defiance of curfews come with the territory of childhood, so, too, impatience, exasperation, and occasional explosions come with the terrain of parenthood. For the parent who catches herself turning on a two-year-old with a shockingly tantrumlike rage, Brazelton has these words of consolation:

> All of us are guilty of turning on the child at times, and the shame which we experience after we realize we've just thrown a two-year-old's tantrum ourselves virtually incapacitates us. Should we feel so guilty? I am convinced that a parent's angry outbursts serve a purpose, too. The child's inner struggles are contained, at least temporarily, by the limits set when a parent can't tolerate him any longer. . . . The role of honestly open reactions from parents in helping a child handle his struggle is a powerful, important one. Definite limits from the outside allow the child to explore himself more freely.

So the limits we set for our children paradoxically give them a greater sense of freedom, and the leeway we give ourselves to have an occasional outburst helps keep us more flexible and forgiving as parents.

Synthesizers are nevertheless aware of the striking difference between punishment and limit setting. This difference is well summed up in a handout from a child care resource center aptly named Bananas (since sometimes our children drive us that way) in Berkeley, California:

> Punishment involves making a child feel guilty, fearful or humiliated. It focuses on the child, not the behavior, and assumes that the child is "bad" and needs to be punished. The best you can expect when you punish a child is that she will stop the undesirable behavior out of the fear of being punished. The goal of [limit setting] is to teach a child to solve problems, make choices, learn to live with the consequences of his or her choices and, hopefully, achieve desired behaviors. [Limit setting] focuses on the action and not the person — it is the behavior that is unacceptable, not the child. When you discipline a child [this way] your hope is that the child will understand your reasons for doing so and make better choices in the future.

In order to understand and implement the differences between punishment and limit setting, Synthesizers also must understand — and teach their children — the difference between feelings and behavior, between feeling angry and slugging a friend, between feeling frustrated and kicking a sibling.

Synthesizers teach their children both to recognize and to label their feelings as naturally as they teach them to label colors or parts of the body. These parents show their children that "You're feeling very frustrated" has a different emotional resonance than "That must have hurt your feelings." Then these parents help their children learn to express or channel their anger without resorting to physical violence. "Use your words not your hands" is a favorite phrase for the nursery school set. Older children can be taught practical skills for resolving conflict like problem solving, negotiating, and compromising and can be guided toward venting frustration by pounding pillows, drawing pictures, or writing in journals.

Synthesizers make enlightened decisions about which issues are open for negotiation with their children and which are nonnegotiable (always sitting buckled into the car seat, for example, or — many years later — never driving after drinking). Early on, they develop simple rules, clearly stated: "You can't hurt yourself, you can't hurt others, and you can't hurt things," for example. Synthesizers learn not to go to the mat with their children on every issue. They have the grace to let their children save face and to win some battles along the way. They save heavy confrontations for really major issues, such as safety or violations of human kindness.

Synthesizers are by no means perfect parents, and they can lose their cool just like the rest of us. But they do their best to make amends by acknowledging when their own behavior screeches out of control and apologizing to their children for it afterward. Such apologies teach children that parents are also imperfect and fallible. Apologizing suggests that there's always another opportunity to make things right. A mother of a three-year-old boy describes the family's disciplinary goals and her own occasional lapses:

▶ We do get angry, frustrated, and at the end of our rope sometimes. We do not spank or hit our son. We do time-outs and countdowns. We try to explain what is going on and give our son a choice he can make. We set limits. We try to get him to see the consequences of his actions and be responsible to correct a wrongdoing. I am more prone to yelling than my partner and will put my son in his room, until we both calm down. After calming down, I talk about what happened with him and admit to my faults (which my parents never did). We hug afterwards.

In a recent essay Dr. Spock recommends as alternatives to corporal punishment taking away a toy or privileges, isolating a child who is out of control — and modeling kindness for children by showing them love and respect. Years of pediatric practice and observation of thousands of families have showed the good doctor that might never makes right:

> What convinced me that spanking isn't necessary was that, in years of pediatric practice, I discovered there were many families in which children were never spanked — and yet these children were cooperative, polite and kind. In some of these families the parents had not been physically punished in childhood, either. In others, the parents remembered the humiliation of being hit or spanked and were reacting to a conviction that the spankings they had received as children had had the wrong effect.

The late child psychologist Haim Ginott believed that the problem with punishment, corporal or otherwise, was that it didn't work. A child who has been punished, Ginott believed, becomes preoccupied with revenge fantasies rather than focusing on what he has done and figuring out how to make amends. "In other words," explain two of his best-known disciples, Adele Faber and Elaine Mazlish, "by punishing a child, we actually deprive him of the very important inner process of facing his own misbehavior." In parenting workshops and several best-selling books, Faber and Mazlish have popularized effective strategies for parent-child communication based on Ginott's work. Their *How to Talk So Kids Will Listen & Listen So Kids Will Talk* is a kind of child-rearing Bible for many Synthesizers. Using dramatic vignettes and cartoon strips to show the old versus the new style of parenting interventions, Faber and Mazlish emphasize straightforward communication, I-messages instead of you-messages, problem solving, and giving children opportunities to make amends. They sum up their humane alternatives to punishment this way:

1. EXPRESS YOUR FEELINGS STRONGLY — WITHOUT ATTACKING CHARACTER.

"I'm furious that my new saw was left outside to rust in the rain!"

2. STATE YOUR EXPECTATIONS.

"I expect my tools to be returned after they've been borrowed."

3. SHOW THE CHILD HOW TO MAKE AMENDS.

"What this saw needs is a little steel wool and a lot of elbow grease."

4. GIVE THE CHILD A CHOICE.

"You can borrow my tools and return them, or you can give up the privilege of using them. You decide."

5. TAKE ACTION.

Child: Why is the tool box locked?

Father: You tell me why.

6. PROBLEM-SOLVE.

"What can we work out so that you can use my tools when you need them, and so that I'll be sure they're there when I need them?"

"We want to put an end to talk that wounds the spirit, and search out the language that nourishes self-esteem," explain Faber and Mazlish. "We want to create an emotional climate that encourages children to cooperate because they care about themselves, and because they care about us." With these goals in mind, they underline the importance of accepting and respecting children's feelings, while also helping them become aware of the consequences of their actions. They look to develop "skills for engaging cooperation" and strive to avoid the "sarcasm, lectures, warnings, name-calling and threats [that] were all woven into the language we heard as we were growing up."

As they struggle to replace the ineffective, humiliating methods of the past, many Synthesizers whom I interviewed have come up with creative and effective alternatives. One mother of four- and two-year-old girls has a family goal that parenting will be "friendly, firm and fun — as Barbara Woodhouse says about training dogs!" Describing her family as a "family democracy", she and her husband use Rudolf Dreikurs's method of setting logical consequences for behavior:

▶ There is no need to yell, scream, or go out of control if logical consequences are set. For example, about picking up toys, we ask our children to pick up their own toys after they've played with them. If their father or I end up having to pick up the toys, we put them in a special green bag, and keep them till the children are ready to have them back — and put them away themselves. Or with our older daughter, we talk about emotional expectations and how it's important to think of others' feelings and say "Please" and "Thank you." If she deals politely with us, she'll be dealt with politely, too.

Another mother, of four adopted children from around the world, two boys and two girls aged two to eight, describes her family as "having more rules than other families — because we have more people." The rules range from always wiping hands before leaving the dinner table to keeping the sand in the sandbox to no TV or swearing. When a rule is broken or a limit is overreached, all the children, from the quiet two-year-old to the rambunctious eight-year-old, know the consequences:

> ▶ When the kids are naughty, they have a process to follow. First we ask them to go sit on the stairs, because they've been showing they can't be with the rest of us. Sometimes they sit and pout. Just removing them from the scene helps us not need to hit them. We think it's too hard to teach kids not to hit each other if we spank them ourselves. We like to remain morally superior! If the stairs don't work, then the kids have to go to their rooms. That usually works, because our kids don't like to be alone.

Another mother of four, ranging from a new baby to an eleven-year-old, admits she likes to think of "clever ways" to organize and set limits for her troops. With mountains of toys, clothes, books, and sports equipment, she and her husband began to yearn for a breath of order in the living room, at least:

> ▶ I was tired of having people spread out their junk. My husband came up with the idea of putting parking stickers on items left around too long. The children have until bedtime to get rid of the item or else it will get "towed." It's working

a lot better than nagging to put a ticket on a tennis racket. And so far, all items with stickers have been put away — nothing has had to be towed!

Inventive disciplinary solutions such as these are most effective when parents have come to terms with their own childhood histories and feel that they can set limits from a place of relative calm and compassion. The mother who resorted to parking stickers had gone through years of unsuccessful and wearing angry explosions before she realized she had to break the negative pattern from her past:

> ▶ I used to get angry at my kids and explode. I learned the explosion mechanism from my Dad, and I was teaching it to my kids. Now my kids, my husband, and I do a lot more talking. That's our generation: we learned that in college as young adults. And it works better than trying to keep it all in or exploding it out.

When confrontation gets so hot that even talking won't help, this mother finds that the "only thing that helps me is to step back and take a deep breath for twenty seconds. I'm silent for awhile before making my next move."

Counselors to abusive or near-abusive parents concur with this mother's instinct to step back from the fray and take her own time-out. Louise McGuire, of the Parental Stress Service in Berkeley, describes the advice she typically gives to desperate parents calling her office for help. Her suggestions are also sound for any of us who have ever feared going too far with our children and those who want to avoid a potentially heart-breaking crisis: "First we let enraged parents vent and complain about their children for as long as they need to. Often these parents feel as if they can't talk with their friends or family, because everyone else's family seems so perfect. If parents are on the verge of hitting their kid, we suggest that they take a time-out themselves — go for a walk (if they have older kids who can be left alone) or put younger kids in their own rooms for a few minutes. There are times to be together and times to take a break."

When the immediate crisis has blown over, McGuire suggests

appraising the big picture: "After the immediate crisis, we ask them to think about their support systems and to open up to other families or join parent support groups to see that problems really are common. We talk about doing something for themselves — both then if possible and on a regular basis — taking a bath, listening to soothing music, anything special to calm themselves down and to remind themselves that they're important, too. Finally, we try to work on building empathy for their child. We ask them to ask themselves, What is my child trying to tell me with his behavior? and, What was it like for me at that age?"

Expert suggestions for breaking the anger cycle run the gamut from tricks of behavior modification (deep breaths, parent time-outs) to techniques for focusing on one's own childhood history and emotional habits. Several ways to recognize and rewrite childhood scripts are offered by Arthur Bodin, past president of the Family Psychology Division of the American Psychological Association and co-director of training at the Mental Research Institute in Palo Alto, California, a pioneering institute in developing family therapy: "To help parents recognize an old anger script, I ask them what was happening in their parents' lives at about the same age and stage. I sometimes use a role-reversal technique in which a parent plays his child and I play the parent coping with an annoying situation. The parent portrays the child whining, for example, and I portray the parent the way I believe the child interprets the parent — angry and demanding quiet. Sometimes the parent will then say something like 'The way you played my role I sounded just like my father!' Often there is a shock of recognition."

Another technique Bodin suggests is to keep a diary of the times when angry situations occur: "For example, a father who got very upset with his daughter for leaving things at school and 'always' leaving the light on at home began to keep a log of when these problems actually occurred. The father was a Depression baby who believed the girl should be conserving energy and money by turning off the lights and called her irresponsible when she didn't. I suggested logging how many times she left the lights on. Through logging, the father became a more accurate observer. He began to realize, 'I was wrong. My daughter only leaves the light on fifty percent of the time!' A week later, after he had told her of his logging, he reported, 'When she knows I'm observing her to log her leaving the lights on, she turns them off seventy-five percent of the time.' "

Beyond resolving these everyday situations as they occur, Bodin suggests that families "improve the family climate: catch your children doing something right." He recommends a pamphlet from Des Moines Child Services called *100 Ways to Say "That's Good."* "Change the family emphasis," he suggests to families locked in angry, unproductive struggles. "Instead of punishing negative behavior, use rewards when children do well — not food or money but something that the parent really enjoys, too, an interactional reward like a special outing or time together."

This "put[ting] an end to talk that wounds the spirit," in Adele Faber's and Elaine Mazlish's phrase, and "search[ing] out the language that nourishes self-esteem" subtly changes the family spirit as well. As the climate shifts from angry storm bursts to sunnier and warmer acceptance, the family's self-esteem improves. Children feel better about themselves when their positive behavior is acknowledged and their feelings are heard and respected. And parents feel better about themselves when they begin to nurture and appreciate the joyful parts of family life and turn an angry, negative cycle between the generations into a positive, nourishing one.

"Before I had my baby, I thought that logistics would be the hardest part of being a single parent," admits *Nina Silber*, who at forty chose to have a baby on her own by artificial insemination with an anonymous donor. Five years later, having singlehandedly weathered the sleep-deprived nights of infancy, the defiances of toddlerhood, and the limit testing during two years of nursery school, she is ready to send her son off to kindergarten. "Now," she says, "I have found that parenting itself — especially issues of discipline — has been the hardest part."

Nina's story could be another negative statistic in the cross-generational abuse column. All the elements of stress are there — abusive parents, single parenthood, few support systems, and a child with a "difficult" temperament. But Nina managed to turn her story around. And though she is not the most typical of mothers sitting around the playground, her process of change, her daily struggles to become a more conscious and sensitive parent — indeed, a Synthesizer — are illuminating and inspiring for any parents.

Short, intense, her occasional prickliness mellowed by her clear aquamarine eyes, Nina was born in Eastern Europe and speaks with a lilting accent. Her family moved to this country when she was still small, and two brothers were born when she was five and seven. Her upbringing was strict and European, especially in the expectation that children should adhere to adult standards of manners and self-control.

Growing up, she was favored by her father but not her mother, who once admitted to Nina that she preferred the boys. Nina strove for academic excellence to please her parents and trained and practiced as an accountant. But affairs of the heart did not go well for her. Were her standards too high? Did she not want to desert her parents? Did she not want another male after her father to tell her what to do? By the time she was forty, desperately wanting a child, she made the complex but finally exhilarating decision to have one by herself.

The insemination process did not work easily, and the pregnancy itself was difficult. But she fell in love with the beautiful baby boy with the big brown eyes which clearly came from the father she never knew. She named him Michael and gave him her own last name. "Throughout his infancy, I adored my child," she says now. "The change came with the terrible twos," she adds. "I was reacting to his being stubborn, and began slapping and spanking him too much."

When I ask her what was the angriest she has ever been at her son, an image from the dog days of two and a half comes painfully to mind. "I threw him down on my bed and suddenly found my hands around his neck. Then I ran out of the room before I inflicted any damage."

She was shocked and ashamed to see "all her negative stuff coming out" in the heat of the moment. "One of the reasons I had a child," she admits softly, "is to get away from the focus on self. I thought I didn't want to grow old being alone and introspective. But instead, everything has come back to me to look at again." As she tried to sort through the debris of her own past as well as handle the moment-to-moment intensity with her increasingly verbal and limit-testing two-year-old, she realized that she needed help.

In the three years since that angry nadir when she came perilously close to abuse, she has been in a support group with other mothers, individual therapy, and Parents Anonymous, a self-help group for parents learning to find alternatives to abuse and violence. During these emotionally charged years, with the aid of skilled professionals and the wisdom of other parents like herself, she has come to a deeper understanding of her own childhood history and has learned a variety of new techniques to channel and express her anger.

When I ask her to describe a recent scene of handling anger and setting limits with her son, a far more even-keeled and humane picture emerges. "Now he's five and he doesn't throw tantrums any more. If he does seriously misbehave, I ask him to go to his room. Then I'll set the timer for five minutes and say, 'I'll see how you're doing when the timer goes off.' " After years of soul-searching and much trial and error, she has managed to replace near violence with a more level-headed alternative, excessive emotional investment with more neutrality. "In the beginning I wouldn't try any intermediate steps. I'd let my son do and do and do something that bothered me, until I exploded. It has always been hard for me to deal with other people's strong emotional responses. So I would just give in to avoid scenes with my son, and then the scenes would get worse."

In the safe context of a mothers' support group — the group led by Leah Potts Fisher and Helen Neville — Nina began for the first time to review and reflect on how anger had been handled in her childhood home. "My father was a very angry man," she began to realize. "He was not an alcoholic or unfaithful. He was a hard worker who had to be in control all the time. He would do the spanking, slap our faces, pull our ears. One of his punishments was to put alligator clips on our ears. He would also play mean practical jokes, like dangling us upside down over a big drop." It was not until she joined the parents' group that she began to see this behavior as anything out of the ordinary, in fact, as abuse.

Paired with her father's abusiveness was a mother who was "standoffish and cold. She was more wishy-washy. She would set us up against our father but then wouldn't stand up for us." With her son, trying to navigate between the rock and the hard place of her family history, she found herself leaning dangerously close to her father's angry mode. "I feared my father but wanted his approval," she says now, adding, "Still do." But when her adored boy began acting out and pressing buttons from the past, she began to hear "my father's voice in mine." As the yelling and slapping and spanking became more and more frequent — and less and less effective — memories of her own childhood pain and fear at her father's hands began to haunt her. She realized she had to get help to learn how to make some changes and save her son from her own suffering.

A pivotal session in the mothers' group occurred one evening when Nina came in at her wits' end. The issue was fighting with Michael, then two and a half, about getting out of the bath and into his pajamas. She turned to the other mothers and the two leaders for suggestions about how to be less "angry and unpredictable," how to set firmer, more effective limits.

Listening to this session afterward on the tape, I saw how it revealed a crucial sequence of steps for making change. The first step is facing and exploring the dynamics of the past and acknowledging the differences between one's new family and one's family of origin as well as strides already made. Then goals for future change can be set, new approaches found by brainstorming with other parents, therapists, or other resources. Deeper but related themes are explored as they come up — the connections between anger and separation, for instance, or anger and self-esteem — because these issues may become either stumbling blocks or signposts for change. The final step is experimenting with new strategies, coping with inevitable resistance and backsliding — and savoring the new behavior as it is integrated into family life.

"Was there anyone in your past you wanted to say no to but couldn't?" Leah Fisher asked her, beginning the session by focusing attention on past history.

"A large number of people," she answered with a tired sigh from years of holding in memories. "I feel tempted to say my parents, but I did say no to them. We had these violent verbal battles. I would lash out, just scream, never analyze. Then I'd either get slapped by my father or he'd stalk off, terribly icy."

"An interesting compromise," Fisher responded, "because you'd communicate your anger, but so vaguely that your parents didn't have to take it personally, and they could dismiss you as being an airhead if they wanted."

Nina nodded in acknowledgment. "In fact I was constantly being told I was crazy. 'What did I do to deserve someone so crazy?' my father would say. 'We didn't have anyone like you in the family before.' They dealt with me as a crazy kid."

Part of Nina's struggle was to separate herself from her own crazy-making past, undo the straitjacket of her parents' criticisms, and begin to see herself — and her abilities as a parent — in a more accepting way. Observes Eliana Gil in *Outgrowing the Pain:*

> Abused children learn by their experiences to expect little of them-
> selves and others. They are not usually taught to trust, and end up
> seeing themselves as bad, crazy, and unworthy of love or attention.
> Just as abused children learned to see themselves this way, they can
> learn to adopt more positive ways of viewing themselves and others.

Soon Nina was shyly but proudly confiding to the group two important differences that separated her new style from her parents': the ability to apologize and the emphasis on showing affection. "If I get angry with Michael, I always go back and say I'm sorry. If he gets angry with me, he comes up afterward and says, 'I love you, too, Mommy.' The fact that we're physically affectionate and that I apologize to him is saving me from being like my father."

But despite some very positive changes in family style, she was still discouraged by the bathtime fights she and Michael were having every night.

"You're talking about the anxiety over separation," another mother in the group offered, pointing the way to a deeper theme. "Part of it is that he's separating from you and not wanting to do things your way. He's saying, 'Hey, I'm in charge here.' "

Nina nodded emphatically in agreement. "Michael does that on all different levels: 'I want my peas on a red plate, no I want them on a yellow plate.' That doesn't bother me if I'm in a good mood, but if I've already put them on a red plate — " She breaks off, rolling her eyes in exasperation. The other mothers in the room groan a collective groan of recognition.

"There's a time you can deal with that and a time you can't," the other mother responded, thinking about the ups and downs of tolerance with her own two kids. "Your kid needs to understand that. It may be reasonable at two, but not at two and a half. If he were my son, I'd pull the bath drain out and let him get cold!"

"What's your own goal?" Fisher asked Nina.

"I'd just like Michael to resist a little less," Nina responded. "I don't want him to be a perfect little boy who hops into his pajamas." She smiled and shrugged. "Sure, in some fantasy somewhere. But I like his spirit. I sometimes wonder if I'm giving him a mixed message: Be defiant. But I'd like both of us to get to the point where the bath-time routine is self-limiting — he bounces on my bed afterward, plays a little, but then goes on without my having to sit on him. Now I have to restrain him to get on his diaper and his pajamas. Some nights he screams bloody murder; other nights he thinks it's a wonderful game."

Helen Neville, the group's other leader, picked up on this mention of a game. "He's very verbal and responsive. If you say, 'We can have a pushing game *after* you have your pj's on,' that might work better. Use his energy in ways you can feel comfortable with."

"Do you try funny things?" suggested another mother. "Sometimes that changes their attention away from resisting."

"I should try that instead of gritting my teeth," Nina admitted with a sheepish smile.

"It's also really useful to separate the joy he gets from jumping on the bed and wrestling after his bath from the frustration you feel around wanting him to get dressed," added another mother. "You have every right to want him to get dressed, and he has every right to want to jump and be playful. But you can acknowledge his needs and have more of a give-and-take."

Leah Fisher again pointed Nina's attention back to a compelling underlying theme that if unexamined could be an obstacle to change. "There are all kinds of separation issues here. One of them is separation for bed."

"Yes," agreed Nina. "He'll say, 'Do I have to go to my own bed?' Also, he's having trouble going to sleep. I hear him in his room banging and reading to himself. It's driving me crazy, because I have no time to myself. It also hurts because on some level I feel like I should be the perfect sacrificing mother who doesn't need that time."

Another mother quickly chimed in. "If you give yourself that evening time you'll have a lot more reserves to enjoy Michael the next day, and you'll actually be closer to being that 'perfect' mother you want to be."

Unraveling the strands of anger and separation, the needs for time alone and time with her child, Nina teased out yet another connection. She had been one of the devoted minority of mothers who nurse their children into their toddler years, and now that intimate bond was gradually changing. "Another separation is that Michael is gradually weaning himself from nursing," she told the group. "I know I have mixed feelings about that — it takes a long time and he bites sometimes, but still, I'm going to miss it. It's my last tie to my baby, and he's been playing baby a lot."

Helen Neville responded to the losses — and potential gains — involved in this time of transition. "As a child pulls away from that physical closeness of nursing, other mothers can say, 'Well, now I can snuggle with this other guy, my husband, who's been wanting some attention.' Now it would seem important for you to think of how you're going to fill that gap — a friend to trade massages with? — some way for you to get that physical contact. Ending nursing is hard for everyone, but especially for you."

"It is going to be hard," Nina answered thoughtfully. "It's also hard for Michael not to have a father to wrestle with. I knew when I made the decision that it would be hard. But in real life it's so much harder than I ever thought it would be. I'm sort of everything to him, and I'm making him everything to me, too. So we're hard on each other."

In the two and a half years since that pivotal evening, Nina and Michael have come a long way to balancing attachment and separation, rage and limits. Nina has continued to get help and support from outside sources and has made huge strides implementing change at home. Learning to be less hard on herself and her son has been a constant theme throughout her struggles to change. Efforts on her own behalf have ranged from practical (relaxation techniques and abdominal breathing to physically "relax the tenseness") to psychological (working on setting clearer boundaries between Michael and herself) to purely pampering (taking one afternoon a month to do something special for herself instead of her usual therapy appointment).

During the times of inevitable backsliding, when she finds herself yelling too much or slapping Michael to control him (often before she gets her period or before a birthday), she does her best to apologize — and tries to forgive herself and carry on. At the same time, she's working on being more accepting and less controlling of Michael. "I'm a lot warmer than I used to be. I praise him, encourage him, and tell him how he's done things well. I've learned that using stars for rewards for good behavior is not awful, and I gave Michael stars for drinking water after he had his tonsils out and even for flushing the toilet!"

As a child, she says, she was simply expected to behave. But now she's learned to see good behavior as a gift — and one that should be appreciated and praised when given. She has also seen the behavior cycle between herself and her son gradually change. Where before Michael misbehaved, was punished, and only misbehaved some more, now she catches his good behavior and praises it, only to see him behave well some more. Ready for kindergarten now and the widening world of school, Michael is a bouncy, curious, outspoken little boy with a strengthening sense of self-esteem. His mother, too, has broken away from the long and damaging shadow of her past and given herself the luxury of being not a perfect mother but a good enough one.

— 8 —

Self-Esteem and Success

THE WRITER

In her room at the prow of the house
Where light breaks, and the windows
    are tossed with linden,
My daughter is writing a story.

I pause in the stairwell, hearing
From her shut door a commotion of
    typewriter-keys
Like a chain hauled over a gunwale.

Young as she is, the stuff
Of her life is a great cargo, and some of
    it heavy:
I wish her a lucky passage.

But now it is she who pauses,
As if to reject my thought and its easy
    figure.
A stillness greatens, in which

The whole house seems to be thinking,
And then she is at it again with a
    bunched clamor
Of strokes, and again is silent.

I remember the dazed starling
Which was trapped in that very room,
    two years ago;
How we stole in, lifted a sash

And retreated, not to affright it;
And how for a helpless hour, through
    the crack of the door,
We watched the sleek, wild, dark

And iridescent creature
Batter against the brilliance, drop like a
    glove
To the hard floor, or the desk-top,

And wait then, humped and bloody,
For the wits to try it again; and how our
    spirits
Rose when, suddenly sure,

It lifted off from a chair-back,
Beating a smooth course for the right
    window
And clearing the sill of the world.

It is always a matter, my darling,
Of life or death, as I had forgotten. I
    wish
What I wished you before, but harder.

Richard Wilbur

There is a certain gleam in my children's eyes when they have done something they are proud of, and nothing makes me happier as a mother than to see it. It is a glow that starts in the eyes and then rushes like elixir through their bodies until they are fairly bouncing balls of pleasure and zest. For my older son, that glint of pride might come with dunking a basketball, reading a story slowly but lovingly by himself for the first time, delivering a joke with punch line admirably intact. For my younger son, an equal gleam comes when he completes a puzzle, catches a ball between two outstretched palms, pees right into the potty. At these moments, their pleasure in their own accomplishments may be fanned by outside approval — mine or their father's, a friend's or a teacher's — but does not seem dependent on it. Their triumph in their own mastery is private and pure, luscious as a good meal, refreshing as a good night's sleep.

There is another look, a disappointed and dejected look that also starts in the eyes, then runs through their bodies like a bad flu, and this one sobers me and chills my heart. This is their pain at disappointments, sadnesses, frustrations. For my older son, it might be losing a game (his own team or the Oakland A's can be equally wrenching); for my younger son, being excluded from a game by his brother and cohorts. Here again, my children's disappointments may be tempered from the outside — by my attempts at empathy or by their father's distractions — but not truly assuaged. Like their pride, their pain has a life force and course of its own, unsettling as a bad meal but transient as a night of interrupted sleep.

As I watch my children grapple with pride and pain, I struggle to find the right place from which to watch them and help them grow. How can I disentangle self-esteem and success, showing them how much I love them beyond their successes, despite their failures, and teaching them to accept and love themselves the same way? How can I nurture their pride in themselves without getting addicted to their accomplishments? How can I help them cope with inevitable disappointments and frustrations without getting despondent about their losses? How can I let them bloom in areas where I have flowered without being overbearing and find their way to places where I have been thwarted? How can I savor their strengths in areas where I am shakier without appropriating those strengths to shore myself up?

If one goal characterizes contemporary parents and distinguishes them from the generation before, it is this newly articulated emphasis on nurturing children's self-esteem. "Self-esteem was not even in the parental vocabulary when we were small," wrote one questionnaire respondent, appraising the shift between the generations. Gone now are the days when children were to be seen but not heard, "modest and helpful," as one thirty-something mother told me of her own mother's goal for her. In eras past, self-esteem meant self-centeredness, pride came before fall, self-praise was no compliment. Now self-esteem is seen as the cornerstone of children's well-being and family health.

The early childhood theorists and family therapists whose work informs my own — Bruno Bettelheim, Alice Miller, Selma Fraiberg, Virginia Satir, among others — believe that self-esteem is fostered by the parents' acceptance of the whole child for better or worse, joyful or sad, achieving or struggling, modest or flashy, like us or different. Family therapist Sheri Glucoft Wong suggests that the two most important insights school-age kids need for self-esteem are first "to know they're special and unique — there's no one like them in the whole world" and then "to know that they're just like everybody else."

For Bruno Bettelheim, the "successful child" is the one who is a success not necessarily in the eyes of the world but in his own heart. This child is

> well pleased with the way he was raised and . . . would decide that, by and large, he is satisfied with himself, despite the shortcomings to which all of us are prey. [He is also able] to cope reasonably well with the endless vicissitudes, the many hardships, and the serious difficulties he is likely to encounter in life, and to do so mainly because he feels secure in himself. . . . [He] possesses an inner life which is rich and rewarding, and with which he is hence satisfied.

For Virginia Satir, "self-esteem is the ability to value one's self and to treat oneself with dignity, love and reality." From this genuine self-love and self-acceptance, love and acceptance for others follow naturally:

> Integrity, honesty, responsibility, compassion, love and competence — all flow easily from people whose self-esteem is high. . . . Appreciating our own worth, we are ready to see and respect the worth of others. We radiate trust and hope. We don't

have rules against anything we feel. We also know we don't have to act on everything we feel. . . . We accept all of ourselves as human.

From earliest infancy on, the growing child builds an internal picture of herself based in part on how she is handled and cared for by mother, father, and other primary caretakers. Every word, impatient or cooing, every gesture, rough or soothing, every expression, approving or disapproving, adds to this internal image. Also central is the caretaker's ability to reflect the infant's cues. The mother who can steadily gaze back at the infant who gazes at her provides a clear and faithful mirror for her child. But if the mother reflects instead her own internal projections or anxieties, then the child never feels truly seen. "This child would remain without a mirror," comments Alice Miller, "and for the rest of his life would be seeking this mirror in vain."

Early childhood theorists like D. W. Winnicott and Alice Miller believe that beginning in infancy, parents' responses determine whether the child will be able to show her true, authentic self or will begin to hide it behind a mask. According to Alice Miller, the inhibiting mask is often many generations in the making. A new mother whose own mother would not let her show her real self will have a harder time recognizing and validating her child's authentic self:

> However paradoxical this may seem, a child is at the mother's disposal. . . . A child can be so brought up that it becomes what she wants it to be. . . . The mother can feel herself the center of attention, for her child's eyes follow her everywhere. When a woman had to suppress and repress all these needs in relation to her own mother, they rise from the depth of her unconscious and seek gratification through her own child, however well-educated and well-intentioned she may be, and however much she is aware of what a child needs. The child feels this clearly and very soon forgoes the expression of his own distress.

Children's accommodations to parental needs, Miller explains, often lead to the "as if personality," or what Winnicott calls the "false self." This is the child who pretends a lot and offers a false front to the world. He masks his real emotions — seething, angry, miserable — with acceptable emotions which he believes the world, especially his parents, need to see. Behaving "as if" this mask is his real self, this child gradually loses touch with what his true feelings are and merges sadly and inextricably with his mask.

But the child whose authentic self is accepted and cherished from the first squawks of infancy to the hottest rebellions of adolescence is allowed to stay attuned to her true self and develop a "healthy narcissism," or self-esteem, as Alice Miller describes:

> I understand a healthy self-feeling to mean the unquestioned certainty that the feelings and wishes one experiences are part of one's self. . . . This automatic, natural contact with his own emotions and wishes gives an individual strength and *self-esteem*. He may live out his feelings, be sad, despairing, or in need of help, without fear of making the introjected mother insecure. He can allow himself to be afraid when he is threatened or angry when his wishes are not fulfilled. He knows not only what he does not want but also what he wants and is able to express this, irrespective of whether he will be loved or hated for it.

"One is free from depression," Miller says, "when self-esteem is based on the authenticity of one's feelings and not on the possession of certain qualities. Indeed, loving a child for what he is rather than for what he can do or perform or accomplish is another vital ingredient in nurturing self-esteem. Valuing a child for who he is allows his creativity to flourish and allows him to take failures in stride and build resources to try again. Valuing a child for who she is does not preclude helping her set goals or encouraging accomplishment. But valuing a child for achievements alone can actually straitjacket long-term success by making a child afraid to risk failure, even afraid to try new challenges at all.

A mother in her mid-forties is trying with her two young teenagers to turn around her memory of being valued for accomplishments alone: "I most value my kids' self-confidence and self-awareness. My parents seemed to most value my accomplishments, which left me feeling that mere effort and trying were of little value."

Another mother who answered my questionnaire thought that her parents most valued her when she was out in the spotlight succeeding, but learned something different when she asked her mother:

> ▶ From my perspective, my parents most seemed to enjoy my successes (such as getting good grades and acquiring good jobs) and least enjoyed my rebelliousness. After talking to my mother about this questionnaire, she told me that she most enjoyed the heart-to-heart conversations that we have. Her answer moved me.

Our parents' consciousness about self-esteem and their attitudes about success — as well as our *perceptions* about their attitudes — have a profound influence on how we value ourselves and our children. Layers of meaning accrue through the generations, and definitions of success and its expression vary dramatically from family to family and culture to culture. What a family values (sports or academics, humor or compassion for others) and how accomplishments are reckoned (with modesty or pride, secrecy or self-promotion) are messages passed both overtly and covertly from one generation to the next. Whether we can take pride in our own achievements or must hide them under a bushel, whether we feel our successes are truly our own or simply feathers in the family cap — all these complexities color each family's definitions of success and each child's feelings of self-worth. And the web of influence extends beyond the triangle of parents and child to include the entire family system: the grandparents who may look to grandchildren to provide them with the honors their children failed to offer (Yiddish has the especially evocative word *naches* for these honors), the cousins held up as exemplars of accomplishment, the sibling who always surpasses the others — or the one who never quite catches up.

Of the four kinds of parents examined in my interviews and questionnaires, the Traditionalist most closely shares the definitions of success remembered from childhood. Usually this means carrying on his original family's emphasis on education and achievement and bringing up his children to value, even idealize, the intellectual sphere. Traditionalists, like their parents, tend to go with a mainstream definition of success. If a child fits comfortably within the constraints of parents' goals — polite and industrious, ambitious and achieving, talented and well-rounded — family harmony is preserved. The Traditionalist parent may have a harder time than many accepting and cherishing the child who veers in an original or unusual direction.

Because the Traditionalist also has a difficult time with separation, he is often tempted to let his own dreams get mixed up with his children's. In particular, this parent may dream of having a child who follows in his occupational footsteps. A mother of two school-age children describes the pressure in this direction that has dogged her children as much from outsiders' expectations as from inside the family: "My husband is a physician, and from toddlerhood on my kids (especially my son) hear, 'Are you going to be a doctor and make Mommy and Daddy proud?' But we tell them to be whatever makes them happy and that we'll be proud of them whatever they choose."

When a parent is unable to separate his chosen path from his children's, the wish may be for more than companionship (wanting to bring Junior into the family business) or a flattering mirror (Junior's same occupational choice confirming Ma's or Pa's). As Bruno Bettelheim explains, the wish that a child follow in his parents' footsteps both ensures that the parent maintains superiority and also continues the relationship in the form that was most satisfying:

> How understandable it is, then, that the parent should wish this bond to continue undisturbed, through the child's taking up the parent's occupation, in which the parent is so much more knowledgeable. Since this wish is largely selfish, it remains unconscious and is replaced by the conscious conviction that such occupational choice is what is best for the child.

"A lot of therapy involves giving people permission to unlock the tight boxes we put ourselves in," observes Chicago psychotherapist Sandra Oriel. According to Oriel, we end up in these boxes because our original family style was either too rigid or too loose and disorganized. The overly rigid parents — some Traditionalists among them — "pass on too high expectations about achievement," Oriel believes; the overly loose parents — and these include some Rebels — "provide too unstable an environment, so that the children end up parenting the parents."

If the Traditionalist sometimes has such a rigid definition of success and limited vision of what is valuable that children's options become severely circumscribed, the Rebel sometimes has such permissive attitudes and such a hang-loose vision that children feel swamped by too many options. Rebels have often vowed to replace the tight ship they resented with a live-and-let-live attitude. But often beneath this laissez-faire demeanor lie the vestiges of the tight grasp in which they were raised. Although Rebels may swear that they will never repeat their parents' psychic intrusions into their lives, their children may have a different story to tell.

A writer friend tells a story of his friend Sam, who confided that he was awed to be around writers because he himself was totally blocked when he tried to write. When my friend asked why, Sam explained that his father had always wanted him to be a writer and from the earliest age had saved everything he had written. Sam's father even made little books of his writing. For his entire childhood an enormous fuss had been made over his precocity at writing — and now he couldn't write at all.

Now, my friend tells me, Sam has a seven-year-old son named Rudy. Two or three years ago, Rudy began to show a rather remarkable talent for drawing and painting, and he, too, is very precocious. Recently my friend went to visit this family, and Sam asked, "Would you like to see this little book?" And indeed, Sam had collected his son's paintings and drawings just as his father had collected his writing. "All the same stuff that drove him crazy as a child," my friend observed, "this father had done with his own son."

This is the classic Rebel, who believes he is fighting back against the intrusions of his parents and then intrudes on his children in spite of himself.

Around issues of success and self-esteem, the Compensator parent finds himself hustling to give his children the kind of support he wished for in childhood. Whatever opportunities were denied him as a child — in education or outside activities, in parents' time or attention — this parent does his best to make up with his own children. But his children may not need exactly what he wants to give, and may have to jockey to take back the reins of their own lives.

Philip Ripstein is a sociologist and a Compensator father in his early sixties with one son in his thirties from a first marriage, an eighteen-year-old son from his second marriage, and two older stepsons. Philip's early childhood was particularly rocky: his mother had lost a baby at three months just two years before he was born, then Philip's father died when Philip was only three. His mother was a woman of grandiose visions but "very self-doubting"; she never fully recovered from the double loss of infant and husband.

"I'm a replacement child," Philip observes. "But the replacement child is not, after all, the other one. Sometimes the parent is even angry at the replacement child. My mother was enormously overprotective; she was also hostile and destructive." After his father's death, his mother placed him in a foster home. Once he was safely out of her jurisdiction, their relationship was cordial; indeed, Philip remembers, "she idealized me." But when he returned to live with his mother in his teens, she became quirkier and more "ambivalent."

"My mother is funny," he offers with an irony that comes easier now that he's in his middle years, a father himself, and has earned the great honor and prestige of being awarded a MacArthur Fellowship. "She doesn't like to hear that I've done well. In fact, she did her best to undermine me. She would try to foster underachievement. She would discourage me from trying for anything. She believed in the evil eye. She was afraid if I were prominent, I'd be killed." Indeed, when I first met Philip and asked him what he did, he smiled mysteriously and said, "I'm still waiting to find out"; he never once mentioned the illustrious MacArthur Fellowship.

Early and tragic loss and disappointment have scarred the Ripstein family tree. Philip's mother, like Philip, was a replacement child. "My mother had an older sister who died. Her mother treated her with the same mixture of overprotectiveness and inaccessibility my mother showed to me. I remember feeling that confusion as a child and saying to my mother, 'I don't feel that you love me.' "

When Philip's older son, Max, grew up to be a troubled young man, brilliant but unable to fend for himself, Philip found himself turning to his younger son, David — the child of his new and more hopeful marriage — as a replacement for Max. "With David, there were times I couldn't hear him, because I was so anxious to have him be Max, whom I couldn't raise because of the divorce."

If Philip's mother tried to trim his sails and discourage accomplishment for fear of reprisals, Philip took a different tack with David. Philip became the eager Compensator, rushing to provide the opportunities for his younger son that he had missed in his own childhood and had missed giving his older son as well. He threw himself headlong into his son's education and activities. He sent David to a prestigious and creative private school, then peered longingly over his shoulder as he chose classes and got involved in the school community. "If I'd gone there, it would have been wonderful," Philip says wistfully. "I was gifted in math and physics and would have thrived there." But the fantasies of the Compensator — that complex mix of selflessness and selfishness — are not always appreciated by his children. "When I said to David how much I would have loved going to his school," his father remembers with both regret and awe, "he faced me directly and said, 'You can't live through me.' "

You can't live through me — with these self-possessed and even-handed words, David has managed to put himself back in the center of his life. He has loosened the triangle that bound his father, his education, and himself and has gently redirected his father's attentions elsewhere. He has taken it on himself to change the family blueprint, to undo several generations of overinvolvement and over-identification between parent and child. A third-generation replacement child, David nevertheless had several advantages that his father and grandmother missed out on. Coming fron an intact and loving marriage, getting an education that was progressive and tailored to individual needs, having two older stepbrothers who provided models and encouragement, David has had the chance to build both internal and external resources. Both because of and in spite of his father, he reached adolescence with a strong sense of self-esteem and a sure sense of autonomy that allowed him to appreciate his father — and to tell him when to back off.

Another kind of compensating parent inadvertently short-circuits her child's self-esteem and circumvents autonomy by looking to the child to compensate for what she lacked in her own childhood.

Parents who yearn for achievements they cannot themselves garner too often find convenient outlets in their children. The mother who lusted for the limelight pushes her baby into TV commercials; the father who dreamed of baseball glory sends his daughter to baseball summer camp; the parents who want to climb the social ladder send their children to an exclusive private school where the parents can hobnob with the social elite. "Some parents love their children so much," Bruno Bettelheim once observed wryly, "that they want them to have everything they missed — including a straight-A report card!" Basking in reflected glory, these parents try to shore up their own rickety self-esteem. In the meantime, they rob their children of the chance to develop their own bedrock sense of self-worth and negotiate an independent course.

The child who is forced to live out her parents' wishes and fantasies must often assume a false self. Alice Miller describes how the necessity for a false self inhibits both separation and self-esteem:

> The child who has been unable to build up his own [internal] structures is first consciously and then unconsciously dependent on his parents. He cannot rely on his own emotions, has not come to experience them through trial and error, has no sense of his own real needs, and is alienated from himself to the highest degree. Under these circumstances, he cannot separate from his parents, and even as an adult he is still dependent on affirmation from his partner, from groups or especially from his own children.

So the reverberations of the false self ripple from generation to generation, along with needs unfulfilled, separation unachieved, and self-esteem shakier and shakier. Often, Miller adds, what parents were unable to find in their own parents, they desperately hope their child will be: "someone at their disposal who can be used as an echo, who can be controlled, is completely centered on them, will never desert them, and offers full attention and admiration." But this wish is a holdover from infantile delusions of grandeur and is inevitably destined for disappointment.

In her haunting novel *Lovingkindness*, Anne Roiphe tells of the complex relationship between a feminist mother, widowed early, and her aimless twenty-two-year-old daughter, who seeks salvation in a rigid Jewish religious sect and an arranged marriage. The novel examines the painful consequences both to mother and daughter when mother tries too hard to push the daughter to live out her mother's dreams — and the daughter tries just as hard to avoid them. In a passionate soliloquy, the mother confesses her early ambitions for her daughter, self-serving as well as self-righteous:

> I had plans of my own for Andrea. They began when she was just learning the words for shoe and nose, table and dog. I thought I saw in her eyes the spark of intelligence, the speed of thought that would have made her a fine lawyer, a civil rights lawyer, who argues for justice. . . . I saw her working into the early hours of the morning writing briefs on school integration and voter rights. I saw my daughter in a suit carrying an attaché case . . . ready to argue for what can be reasoned, what can be used to improve the landscape and make more comfortable the social domain.

As Andrea grows to adolescence, her mother begins to observe that her gifts are not intellectual and humanitarian but intuitive and creative. She adjusts her own dreams accordingly:

> As her breasts grew . . . as her interests turned away from the stuffed animals I had bought in such profusion, it became clear that she might in fact not even graduate from high school. Her gifts were not so much analytical as they were spontaneous, responsive, sensitive. It occurred to me that perhaps she was an artist, a painter who would astonish with a new vision of politics and form combined to awaken the sense and the conscience.

But despite the sketchbooks filled with art, Andrea remains resistant to her mother's plans: "She wouldn't talk about art. She wouldn't go to a museum with me. She didn't want to be anything. She drew but she stopped showing me her drawings."

Watching her daughter withdraw further and further into her own pain and anomie — hours playing music in her room by herself or rocking infantlike in front of the TV — her mother is slowly and painfully forced to face her daughter's insistence on her separate self:

> Between mother and daughter the affair is fraught with small needles, little pinpricks, an occasional bloodletting, a wrenching away from exactly the unity that was once so desired, so needed, so always imperfect. As the mother withers, her need for her daugh-

ter mounts. She pours herself into her child. Each triumph, each flash of beauty, each step in the wider world is enjoyed as if it were one's own. But exactly this stickiness, this glueing of completeness onto incompleteness, drives the daughter to secrecy, to abandonment, to a ferocious fight for her own skin, her own destiny.

In such a relationship, success and failure are both perpetually sullied by the parent's need for the child to complete his own dreams and the child's need to pursue her own destiny. Even with children only five and two, I can see the temptation to dream through them. Last year at nursery school, my older son's class was asked to perform a rousing spiritual at a local senior center. My son adored the song, sang it to himself around the house, and knew the words so well that the other children turned to him when they faltered. But when the children were given the choice of performing for the seniors or staying at school, my son chose not to perform and spent that morning with a few others at school. I tried to understand his point of view (later he told me that he had been scared off by hearing of a rickety stair to the stage), but inside I was surprisingly disappointed. Before the performance, I tried to discuss his decision with him, and so did his teachers, but he would not budge from his position. For a long time afterward, I brooded about mine: how much I wanted him to perform, how I knew he would shine, how I'd bask in the reflected rays. Finally I stopped myself: this was only nursery school! The experience was a sobering glimpse into the tenacity of our dreams for our children — and the awesome force of our children's resistance, the steadiness of their surge toward selfhood.

So I was comforted to come upon an essay called "Keeping Up with the Joneses" by Anne Roiphe, in which she admits she has not resolved this issue even after twenty-six years of trial and error:

> My first child was born twenty-six years ago and I still find myself unsteady on this issue. I'm not sure that it is possible to be entirely realistic and not wager one's ego on a child's success. I'm not sure we *can* compete within the bounds of sanity. I only know we have to keep trying.

That we almost invariably take pride and pleasure in our children's success we readily admit; that we are also tempted to claim those successes as our own can be more complicated to acknowledge. For a black working-class single mother who has struggled for years to raise four boys on her own, seeing her oldest son about to graduate from high school feels truly like a shared achievement. From her point of view, certainly, her unflagging support for her son and her years of sacrifice help justify this mixture of pride and possessiveness in her son's diploma, a degree she feels will be as much hers as his: "One of my biggest dreams is to see my boys finish high school and college. My dream is to see my kids in caps and gowns. If you give me that degree, I'll truly feel I've accomplished what I was meant to do."

In other families, parents may view their children's success as compensation for their own dreams squandered or unfulfilled. A mother who feels she was a disappointment to her mother still holds on to high hopes for her own daughter:

> ▶ I feel I turned out "average." I hope my daughter will excel in something, but only if she finds her place to excel. My mother has never expressed this, but I feel she's disappointed because she's not "great" and neither am I. She always wanted me to be "somebody" — perhaps the "somebody" she never was, because she gave up a career to be my mother.

If we are often tempted to appropriate our children's successes as our own, we also tend to take their failures too personally. "When my eight-year-old daughter was put in a lower reading group at school, *I* felt demoted," admits a mother who had agonized as an early reader and was not diagnosed as dyslexic until she was eleven. "Dinner time was always a strain during our son's high school years," remembers another mother, whose son has finally found himself at twenty-five as an outdoor adventurer. "I read our son's lack of success academically as my failure and my husband read it as his."

All too often we tie our own success or failure as parents to our children's success or failure. But the child receiving honors in cap and gown may not have been lovingly encouraged and supported by the beaming parents; she may owe her success to independent perseverance, some dedicated teachers, good genes, or a mysterious combination of all these influences. The child who never makes it to graduation may not have been impeded by neglectful parents; she may have floundered quite independently, or had poor teachers, bad luck, or an equally mysterious combination of other circumstances. Overdoing our responsibility for our children's setbacks may be just as hazardous as overemphasizing our contribution to their glories.

Still, watching our children reconnoiter with success and come to terms with failure can give us an opportunity to revise our own childhood scripts, providing healing and insights about unfinished business. A mother of three girls feels a particularly nagging identification with her oldest daughter's "social problems." At eleven, this girl "wanted to be part of the group," just the way her mother had ached to belong to the popular group in her school days. But the mother now realizes admiringly that her daughter is a "real original thinker, she sees things in odd ways." And the mother has also stood by and applauded her daughter's growing acceptance of her uniqueness and individuality. "My daughter has now told me that she doesn't expect to be part of the popular group," her mother explains, crediting her daughter with "a more mature attitude than I had." Even now, appreciating her daughter's evolving maturity and self-acceptance has also helped this mother lay to rest old slights and redefine her notions of success both for her daughter and for herself.

Another mother with a teenage son and daughter has learned similar lessons from her children about winning and losing and taking rejection in stride. "One of the most painful things for me as a mother has been to experience my children's rejections and defeats," she admits. From her daughter's sobs when she failed the Red Cross swim test to her son's despair when his eighth-grade girlfriend jilted him, this mother was at first anguished to see her children's disappointments. "I was terrified of rejection as a young person, so I avoided it either by being first or by not trying at all," she remembers. "When my son was in Little League, I'd be all atremble watching him. I'd try not to let him know how much I cared, but of course he knew." But now, she says, although both her kids are "very competitive," she can see them finding an equilibrium that she, too, has learned from. "I can see my son playing squash now, and he can win or lose and be okay with it." Watching her son "be okay" with winning or losing has helped this ambitious and competitive mother find a better balance in her own life. Sometimes now when she flubs a challenge at work or loses a hard-fought tennis match, an image of her son comes to mind, and his equanimity helps her find her own.

Ironically, if more parents than ever before are aware of the importance of nurturing their children's self-esteem, more parents are also pushing their children too early and too fast. Enlightened early childhood psychologists and pediatricians may speak out for nurturing the whole child, and each child according to his own talents and pace. But "Superparents" desperately seeking success are nonetheless using flash cards with their babies to teach early reading, sending toddlers to karate and Suzuki violin classes, and hiring tutors for preschoolers to vault them ahead when they get to school. In a *New York Times Magazine* article called "Kids in the Fast Lane," Sara Davidson, author of the best-selling sixties chronicle, *Loose Change*, and, in her forties, the mother of two young children, tells a story or two on herself, her children, and her peer group of fast-track families. In this subculture, scheduling play dates is as high-powered a negotiation as the hottest Hollywood deal:

> The booking of a five-year-old is, in their word, "awesome." Consider Joshua. His parents leave for work at 8 A.M. and rarely come home before 7 P.M. They live with a Spanish-speaking housekeeper in the Hollywood Hills, where there are no other kids nearby. If Andrew [my son] wants to play with Joshua, I call his mother's secretary and learn that Josh's only opening is Wednesday. On Monday, he has computer class. On Tuesday, music. On Thursday a tutor comes to the house to coach him in reading and math. Joshua doesn't "need" a tutor, but his mother, Laurie, wants to make sure he feels "superconfident in class." This makes me nervous. If the other kids have tutors, will Andrew need one too?

For fast-track parents and their kids, the line between encourage and push is also hard to negotiate. Watching four-year-old Andrew in a karate demonstration, Davidson sheepishly checks out her own reactions:

"Support" is a trigger word, which we hear every day. At school, at the doctor's, we are told the most important thing our children need is a good self-image and self-worth. So, dutifully, at the next group class, when it's Andrew's turn to fight, I elbow my way to the front of the parent group and force myself, half cringing, to yell, "Hit him, Andrew, good!"

"In a generation where it is no longer acceptable to make your kids a career, parents may do it anyway — but covertly," observes therapist Leah Potts Fisher. Speculating about the proliferation of lessons and activities for children, Fisher asks, "Are these lessons for the kids or are they to help out overloaded parents? Is a child in an activity because she wants to be — or because her parents want it? And are parents giving children lessons out of concern or guilt — buying time and interest for their children when they're too busy to give it themselves?"

Sara Davidson testifies to the ways high-powered parents use their finely honed professional skills to turn their children into yet another career venture:

> We are, I am told by educators, the most difficult group of parents they've ever had to work with. We worry about everything; we analyze and stew and get second opinions and read books and come to each situation prepared with lists of questions. . . . What has happened is that we have brought the tools that helped us gain success in careers to the task of parenting. We are competitive, time efficient; we run on schedules and so do our kids; we believe in doing things right and want our kids to have the right tools; and we're concerned that with children you can never start anything too early.

David Elkind, child psychologist and professor at Tufts University, has made a name for himself as the impassioned prophet of slowing down the "hurried child," a term he coined in his book of that name. In formal learning, he insists, "the whole idea of earlier is better is just wrong." Scoffing at flash cards for babies and reading tutors for preschoolers, he maintains that decades of research on intellectual readiness for reading, arithmetic, and other skills "shows that children at an older age can master skills better, with greater ease." Recent studies show, too, that small children introduced to reading and other academic subjects too early may show an initial burst of skill and enthusiasm, but this boost soon peters out and is replaced by resistance.

Not only does hurrying backfire intellectually, it also stunts young children's emotional development. The short-term consequences of hurrying children run the disturbing gamut from stomachaches to headaches, sleep disturbances to behavior problems. And from Japan — where hurrying children is a national mandate — we are even beginning to hear shocking statistics of school-age children committing suicide over fear their grades won't be high enough to satisfy parents.

The long-term consequences of pushing children too fast may be deep and lasting psychic injuries and problems establishing a secure sense of self. An overemphasis on achievement for its own sake, on doing rather than being, can also gravely injure children's self-esteem. David Elkind describes the middle-class phenomenon of "achievement overload":

> So much emphasis has been placed on achievement that young people overload their schedules. . . . When young people assume that parents are concerned only with how well they do, rather than with who they are, the need to achieve becomes addictive. True meaningful support should communicate to children that achievements are supported because they are *good for the child*. Then children recognize that what they are doing is for their own good and not just for the parents.

Gata Kamsky is a fifteen-year-old Russian chess prodigy who defected to this country with his father, Rustam. Together they have had the single-minded purpose of taking on the American chess establishment. From the time the boy Gata was eight, his father has seen to it that he has done nothing but play chess. No recreation, no entertainment, no sports, no friends. Just chess day and night, until Gata's only laughs come from admiring a sleek chess move in a book, and his dreams are only of chess. Father and son live in a small apartment in Brooklyn on a yearly subsidy from a wealthy chess lover and benefactor. (Mother left the family when Gata was a small child.) Except when he is playing in a tournament, Gata does not make a move or utter a word without his father's prompting.

"His father's pawn," writer Fred Waitzkin called him in a *New York Times Magazine* article. Gata Kamsky is the hurried child carried to the most disturbing extreme. His individuality has been sacrificed for the success his father craves; his hothouse existence is a tragic commentary on the way parents who live for and through their children's achievements constrict their children's growth.

Waitzkin is also the father of a chess prodigy, a thirteen-year-old who has won the scholastic national championship three times. As he watches the senior Kamsky watching Gata in an intense chess tournament, the writer is both critical and sympathetic:

> While Gata played with detachment, Rustam, the father, paced around the periphery of the room, his war-torn prizefighter's face — he had been a boxer in the Soviet Union — showing first sadness and then inexplicable fury. A child's prodigious chess talent can be both a joy and a trap for his parents, who sometimes become so intoxicated by the child's magical accomplishments, so overwrought during games, that little else seems important.

Still, Waitzkin can't help but compare:

> For me, it was very strange entering into the world of Gata and Rustam, for with different details and textures their life has been my wicked fantasy. Like the parents of other chess-talented American children, I have often wondered how well [my son] Josh would play if he studied chess for five or six hours a day, like the top Eastern European kids, instead of attending a very demanding school, playing sports in the afternoon and pursuing an active social life. Like Rustam, I've also fantasized about my kid winning the world championship, and it frustrates me that in our middle-class life there isn't room to make a run at it. The American ideal of the well-rounded child precludes bold sacrificing for excellence.

So the American father looks at the Russian boy — stiff and single-minded, successful in his groove but stunted out of it — and at his own son — active and well-rounded, chess-talented but not quite so often victorious. And he looks at the Russian father, driven and desperate and dreaming out his dreams through his child, and at himself, coming to terms with the same temptation in part by writing about it. And though he sees his own son as thriving and the other man's son as stymied, and he calls his fantasy "wicked," he still has to reshuffle his dreams and put his fantasy to rest.

"Each of us sees our children to some degree through a haze of filters born of our past experiences, personal needs, and cultural values," observes Dorothy Briggs in her classic *Your Child's Self-Esteem.* "These expectations become yardsticks by which we measure a child."

Synthesizer parents constantly question their expectations in light of both their own needs and their children's needs and capabilities at different stages. As one such mother confided, "The hardest thing about parenting is keeping my own baggage at bay, and remembering my child is only four and not expecting behavior she is incapable of giving." Another mother describes how she is trying to combine the best of her parents' encouragement with her own less intense perspective:

> ▶ My parents raised us with a very "can-do" attitude and always taught us to try again if we didn't succeed at first. "Nine doors may close in your face before the tenth will open," my father always said. I now share this philosophy with my own children and feel proud when I see their determination. But at the same time, I try to convey that I love them just for being who they are, whether they succeed or fail, whether they try their hardest or not.

Dorothy Briggs suggests that parents periodically go through an "expectation inventory":

Why do I have this expectation?
Where did it come from?
What's in it for me?
Is it based on my needs or my child's?
What purpose does it serve?
Does it realistically fit this particular child at this particular age?

Expecting too perfect behavior too early — "rapid scholastic achievement, respect for property, cleanliness, sociability and sexual control" — makes our approval dependent on the impossible, adds Briggs. "Then, we involve a child in a rat race that undermines self-esteem. *How early* and *how fast* we press for these goals affects each child's view of himself."

Part of the Synthesizers' balancing act is the ability to appreciate and encourage the flowering of the whole child. Sometimes in the whirlwind of hurrying their children toward achievement, parents lose sight of them as individuals. But Synthesizer parents do their best to value each child's uniqueness and complexity. These parents embrace their children lovingly in private moments just for the shared pleasure in being together, not only to offer accolades for achievements. Comparing himself to his own hard-driving parents, a musician father describes his striving for "more acceptance and appreciation of simple pleasures (e.g. sports, popular arts, 'non-productive' — a misnomer, I think — relaxation). My parents are achievement-oriented and were very judgmental about what leisure pursuits are good or bad, that is, a waste of time."

Laura Markham, the wife of this musician, is a Synthesizer mother in her mid-thirties. Their daughters are five and two. She, too, is accommodating the cross-generational reverberations around success on her side of the family, as she does her best "to appreciate my children for what they are now." Even with children this young, she finds herself getting "caught up in the narcissistic trappings of parenthood." As she says:

> ► I do get a certain thrill if I'm told my child is clever or cute or nice. When I'm told something positive about my children, I sometimes have several reactions: don't express your pride, it's immodest; appreciate your children for their accomplishments *and* for who they are. I don't want my children to feel my love is contingent on certain behaviors or acquired skills.

As she digs back into her family history, Laura explores the web of messages and double messages linking her parents, grandparents, and siblings. A middle child with a high-achieving older sister and an easygoing younger brother, Laura describes a warm and encouraging family atmosphere with an emphasis on social service and tolerance for differences:

▶ My two siblings and I received plenty of attention and warmth from both parents. They provided us with opportunities to try lots of things, and they believed and acted on a strong sense of justice for others. I have clear memories of my mother's involvement in the civil rights movement: she took us on various civil rights marches, including one historic event led by Martin Luther King. In retrospect I also appreciate my parents' ability to let us find our own way as teenagers. In high school, I wore incredibly outlandish outfits to school, and my mother never criticized my choices, although she was a counselor in my school and later told me other staff ridiculed my clothes in front of her.

At the same time, her family highly valued achievement and worldly accomplishments, the wider ranging the better:

▶ My mother, her sister, and father all received doctorates from Ivy League schools. While my mother denied that the status of a school meant anything to her, I did get the message that my worth was tied to attending a prestigious college. Two years after my sister started at one, I was put on the waiting list there and accepted at her second-choice college. The rejection underlined my feelings of low self-worth; I was second daughter and second best (I still recall my father calling me his "number two girl," which I interpreted in a different sense than I now believe he intended). My teens and early twenties were overshadowed by a conflict between trying to catch up to my sister and trying to achieve an identity in other ways (dropping out of school, working in a factory, hitchhiking around the country; all badges of my countercultural identity).

Laura also found herself trying to match the wide sweep of accomplishments set by a revered aunt:

▶ My mother and her mother (a very powerful and present figure) strongly admired people with a range of accomplishments. My aunt, who is an extremely talented musician and artist as well as a professor of anthropology, was idealized.

Despite all our lessons (including French lessons at dinner every evening) and the usual music, swimming, and art lessons, I never felt accomplished enough. My self-worth was directly tied to my achievements, and for years I struggled with a sense that I was less good than my sister.

Years later, a conversation with her mother suggested that these same issues had also bothered her mother as a young parent. But her mother believed that she had made some changes in raising her own children:

> ▶ Interestingly, my mother says now that she consciously modified her upbringing, which was even more family focused, more achievement oriented and less emotionally open than my own.

When I speak with Laura's mother, Joyce, she mentions the difference between her own upbringing and her children's as a matter of more doors flung open to the outside world:

> ▶ I would like to have had more horizons opened to me as a child, more friends encouraged to play with me, more attempts made to give me self-confidence in varying activities. One minor example was that I was never taught to cook, to iron or allowed to baby-sit. I tried to open up many activities for my children, hoping they would learn to cope and learn self-confidence. I think we encouraged the children in their intellectual, creative, and social pursuits. We tried to open new horizons to them — tennis, skiing, swimming lessons, piano and instrumental lessons. If they took on new interests not advocated by us — such as Laura's pets, her treehouse, her interest in helping Dr. Schweitzer, her plan for an alternative high school — we did not back away and mostly encouraged them.

For her part, Laura can acknowledge the effort her parents made to help the children "feel good about ourselves." As a Synthesizer, she appreciates, and wants to continue, the way her parents:

► praised me for being a good friend, for taking initiative at school, for being creative. That my mother was generally available to us and respected us both increased my sense that I was and am important to her and my father. I let my daughters know that they are appreciated and try to spend time enjoying them. All in all, if I can do as good a job as my parents did in parenting us, I will feel I have done quite well.

Despite her appreciation, she still grapples with contradictory childhood messages about pride and accomplishments and thinks about how to resolve these conflicts with her daughters:

► On the one hand, learning skills (especially in school or music lessons) was rewarded. On the other hand, expressing pride in our achievements was subtly discouraged. My mother has told me several times that she was glad when I was born, because my sister, then two, was so full of herself. I would expect a two-year-old to be self-centered — it seems developmentally appropriate — but, for my mother, it was something to be squashed.

Pride in accomplishments versus narcissism, comfort in who you are versus worry over what you can do, pleasure in special talents versus having to be good at everything, efforts for their own sake versus efforts purely for approval — these are the dilemmas that have followed this family through several generations. Where Laura's mother, Joyce, modified their intensity without necessarily articulating them, Laura is doing her best to make the dilemmas conscious. This making conscious the past is the Synthesizer's gift to her children and gives them a wider and freer territory in which to discover themselves.

Parents and children can be matched and mismatched in many complex ways — the hard-driving parent whose child would rather stop to smell the flowers, the intellectual virtuoso whose child is more interested in sports or art or nonverbal pursuits, the high achiever whose child has a learning disability and struggles all the way through school, as well as the parents of modest talents whose child's accomplishments outshine their own. Where the Traditionalist views these discrepancies with disappointment that family ideals are not being carried on, the Rebel keeps expectations low if he felt he was pushed too hard or may push too hard if he felt ignored. With a low-achieving child, the Compensator anguishes over the narcissistic loss to his own projected dreams of glory; with a high-achieving child he may perversely envy the success he wishes were his.

But when Synthesizers experience these parent-child mismatches, they are able to redefine their notions of success in order to appreciate and guide a particular child and take her explorations as a cue for their own growth. Like Harvard education professor Howard Gardner, whose *Frames of Mind* explores the theory of multiple intelligence, they have stretched their definitions of intelligence and competence, learning to value many kinds of skills, from linguistic to logical, from spatial to musical and physical, from the art of understanding others to the wisdom of understanding oneself. Expanding their notions of skill and success, Synthesizer parents have learned to let each child's special light shine, widening their own world in the process.

In a high-achieving black family — the mother a professor, the father a doctor whose parents had such high expectations for him that they called him "Doc" as a child — the eighteen-year-old son is "not ambitious, which is the cause of some tension," admits the mother. But she calls the family "very close" and values her son as "one of the most well-adjusted people I know. He is flexible, sensitive, and fair." "My husband is very driven," she adds, "but our child is just happy to be." This mother is able to appreciate her son for an intelligence that shows itself in his special qualities of character, and realizes that his is a personality that would rather be than do. She also sees the generational differences in economic terms. "Money doesn't have to control his decision about a profession the way it did for my husband and me," she says.

Synthesizers seem able to nourish their children's self-esteem whether or not their children bring home the classic regalia — good grades, diplomas — of success. These parents may get a welcome chance to ease up on their own internal pressures and boost their own self-esteem. A mother in her mid-thirties, for example, com-

pares her parents' constant push for academic excellence with the
tolerance and appreciation she has discovered raising her learning-
disabled son:

> ▶ I was always the one in the family who brought good grades
> home on report cards and the one who heard "you can do
> better." *Now* even the smallest achievements are noticed and
> spoken of. Having a learning-disabled child, we know that
> even the simplest of things like tying a shoelace can be a major
> accomplishment.

Another Synthesizer mother, also from a family where good
grades and academic success were simply expected, has had to
"redefine her priorities" with a dyslexic son. Although the redefinition has not been simple, the challenge has deepened and sweetened family life. With this son and their three other children, the
parents are also teaching another invaluable lesson about success
and self-esteem. They are helping their children learn the graceful
art of failure:

> ▶ I hope our children can be more flexible than I was. I
> followed a straight plan after graduation from college. I refused
> to see the reality of a really bad first job. I hope my children
> can make better decisions. I'm still sorting out why those years
> were so unhappy for me. I realize now that we have to teach
> our kids to learn to live with failure. We want them to succeed,
> but they have to learn to fail to avoid the onslaught later.

Appreciating each child's unique unfolding, setting realistic expectations for different children at different ages and stages, being
open to wide-ranging definitions of intelligence and skill, letting
each child find self-worth and success on her own terms, and knowing that failure is often a necessary traveling companion to success — these are some of the building blocks of self-esteem revealed
by my interviews with Synthesizers. Virginia Satir's definition
elaborates on my own and sees self-esteem as the cornerstone of
healthy families:

Feelings of worth can flourish only in an atmosphere in which individual differences are appreciated, love is shown openly, mistakes are used for learning, communication is open, rules are flexible, responsibility (matching promise with delivery) is modeled and honesty is practiced — the kind of atmosphere found in a nurturing family. It is no accident that the children of families who practice the above usually feel good about themselves and consequently are loving, physically healthy, and competent.

Satir contrasts this healthy family, highly nurturant of self-esteem, with a troubled family where self-esteem is stymied:

> Conversely, children in troubled families often feel worthless, growing up as they must amid "crooked" communication, inflexible rules, criticism of their differentness, punishment for their mistakes, and no experience learning responsibility. Such children are highly at risk of developing destructive behavior toward themselves and/or others. Much of an individual's potential is held in abeyance when this happens.

Parents, Satir says, are "the initiators, teachers, and models for self-esteem." "However," she cautions, "we can't teach what we don't know." If we are critical and dissatisfied with ourselves, chances are we will be just as critical and dissatisfied with our children. If we feel empty and undernourished, we will not have anything left over to nourish our children and encourage their self-esteem to bloom. So part of our responsibility is to nourish ourselves, to fill up the holes left over from childhood, to meet our own needs, whether through journeys or activities of personal exploration, through the give-and-take of friendships or marriage, through guidance or therapy.

Here again the healing potential of parenthood helps catalyze change. As Virginia Satir observes, "When people arrive at parenthood without high self-esteem themselves, they have new opportunities to gain it as they guide their children. The fortunate part is that self-worth can be reshaped at any age."

Rafael Yglesias, the father of two young sons, is a writer in a family of writers, an early and questioning achiever in a family of achievers, a family where even the most ordinary children's acts are embraced as extraordinary. His father and mother, José and Helen Yglesias, are novelists based in New York City (the family name, pronounced Eeglayzeeas, is Spanish). His half-brother and half-sister from his mother's earlier marriage, Lewis and Tamar Cole, are writers as well. Rafael wrote his first novel, *Hide Fox, and All After*, at fifteen, published it at sixteen, and dropped out of school soon after to become a full-time writer.

Now, at thirty-five, he has published his fifth novel, *Only Children*, and much of its intensity and immediacy comes from a story that is close to home. About parents and children, it explores the questions Yglesias himself is exploring as a parent, the questions of success and failure, of what is ordinary and what is extraordinary, of loving children for who they are and for who we so desperately need them to be. The title itself is a double entendre. Each of the novel's two ambitious and well-heeled couples has only one child, a boy. But all of the parents are still, in a deep sense, only their parents' children, not yet fully grown-up adults.

"I felt that pregnancy, birth, and child rearing had been sentimentalized terribly in drama, that it had been written about by men who didn't know anything about the experience or were determined to make it seem like a Hallmark card." On a slushy winter afternoon, Yglesias sits and talks about his new book, and about being a father, in his Greenwich Village office, where his children's artwork takes its comfortable place on the shelves with his novels. Intense and thoughtful, Yglesias could be a persuasive spokesman for the "New Father." But like many nontraditional fathers, he, in fact, combines insights from the new with vestiges of the old. He has been a lot more involved with the daily care of his sons than his father was (particularly when his children were younger and his writer wife, Margaret, worked long hours at *Newsweek*). But he took over mostly at night, leaving the daytime care to a full-day baby-sitter. He is a lot less competitive than his own family was, but still he was relieved when his older son got a tricky question right on parents' visiting day at school.

About his focus in *Only Children*, he explains, "I always look for ways in fiction to discover ordinary experiences and write about them in a way that is very real to people who have lived them but hasn't been made real before. Sometimes I go through trouble as a writer, because people tend to like their experiences to be made nicer than they actually are. Here I thought that I had, because I felt that there was something glorious about being a parent, but that it was not what people make of it." He pauses as if searching through a file of images from his own past. "It was not the sentimental notion that you find a creature who loves you, but that you work through your own problems as a kid by the way you raise your own kids.

"I remember the first time I saw my older child being played with by my parents," he continues. "I realized that what they were doing with that kid was probably pretty much what they did with me." What he observed was "a mother who to my surprise is not as good at mothering as I thought she might have been. I tend to think of her as the fabulous mother who knows how to do everything, but she seemed to me a little bit panicky at times when she shouldn't have been. On the other hand, she also seemed very soothing in a way that my father is not."

What he saw in his father, and has seen reverberating to his sons' generation, was a familiar quickness to pounce on a new recruit for the family's literary dynasty. "My father from the very beginning was determined to convince himself that my son was a writer," he remembers with a wry smile. "He was determined to convince himself that my son was literary and understood stories and liked to pretend."

Still, Rafael catches himself being similarly quick to uncover artistic potential in his growing boys. Already he has earmarked his older son, Matthew, as the potential writer ("It is true that my older son very obviously loves plots; he loves stories. He's very good at remembering, he loves to read, and he's very careful about language when he expresses himself") and his younger son, Nicholas, as the potential director ("He has that personality.") But then again he adds that Nicholas, too, "loves plots and stories and expresses himself with colorful passion and honesty."

Though gently critical of his father, Rafael is psychologically-minded enough to admit that he shares his father's ambitious instincts for his sons — and honest enough to admit that he may not be able to change these instincts. "I spend a lot of time making fun of the fact that my father's way of expressing his affection for me is in terms of praising me for my achievements: 'You're so bright, you're so this . . .' Now I am very aware of that, and I am very aware that I shouldn't do that with my sons. And yet there is a tremendous urge to — it's like holding back the desire to have a cigarette or something! It's really hard not to praise them for their achievements, because in my mind that's a way of saying 'I love you.'

"I don't know if this is particularly typical of Jewish families — my mother is Jewish and my wife is and a vast majority of my friends are — but it seems particularly true at least in New York City," he explains, speculating on the wider context. "Maybe it's because they were immigrants and children of immigrants. But it's almost as though they don't feel they're entitled to love their kids unless their kids are brilliant. It's like, 'I have to have this brainchild, otherwise what's my justification for this effort?' In a way, I got easier on my Dad about it in my own mind when I realized that for a lot of people it was that cold. Because with my father it's almost something else. He wants to believe that everything I do is extraordinary whether it is or not, which in a funny way is better, because that's closer to blind love, closer to just acceptance."

What spooks Yglesias — and in part what he wrote his novel to work out — are the parents who seem to love their children only if they're brilliant, only if they're out in front, only if they're doing things first. These parents, he believes, seem to be saying, " 'I'll love you if you are better than the other kids in school. I'll love you if you go down the slide first. I'll love you if you learn to feed yourself first. I'll love you if you're out of diapers first.' Although it's not abusive in any way that anyone would recognize, it's really kind of emotional abuse. It's really, 'I don't love *you*, I love what you can achieve.' It's almost invariably someone who is raised that way who feels that about himself, that feels he's unlovable unless he's very successful."

Yglesias uses the two families in *Only Children* — Diane and Peter Hummel and their son, Byron, and Nina and Eric Gold and their son, Luke — to explore the dimensions of the conflict around success and love. The novelist shows each of the parents coming to terms with the shadows of the past and evolving a personal definition of success and self-worth and a special way to cherish and nurture their sons.

Peter Hummel is a foundation executive in charge of theater grants, whose "lack of interest in fatherhood [is] unfashionable." After the birth of his son, he is determined to keep up his frantic pace at work, his social life, and his extramarital sex life. But eventually and almost in spite of himself, he gets caught up in the heady and complex rush of parenting. Raising young Byron stirs up bitter memories of being abused as a child and gives him a second chance to resolve his anger and grief.

His wife, Diane, in spite of new motherhood, tries not to break her relentless stride toward partnership in a prestigious law firm. When at length, frayed to breaking, she lets go of her tenacious goal, she feels her "identity float up, away from impossible standards." Instead, she inflicts generations of impossible standards on Byron. In the classic Superparent tradition, she drags her two-year-old to an IQ test and to Suzuki violin lessons, until the intensity of his resistance forces her to begin to let him be his own person.

In the other couple, Nina Gold, the daughter of a wealthy New England family, has never felt valued or accepted until she produces an heir. Though luxuriating in early motherhood, she wants to "do something besides be a mommy" and finds a new direction by going to art school to become a designer.

Her husband, Eric, a stockbroker from the Bronx, strives hungrily to make a killing on Wall Street while feeling failure dog his every move. Eric is shamelessly devoted to his son. But in his wife's eyes, he loves Luke like a possession, "THE possession": "Eric loved only through ownership, so for him the emotion wasn't false, it was real love. Nevertheless, it required performance, that Luke, like some stock, gain in value and popularity."

From Peter's painful but healing confrontation with the abuses of his past to Diane's mellowing of ambition for herself and her son, from Nina's gaining of confidence as a mother and an artist to Eric's acknowledging his own failures but allowing his son to move beyond him, the novel shows a deep belief in the ameliorative power of parenting, its ability to rewrite old scripts and heal old wounds.

Near the end of the novel, in a poignant and symbolic scene, Eric takes Luke, just turned five, to the park to learn to ride a bicycle. Eric's father, Barry, a well-intentioned but unsuccessful businessman, comes along for the ride. In a subtle point and counterpoint that shows the shifting of gears between the generations, the father and grandfather offer their differing lessons to the boy as they run alongside the bicycle.

When the grandfather says, "Just pedal fast," the father counters, "Pedal as fast or as slow as you want." When Barry urges Eric to "let go of Luke," Eric promises his son, "I'll hold the bike until you ask me to let go." And when the grandfather's counsel is, "The better you become, the more likely you are to fall," Eric reassures Luke with his own wisdom: "The better you are, the faster you go, the more sure it is that you won't fall. And if you do fall — " Here, he breaks off, and his son picks up the thread with a confidence born of trust in his father and in himself, "I can just get back on and ride, right?"

And with that, Luke jumps on his bike and skims away, "riding on the world," his face shining with joy and pleasure in his competence, his achievement, his newly unfolding separate self, linked to the generations before but ready to move ahead. He flies past and beyond his grandfather and father, finding his own balance, his own momentum, feeling "alone and proud and very good."

— 9 —

Becoming an Extended Family: Grandparents, Parents, and Grandchildren

GENERATIONS OF SWAN

Sex, the invisible treasure
that sighs from a baby's fingers,
governs her gestures as wholly
as form commands the swoop
in the neck of a swan.

. . . .

Long anticipating her body,
the clans will have nudged her
to transform baby into child,
child into gap-toothed girl,
girl into woman, every ancestor implicit
in every gesture, each grief,
each amazement — just

as in middle life she may fail
to recall (surviving perhaps
as a haggard bent-kneed crone,
perhaps as a thickened matron)

whether the touch of her mother's hands
fondling her infant body
had whatsoever to do
with the colors she would wear
or the way she chose to walk.

How could this tottering baby
who lurches across our carpet
to bestow on her grandfather's lap
the ultimate gift of a spoon

anticipate the flush of desire
that young men two decades hence
will feel bulge in their throats
at the grace of her deep breasts,
that ancestrally curved neck,
and the legendary blue eyes?

Peter Davison

My four years of work on this book were first joyfully and then sadly bracketed by the birth of my second son, Will, at one end, and the death of my father-in-law, James Houghteling, at the other. I began with the high spirits and high expectations that accompany new life, both babe and book. But I come to the end now in a more tempered mood. The full spectrum of the life cycle has unfolded alongside me while I tried to keep this book on its course. Now it seems that the only fitting conclusion must begin with this death in our family, which we needed to grieve for and integrate just as surely as we needed to embrace our new son and draw him into the family fold.

For if our children's young and unfolding lives are mirrors to our own, reflecting both what we value in ourselves and what we would rather hide, so, too, are our parents' older lives mirrors to our own. In their worries and wrinkles, in their sweet successes and inner reckoning, our own aging is foreshadowed. And in their deaths, ours inch that much closer. Our children give their grandparents a sweet glimpse at immortality, and our parents give their grandchildren a soulful peek at mortality.

Our son Willy is William James, his middle name honoring both of his grandfathers. My father he calls Jimmy and runs madly to keep up with him and Nate on the softball field, on the tennis court, dodging the waves in the summer ocean, pedaling bikes and trikes around the block. A loving and devoted father to two girls, my father had been sitting on almost seventy years of athletic energy that my sister and I managed to bypass entirely. Now that he finally has a chance to unfurl this exuberance on his grandsons, it is hard to say who is the most enthusiastic when the games are played.

If my father joyfully staked out the great outdoors as his territory, my father-in-law's domain was most often indoors. A large and gentle man, humorous, scholarly, and contemplative, Jim was a law professor who was happiest in the world of books and ideas; he would excuse himself from the social whirl of a large family to the peace and quiet of his upstairs study. As a grandfather, he was playful and imaginative, perfectly capable of getting down on the floor on all fours or reading to a grandson perched on his shoulders. Willy saw to the heart of the man, his sweetness and playfulness, and gave him the nickname "Jim Babydoll."

Our last visit was at Christmas, and on New Year's Day he and my mother-in-law drove us to the airport and we hugged goodbye. The next day he had an aneurysm in his aorta that would prove fatal a month later.

During this last month, while doctors struggled to save his father's life, Bob flew back and forth across the country from San Francisco to Boston to sit at his father's bedside, take comfort in being with the rest of his family, and finally say good-bye for the last time. I stayed at home with the boys, absorbed in our family's grief, trying to comfort and explain the unexplainable to my sons. And while my husband and I and every member of the family struggled with a welter of emotions — rage and despair, loneliness and sadness — I watched my sons go through their own stages of loss.

At first, they could not and would not accept the gravity of their grandfather's condition. "Is he better today?" they would ask, and, "When is Jim Babydoll coming home from the hospital?" Denial was a comforting shawl over the news that was still too raw and painful to believe.

Anger at the unfairness of what was happening came next. When my husband called from the East Coast to say that his father's death seemed imminent, Nate wept and raged that his grandfather was going to die before another older and cherished relative who had been ill and hospitalized for a long time. "Is Jim going to die first?" he kept asking, as if the rules of the game had been abruptly and unfairly switched. That the younger elder should die first made no sense to him, and he wept over a game he could not control.

When the word came that their grandfather had died, both boys were somber but contained. But shortly afterward, they tried to undo the inevitable with their own magical thinking. Crawling into our bed one morning, Nate mused, as if shaking the last shreds of a dream, "Wouldn't it be good if when you got to be seventy" — Jim was almost seventy when he died — "then next you'd be sixty-nine and then sixty-eight and then sixty-seven?" Willy's voodoo was even more primitive. Sitting in the yard one day, the boys asked where their grandfather's body was, and we explained that his remains, after being cremated, were being buried in the ground. Without a second's hesitation, Willy began digging in the dirt, searching for his lost grandfather.

I remember how hard it was to accept the finality when the first of my grandfathers died. For a long time afterward I would see the familiar shock of white hair, the tortoiseshell glasses on an older man and believe it was my grandfather come to life again. For me, as for my sons, the memory of my delight in a grandfather's wise and kindly presence was forever after tempered by the memory of this early loss, by the stinging recognition of the sudden finality of death.

Most of the gifts their grandparents have given my sons have been a delight to receive — my mother's cuddles and family stories, my father's loving teases and endless hours of ball games, my mother-in-law's gentle kindness and lessons about the world, and my father-in-law's thoughtfulness and playful humor. But along with these most welcome gifts comes a gift that is far harder to accept. This is the knowledge, which comes when a grandparent dies, that these bonds are finite, and we must learn to treasure the moments we have.

The period when grown children become parents and older parents become grandparents can be a critical opportunity for rebalancing the family system. For most families, it is a time of many transitions, a time of numerous entries and exits and a chance to renegotiate boundaries and relationships.

In just over a decade, ten members have been added on my side of the family (spouses, in-laws, and grandchildren) and in about the same time, eighteen have been added on Bob's side! We have observed how all four of our parents have balanced home life and work life, making critical career shifts and coping with retirement by making it semiretirement. We have ached for family members confronting illness, and we have mourned several deaths.

How a family copes with each of these transitions will depend, in part, on how the family has coped with turning points in the past, how well they have redefined boundaries at each new stage of family life, and how they have dealt with the complexities of separation and interdependence, of loss and renewal.

Only since the middle of this century has the older generation lived long enough even to expect many grandchildren. The length of the "launching stage" — the time between the marriage of a family's last child and the death of one of its parents — has increased from less than two years in 1900 to about thirteen today. And the relationship between an adult daughter and her mother may be the longest lasting they will ever have. As the entire population ages, the adults in the middle have become a kind of "sandwich generation," caught between raising their own children and caring for aging parents. According to a 1988 United States House of Representatives report, the average American woman will spend seventeen years raising children and eighteen years helping aging parents. In some extended families, midlife women may find themselves shuffling between the "mommy track" and the "daughter track." "I remember leaving my twenty-fifth college reunion early, because I worried that my children might be in trouble," remarked one midlife mother whom I interviewed. "Ten years later, I left my thirty-fifth reunion early, because I was worried about my elderly parents." Borrowing the image of "invisible loyalties" from family theorists Ivan Boszormenyi-Nagy and Geraldine Spark, I see the challenge of this period for the adults in the middle to find the equilibrium between old loyalties to aging parents and new loyalties to growing children.

For Erik Erikson the eighth and final stage of the life cycle is a time of "ego integrity versus despair." For the older generation, this is a time for "the acceptance of one's one and only life cycle as something that had to be and that, by necessity, permitted of no substitutions: it thus means a new, a different love of one's parents." Most significantly for my inquiry here, Erikson highlights the link between the earliest stage of the life cycle, the stage of basic trust versus basic mistrust, and the last stage this way: "It seems possible to further paraphrase the relation of adult integrity and infantile trust by saying that healthy children will not fear life if their elders have integrity enough to not fear death."

Seeing grandparents meet the end of their lives without fear helps grown children and grandchildren greet the rest of their lives with greater trust as well. On the New Year's Eve before my father-in-law fell ill, he spoke to my mother-in-law about having a sense of completeness about his life. Not that he wanted to die, by any means, but that he could accept the possibility of death. This conversation turned out to be, in some sense, premonitory. It was also a deep consolation to the rest of the family to know that Jim had reached this equanimity before he died. The knowledge helped the rest of us carry on.

For grown children and their older parents, renegotiating the boundaries is the first and most far-reaching challenge of this stage. We still have no words to distinguish between the parent of a two-year-old and the parent of a forty-two-year-old, nor between the toddler and the middle-aged child ("adult children" is the term most frequently used, but even that conveys the contradiction inherent in our language). But even without the appropriate words, this period requires rebuilding relationships on the basis of mutual adulthood rather than on that of adult to child. For both generations, this redefinition can mean liberation to explore life's next set of opportunities. For the older parent this stage can be a time to look beyond the daily demands of parenting; for the adult child, it can be a time to survey the options, including parenting, that lie ahead.

Redefining the boundaries means acknowledging the ongoing interdependence of the generations as well as allowing increasing autonomy. "When you come to accept yourself, you will stop picking on your mother," said a thirty-five-year-old woman in Rosalind Barnett's Wellesley College Center for Research on Women study of adult mothers and daughters. "Conversely," adds Barnett, "when mothers come to accept their own lives, they will stop reacting so strongly to their daughters." When the adult child leaves home for the wider world, she begins to relinquish her dependence on her parents, both for economic support and, even more critically, for emotional validation. "The essence of being an adult," explains family therapist Donald Williamson, "is to have given up the need-to-be-parented. . . . Being able to embrace the [older] generation exactly as they are, and to value this, is the very essence of giving them up as parents." The goal for family well-being continues to be autonomy with mutuality, rather than either distant cutoff or clinging dependence.

Family therapy uses two approaches to help the older and younger generations renew their relationships and begin to accept each other "exactly as they are." Both were developed within the context of therapy but can be meaningfully adapted beyond it. Murray Bowen's family-of-origin work is one path. Here the adult child returns to his original family home and works to define an adult-to-adult relationship with each of his parents as individuals and allows each parent to get to know him. In sessions with a trained coach both before and after the visit home, the adult child is encouraged to take responsibility for his behavior by using a strong "I" position and to prepare for the family's possible attempts to pull him back into old patterns.

Adult children who return to their roots and successfully work through their earliest relationships often report encouraging changes in other corners of their lives — in relationships with spouse and children, employer and friends. One woman who sees the vulnerability beneath her aging father's bluster comes away better able to deal with an argumentative boss. A father embroiled in battles with his teenagers belatedly settles some old accounts with his parents and comes home less demanding and more willing to compromise with his children.

"Life review" is another helpful route back to the past that helps clarify understanding and shift the balance between the generations. Here older parents go beyond the process of reminiscence to examine what their lives have meant over time, their successes and failures, their significant relationships and personal watersheds. According to Myrna Lewis and Robert Butler, who use life review in group therapy with both older and younger clients, the process helps the "older person [reflect] on his life in order to resolve, reorganize, and reintegrate what is troubling or preoccupying him." Family albums, scrapbooks, written or taped autobiographies, clippings, genealogies, reunions, and pilgrimages can all be aids to this process. A man nearing seventy, Lewis and Butler report, journeyed back to his childhood town where he had been orphaned at the age of nine. After talking with townspeople who had known him as a child, he began to see how he had purposely adopted a "noble image," faithfully attending church and Sunday school and doing good deeds for people so they would like him. People told him that he never grieved openly or raged over the loss of his parents. Suddenly, he got a flash of insight into why he was such a "damn nice guy all the time." In the final years of his life, he gave himself permission to show his authentic feelings.

During this life review, the role of the younger generation is to be a friendly and accepting listening audience rather than to persuade their parents that things were different or better. The sense

of continuity and the transmission of family history are also meaningful benefits for the younger generation. Given this privileged
glimpse into the sweep of their parents' lives, they can begin to see
them as people.

In a revealing essay called "The Therapist's Own Family," family
therapist Jeannette Kramer describes her own emotionally charged
yet healing journey to change relationships in her family of origin.
Her story dramatizes the impact of both family-of-origin work and
life review.

Jeannette Kramer's parents were hardworking midwesterners:
her mother a housewife and a dominant presence in the family, her
father a university professor, a "man of few words" but with an
unexpected flash of humor. A series of traumatic events in Jeannette's childhood had gone unacknowledged and unmourned: the
death of her father's mother, her mother's difficult third pregnancy
as she neared forty and then the death of one of the just-born twins,
her mother's subsequent "nervous breakdown," and Jeannette's illness, most likely stress-related, at nine, which required five months
of bed rest. These events had forever altered the tone of family
life.

When Jeannette's mother returned from the hospital after her
postpartum collapse, her father warned the children "not to upset
her." Jeannette heard this as a clear directive: "Don't upset your
mother or she may die," and it shaped her adolescence and much
of her early adulthood. Her marriage to a more confrontational
partner whom her parents did not like kept her in an uncomfortable
triangle for almost twenty years. When her husband opted out of
the triangle by refusing to visit her parents when she went home,
she was left to confront them and rebuild her relationships with
them on her own. As she describes it:

> Thus began the slow and painful reintegration of myself — pulling
> together the adaptive child my family knew with the effective adult
> I could be away from them. My plan was to talk about the unspoken
> tensions with each of my parents, to establish firmer boundaries
> with my mother, and to move closer to my father and siblings on a
> one-to-one basis.

Kramer initiated a series of letters and visits, detailing subjects
long declared off limits — old family memories and habits, atti-

tudes about the church and about smoking and drinking. At first her father answered all the letters, even the ones she addressed to her mother. But over the course of several years, she began to reestablish her connections with each of her parents separately and to establish for the first time a climate of greater family honesty. Here she outlines the many things she learned in the course of her family-of-origin search:

1. To untangle one member from another. I had been angry at Mother, while Dad had been the "good guy." I learned that people who stay in relationships bear equal responsibility for the outcome.

2. To make the covert overt; to talk openly about matters no one talks about.

3. To make myself vulnerable while remaining in control of myself. This meant being able to tell Mother or Dad about problems without having to accept their solutions.

4. To stop being oppositional and live the same way with family members as I did in the rest of my life.

5. To use humor to get my point across, and to laugh at myself and at my own seriousness.

6. To respond immediately when an answer was called for. . . .

7. To make decisions carefully and then to stand firm, expecting reactions and therefore not being overly affected by them.

8. To enlarge the field when I reached an impasse by adding family members. My sister provided insights from a different perspective; I was beginning to plan interventions involving aunts, uncles, and cousins.

When her mother died suddenly of a cerebral hemorrhage, Jeannette mourned deeply but also felt deeply glad that she and her mother had made peace with each other. Following her mother's death, as other family relationships shifted to fill the void, Kramer intensified her commitment to understanding her father's "life as a man and my life in respect to his." She undertook to help him in a life review they had begun years earlier by working on genealogical charts of his extended family. Now she offered to help him reconnect with his own siblings, both in their eighties and relatively healthy, a project that would broaden the family support system for her father, and give father and daughter a mutual focus. "Reconnection with his siblings gave him continuity with his own generation and gave me an understanding of their life together,"

Kramer realized. Where her mother's death was sudden, her father's life ended with a slow and painful deterioration. Still, Kramer was able to accept his death with equanimity because she had finally forged an authentic relationship with him. "There is no ideal way to end a life," she concludes. "If one can see death in a transgenerational context, however, one can keep the emotional forces fluid, allowing growth to occur."

Rebalancing the relationships between older and younger generations and coming to terms with a parent's aging and death are both profoundly affected by the presence of a third generation. With our first son's birth, my husband and I first experienced our own rebirth as we stared adoringly at our newborn in his crib. Five and a half years later, when my husband's father died, we felt more keenly than ever how blessed we were to have the ongoing connection that our young sons provided. Many times during the grim January of my father-in-law's illness I saw how our children helped us cope with our grief. Their humor, their buoyancy, their unrelenting liveliness gave us another focus and took the sharpest edge off our pain. I shuddered to think how much more painful our mourning would have been without them, and I held them all the closer while letting their grandfather go.

The intensity and vulnerability surrounding the death of a grandparent only highlights the many meanings that grandchildren have for the family system. In a variety of connected ways, having grandchildren means a kind of second chance for the entire family. The new generation ensures that the grandparents' lives will in some sense endure beyond their deaths. A grandson carries on his grandfather's last name, the shape of his head, his grandmother's love of music, perhaps played on his grandfather's violin. A granddaughter carries on her grandmother's first name, her wavy red hair, her recipe for kugel, her grandfather's knack for puns.

Then, too, when grandparents die and the earliest parent-child chapter is closed, the new generation provides the parents with an open-ended sense of possibility. Grieving for what might have been in the relationship that has ended is softened by the knowledge that there is still time to improve, or just appreciate, the parent-child relationship that remains. As Stanley Cath and James Herzog also point out in an essay about the dying and death of a father, assuming the parent role *after* one's own parent dies can mean "grieving through the loss by becoming that which was lost."

For the grandparent generation, the presence of grandchildren can mean revitalization in their later years. "Whom does she have to live for?" a probing nurse asked the family sitting around the bedside of an older woman severely riddled with cancer. "Does she have any grandchildren?" The implication that the love of a grandchild can rouse a sick woman from her deathbed may be part wishful thinking. But anyone who has seen a world-weary older face melt into smiles over a baby will not entirely doubt the medicinal power of grandchildren. Basking in the uncritical love of young grandchildren brings back the rosy glow of long-forgotten early parenthood and can be a balm to many an oldster's wounds.

Grandparenthood can be a kind of ongoing life review, as grandchildren give grandparents an opportunity to relive and come to terms with their own experience of being parents. Were they too strict or critical, too intrusive or standoffish with their own children? Being a grandparent gives them a chance to get it right. "As you grow older, you realize that some things you thought you had to stress weren't that important," remarked a grandmother of ten, who joked that she had so many pictures of the grandchildren on her piano that she'd soon need a new piano. "Danger was something I used to obsess about. Now I realize that children can climb trees and even if they fall, they'll be okay."

"If I'd known grandchildren would be this much fun, I'd have had them first" boasted the red sweatshirt of an older man I passed on the street recently. Most grandparents I interviewed agreed that children are easier and more fun the second time around — and without the daily burdens and doubts that go with the territory the first time. "Becoming a grandparent is a second chance," observed Dr. Joyce Brothers for a magazine article I wrote on the unexpected joys of being a grandparent. "For you have a chance to put to use all the things you learned the first time around and may have made a mistake on. It's all love and no discipline. There is no thorn in this rose." Or as Dr. Spock remarked, "When you're a grandparent . . . you can take a parent's pride and pleasure in a child's good qualities, yet not feel responsible for his every act and trait." And having grandchildren means one last peek in the flattering mirror that children provided and one last chance to live out a vicarious fantasy that one's own lifetime did not offer.

If grandchildren give grandparents a welcome second chance, grandparents also offer a kind of second chance and a crucial backup to their grandchildren. Grandparents can embellish everything positive in the relationship between parents and children and sometimes be a buffer against the negative. Grandparents can be a vital source of emotional support. Often they can offer the sense of limitless time and attention when parents are too busy or preoccupied to notice a child's small thrills or heartaches.

More often than not, grandparents' love is unconditional, as liberally forthcoming as their cookies or birthday gifts. As psychoanalyst Therese Benedek points out, "The love of grandparents gives the child a sense of security in being loved without always deserving it. Thus the undemanding love of the grandparents preserves for the child a piece of the self-indulgent sense of omnipotence experienced unconsciously during infancy."

Adding grandchildren to a family can heal some old conflicts and bind the generations more closely together, as when a wayward daughter is embraced as the mother of young children or a previously rejected spouse is accepted into the fold as a new parent. Grandchildren can be a welcome new focus, becoming what family therapist Jack Bradt calls "hostages to reduce intergenerational tension." But in expanding the family system, grandchildren can also exacerbate tension, reactivating old conflicts and triangles and introducing troublesome new opportunities for friction. Not surprisingly, nagging unfinished business left over from childhood is often replayed by triangling in our children with our parents and ourselves. In many families, triangles carry over from generation to generation — the participants change but underlying tensions remain unresolved. A father of two young girls describes how the triangle of himself, his siblings, and his parents is repeated in the triangle of himself, his *daughters*, and his parents:

> ▶ What is most interesting to me is how my parents seem to be repeating some of the approval/disapproval patterns with

me and my siblings that occurred when we were children. I think my children and my parenting are being favored over those of my older brother and sister, just as I was favored as a child.

A mother of a young son confronts the troubling way that the triangle of herself, her parents, and her son mirrors that of herself, her parents, and her husband: "I had tried for fifteen years to get my parents to like my husband, and then I felt I was going to have to try to get them to like my son. I didn't want to have to do it."

Having suffered the hostility toward her husband in silence, she was determined to clear the air between her parents and her son. Eventually she sought professional help to understand and come to terms with "her parents' limitations," as she put it. She began to adjust her expectations and to appreciate what her parents were able to give. After a short "moratorium" during her therapy when she did not see her parents at all, she reestablished contact, and together they evolved an agreement to visit every six months. Now when her parents come from out of town, they stay with her instead of at a hotel, and she gets a chance to give them some nurturing attention as well.

In many cases, being able to recognize and acknowledge the hurtful continuation of old griefs can be a first step to interrupt the cycle. As always, strengthening the two-person bonds within the triangle and maintaining a separate self-focus and identity can be pivotal ways to break free of old constraints, build positive rapport, and nurture family harmony.

Grandparenthood brings with it the opportunity for triangling in other family members in numerous ways — which set of grandparents, or grandchildren, is the favorite, who gives the better presents, who gets the grandchildren for the holidays, and so on. Relationships within the triangle can contain the tension of the family system in a variety of ways. Sometimes new parents and their children draw tightly together, making a rigid boundary around their nuclear family and shutting grandparents out. Or grandparents and grandchildren may unite against a common enemy and shut the parents out.

The sometimes unlikely but nevertheless passionate alliance between the oldest generation and the youngest is succinctly captured by poet Fred Marchant in this verse from "A Baptismal Photograph." Studying the "grim Irish grandfather" holding his lace-swaddled baby grandson — the poet-to-be — Marchant observes:

> Certain of where he is going,
> and of what I need to get there,
> he will not smile.

> He would rather die than drop me.

Grandchildren can indeed be hostages for tensions between older parents and their children. And grandparents can be emotional safety valves to help discharge marital tensions between the parents. Beverly Shaver, a sixty-five-year-old grandmother and writer, tells poignantly of helping her two granddaughters, eleven and nine, through a time of marital crisis for their parents. When the call came from their daughter-in-law that their son, the girls' father, was threatening to leave the family "to fulfill his inner potential," the Shaver grandparents did not hesitate to take the girls for a couple of weeks. Watching the girls battle their sadness and guilt ("Maybe if we had been nicer, Dad would have wanted to stay with us at home"), both grandparents ached for them and hunted for ways to ease their pain.

One of the first evenings, Grandpa told the story of their Labrador, who took off one spring "because that was what male dogs sometimes did." He came back eventually and found out that the rest of the family had carried on fine without him. Admitting to the girls that dogs and daddies don't always come back, Grandpa reassured them that "the important thing is that life goes on and can be good for those who stay behind."

Together the grandparents helped their grandchildren face their disturbing rush of feelings (making a collage of "Things We Can Depend On" was one way). And then they set out to help the girls feel that they were in control of small parts of their lives and could learn new skills to build their competence. Cooking their own spaghetti sauce, planting bulbs, piping "Yankee Doodle Dandy" on a new harmonica, doing their own laundry, writing a story and reading it to an eighty-year-old friend in a nursing home — each new project boosted their self-esteem and their bond with each other. When they left their grandparents to fly home to an uncertain future, they held up joined hands. "In unity there is strength," their grandparents had emphasized, reinforcing their sisterly bond and helping them face what lay ahead.

Just as children provide both flattering and critical mirrors to their parents, so, too, do grandchildren hold up the same double-sided mirrors to grandparents. In a granddaughter's welcoming hugs or a grandson's verbal precocity may be reflected a grandparent's best traits or those best remembered of their children. These positive reflections amplify the grandparents' approval of their children as parents — and indirectly enhance their memories of themselves as parents as well. But in a granddaughter's cool rejection or a grandson's verbal cockiness grandparents may see things they would rather ignore. These unsettling observations may reflect badly on the children's parents and thus, indirectly, on the grandparents' shortcomings as parents. In this way grandchildren may offer up a painful as well as a positive life review.

Family therapist Betty Paul describes some of her pleasure as well as her ambivalence as she observed her grown son, his wife, and their young daughter set up a different kind of family from the Pauls' original family. She starts on an enthusiastic note but ends by facing a haunting disappointment. "My son and daughter-in-law do a fabulous job. They parent totally differently on the surface. My daughter-in-law had her daughter with a midwife and came home from the hospital right after. Now she wants her Ph.D. She and my son have an agreement that he will share child care: their daughter will have twenty hours with her mother, twenty with her father, and twenty with a sitter. I didn't start my career until ten years after she'll be starting hers. But I centered my life around my children and was disappointed when they didn't center theirs around me."

So grandparents may see unflattering as well as flattering reflections, ambivalence about the past as well as acceptance of it in the mirror of their grandchildren's lives. And grown children may look at their parents as grandparents and be either pleased or disappointed with what they see. In their parents' comfortable or awkward relationships with their children, they may see images from the past that they cherish — or would rather turn away from.

At the outset of this book, I reflected on the way many of us grapple with an internal image of a perfect parent — the one we wish we had and the one we struggle to be, creative and energetic, patient and calmly centered, ceaselessly loving and empathetic. Now, in conclusion, I look also at the internal image of a perfect grandparent that many of us still cling to — perhaps the one we had, the one we wish we had, or the one we want our parents to be: devoted but not intrusive, supportive and available but never domineering or contradictory. But just as we rarely live up to our own internal standards of perfection, neither do our parents fulfill our fantasies of perfect devotion. One of the special challenges of becoming an extended family is figuring out a comfortable balance among grandparents, parents, and grandchildren, between too little grandparenting and too much, between intergenerational over-dependence and estrangement.

Surely the media image of the apron-clad, cookie-baking grandma and the overalls-clad, fish-hook-baiting grandpa die hard. With today's longer, healthier lifespan, geographic mobility, and economic pressures, our children's grandparents may still be working or absorbed in their own interests and may live at great distances from where we end up. The increasing number of teenage mothers means that many grandparents are still in the prime of their working lives; at the other end of the spectrum, the increasing number of older mothers means that some grandparents are too elderly or infirm to chase after toddling grandchildren. And the grandparents in between — old enough to be liberated from nine-to-five pressures but young enough to pick up a squirmy grandchild — may be too excited by the possibilities of their own lives to make much room for grandchildren.

"The reluctant grandmother" is a more common phenomenon than the stereotype of the grandma gushing over her grandchildren's pictures may have us believe. *Alice Lydoff* is one such grandmother, who spoke freely about her ambivalence and reluctance about her newest role while insisting that most people "wouldn't be this honest about grandparenting — even though most of my friends feel this way." Trim and vital at sixty, Alice is married to an obstetrician and is the mother of five grown children (three of them doctors and one married to a doc). She has seven grandchildren. She is also a public health nurse and administrator who got her degree in her early forties when her oldest son graduated from Harvard. "My life is so much more interesting now compared to what it was when I was a mother," she observes and then sighs. "People just get tired of parenting after a while."

Although she describes herself as once "dying to have grand-children," she admits ruefully that she was disappointed, even bored when they came along. For her, the introduction of grand-children derailed her relationships with her adult children. "I was beginning to have an equal relationship with my children, which I really was enjoying. But when they had children, the conversation went from interesting subjects to diapers and nursing. I was very bored. Initially I was not as ecstatic as I should have been — if there are shoulds, and I try to keep shoulds out of my life, but they still creep in.

"As my kids get older and have two kids of their own, things have become more interesting. Still, they understand I can't do much baby-sitting. I have a bad back, so I can't pick my grandkids up. Some of my children resent this more than others. And when all my children come over with all their children, it's so noisy, it's bedlam. If there's a major upset or tantrum, I go off into a different room."

The reluctant grandparents pride themselves on remaining faith-ful to their feelings. But their grown children and the grandchildren have a different story to tell. A friend reported sadly and angrily about a long summer visit to her parents' home with her husband and three small daughters in tow. Usually a nanny helped lighten the load, but that summer the nanny was off. My friend felt sure that her parents, still active but no longer working, would occa-sionally provide an extra pair of hands or a night off for her husband and herself. But the grandparents were stunning in their ability to ignore the signals that help was needed. My friend described her father, deep in his newspaper, with his baby granddaughter in her bouncy seat on the floor beside him. After a considerable time, the baby started to fuss, then bawl loudly to be picked up. Grandfather languidly raised his head from his newspaper and announced

"Crying baby" to alert the parents to run to the rescue from the other side of the house. With such grandparental reluctance, the younger generation is not too quick to make return visits.

Nevertheless, despite such occasions when the generations are severely out of sync, it is still my premise that grandchildren provide a second chance, an intergenerational bridge, and a healing rapprochement between the generations. What the presence of grandparents and grandchildren means in a particular family has much to do with that family's style and their approach to repetition and change across the generations.

For the Traditionalist parent, becoming an extended family provides the deep blessing of transgenerational continuity, a chance to carry on the beloved family traditions of the past. Seeing her older parents as grandparents revives the warm memories from her own childhood and renews that early bond, as this mother describes:

> ▶ My parents are very close to my children. My mother is there for love; my father for play. It was pretty much the same with my brother and me. Mom was always there for love, reading, games, etc., while Dad was more for jumping on and knocking over.

Almost in spite of this mellow harmony, the Traditionalist may need to struggle to delineate a new family style, honoring the connections with the past but not subsumed by them. As long as the grandparents' involvement does not become intrusive or inhibiting to this new style, all three generations benefit from the interdependence and continuity.

For the Rebel parent, seeing his parents as grandparents can be yet another source of irritation or an opportunity for rapprochement. In Rebel families there is often a disconcerting resemblance between the oldest generation and the youngest. But sometimes a trait that was unnerving in a mother can be endearing in a daughter, a habit that was insufferable in a father can be tolerable in a son. So the Rebels' children can provide a bridge between parents and grandparents, a new opportunity for acceptance and compassion.

Then, too, seeing their older parents through their children's eyes gives Rebels another chance to look at the childhood scenes they have spent so much of adulthood running from. And that second look sometimes dissipates some of the power of the past. Here a mother at midlife whose two children are teenagers looks back at her own past and revises the script in light of her new observations:

> ▶ My parents are similar as grandparents to the way they were as parents. They have VERY high expectations of a child's behavior. But now it's a relief to see that what I took to be my incompetence as a child was in fact a reflection of excessively high adult expectations. Fortunately, my kids can see their grandfather and say, he's a perfectionist, whereas I just felt badly about myself and developed an ongoing concern that my best was never enough.

For Compensator parents, seeing their older parents with grandchildren may exacerbate the old sense of loss but also help repair it. For just as Compensators may lavish on their children what they missed in their childhoods, so, too, may their parents finally find themselves able to give to their grandchildren what they were not able to give their children. Sometimes behind the most gift-laden grandparents hide the ghosts of parents who were too busy, too distracted, or too inexperienced to give much the first time around. Such attention or largesse visited on grandchildren when it was not available years before may not be a completely welcome gift. Here the mother of a toddler describes her jealousy when her parents delight in her child:

> ▶ My parents are very indulgent since this is their first grandchild. Sometimes I think they go overboard. Sometimes I think that when I'm talking to my mom, and she's holding my son, she doesn't even hear me. What I say goes in one ear and out the other, because she is paying so much attention to her grandson.

But for other Compensator parents, the attention is welcome even one generation removed. Seeing and appreciating what their parents are now able to offer their children heals old childhood griefs and strengthens their present bond.

For the Synthesizer parent, becoming an extended family provides a welcome opportunity to integrate the best memories from the past with the new resources of the present. Synthesizer parents feel secure enough to accept help from grandparents without feeling overwhelmed by it. But they can also accept hesitation or reluctance without feeling neglected by the grandparents.

The central issue for the Synthesizer is building a relationship with older parents of mutual interdependence rather than childish dependence. Here the father of two young girls acknowledges and applauds how his having children helped change a structure in which his parents tried to control him to a more egalitarian one in which his parents could share the pleasures of the new generation:

> ▶ My relationship with my parents has been enlivened by my children. I had become a little bored with my parents' focusing on my plans, achievements, and opportunities. It's more enjoyable for me now, seeing my parents enjoy my kids and vice versa, focusing on simpler joys and away from me as their child. It feels less like a parent/child relationship and more like big brother/big sister: comparing experiences, more accepting of differences, no power struggles — fewer agendas with each other.

For most parents — whether Traditionalist or Rebel, Compensator or Synthesizer — a moment comes amid the joys and heartaches of parenting that is a kind of healing epiphany between the generations. It might come at a moment of inner peace when a loving ritual from the past is performed again. Or it might come at a moment of intense exasperation when he hears his parent's words pouring in a torrent from his own mouth. It might come after the soul-searching of therapy, as it does for Peter Hummel in Rafael Yglesias's *Only Children:* "I realize Mom is just a person. She is not a monster. She's just an ordinary person, who made ordinary mistakes. She thought of herself first. Everyone thinks of themselves first."

Or the healing epiphany might come in the ordinary course of daily events, with the unexpected dazzle of a toddler's sticky kisses, an older child's shy hugs. Here a mother in her late thirties with children about to leave home finally understands what her parents went through and forgives them their imperfections: "I finally forgive my parents for all the things they did 'wrong.' I now know what it's like and how even a saint can lose patience, leave you with a sitter, not co-sign a loan so you can buy an MGB, etc. We are very close and I count them among my best friends." The moment of insight, of forgiveness, of reconciliation is the moment we realize that our parents did the best they could and that is all we can now ask of ourselves.

"Do Newborn Babies Shape Their Parents?" asks a poster advertising a talk by T. Berry Brazelton several years ago. Now the poster hangs in the basement office of his yellow frame house, a national historic landmark, in Cambridge, Massachusetts. Like his hero, Benjamin Spock, for our parents' generation, Brazelton, at seventy, is a household name among today's generation of parents. Nobody has been more influential or informative in linking medical and psychological insights, in appraising the infant's and then the child's impact on his parents — as well as parents' impact on infant and child — and in explaining how each member's feelings and needs affect the well-being of the whole family. His thinking both reflects and has deeply influenced the changes in perspective from our parents' generation to our own, while at the same time providing a bridge in both directions.

Brazelton estimates that over the years he has taken care of some 25,000 children; three of Dr. Spock's grandchildren were among them (and my husband's two older brothers as well). Countless public appearances and many medically sensible and psychologically sensitive books (including *Infants and Mothers*, *On Becoming a Family*, and *Working and Caring*), and his cable TV series "What Every Baby Knows" have forged him an international reputation.

Despite his prominence, in appearance and manner he seems more like a country doctor than an international pediatric authority. His style is gentle, touched by humor and whimsy. The story goes that when he was waiting recently in a crowded airport for a plane, standing next to a sprightly four-year-old girl, she suddenly turned a somersault. Without further ado, the pediatrician got down on his hands and knees and turned a somersault, too.

On the day we meet, one of the hottest August afternoons that year, he is wearing a rumpled madras shirt and a beige summer suit. A small fan of questionable vintage hums while we talk in his pediatric office, where he still sees patients about one week each month. The spacious waiting room seems untouched since the fifties, with its molded plastic chairs and Danish modern sofa, its fish tank and old rocking horses, its dollhouse, blocks, and puzzles. There must be a familiar feeling of comfort — and déjà vu — for Brazelton's former patients who now bring *their* children to see him.

Brazelton's personal story makes vivid the healing ties that are possible between grandparents, their grown children, and grandchildren. In the house upstairs, the youngest of his four children (three daughters and a son) plays with her three-year-old son, Brazeltons' only grandchild so far. His daughter's family is camping out with him and his wife, Christina, while their own house is being painted. When Brazelton's grandson comes into his waiting room and sees the young patients playing with the toys, he eyes them suspiciously. "What are you doing playing with *my* toys?" his grandfather imagines the boy saying.

Brazelton credits his youngest daughter with changing his long-held position about working mothers. Like Dr. Spock, Brazelton has revised his out-of-date conviction that every child needs the full-time care of an at-home mother to prosper. "The reason I wrote *Working and Caring* was because my own daughter, as well as the mothers of many of my patients, would say, 'I don't have a choice about going back to work and you're not helping me.' I realized that I had a bias of my own, that I wasn't responsive to what they needed." The new position he evolved landed him on the cover of *Newsweek*, heralding an article that advocated juggling work and family life by, among many things, "enjoy[ing] the pleasures of solving problems together" and "establish[ing] a pattern of working as a team."

Brazelton also credits his young grandson with inspiring a long-overdue rapprochement between himself and his youngest daughter, and he will be forever grateful for it. Her baby was born twelve weeks early, then stayed in the hospital for months. Grandfather was more than willing to be there for his daughter and her son. "With a sick preemie, she needed me a lot. After a stormy adolescence, her relationship with me changed dramatically. Now we've come back together in mutual need."

Watching with pride as his own family knits together, Brazelton portrays the interdependence among the generations this way: "I see my daughter hungry to see my wife and me nurturing her baby as a way of recapitulating her past as well as to see our affection for her son. My daughter also nurtures me when I'm stressed out the way I nurtured her. So I've seen her development as very gratifying."

For his own family, as well as for the larger picture, Brazelton believes very strongly that all three generations deeply need each other to learn and thrive. "I have a strong bias that your own experience is all you have to start with as a parent," he explains. "Later experiences don't dominate nearly as much. All parents fall back on their own parenting. Therefore, I wish that most parents today had more experience seeing the older generation with their grandchildren. I keep hearing young parents saying that they don't want their parents around when there's a new baby. But I disagree. I think it's an asset to have someone to bounce off against."

He reflects and continues. "Sometimes a young parent will say to me, 'My mother doesn't approve of what you said or what you wrote in one of your books.' To that I'll say, 'Then do what your mother feels is right, because that's the connection you'll always have.' " He shakes his head. "The generation gap is hard. We may have fostered it when it was not in our best interest."

Indeed, his conversation becomes most passionate when he argues for repairing the generation gap, "seeing two sides of the coin," and recognizing the mutual needs between the generations. "Every parent tries his or her best to introduce things missed as a child. They're not always successful, but the effort to do it is positive. And learning to parent is learning from mistakes, not successes. Still, it's a mistake to try to change the past too abruptly or intellectually. Parenting is not intellectual. And the repetitions from generation to generation carry strength and experiential value."

Comparing this generation of parents with the last, Brazelton sees, as I do, greater complexities and demands but also greater awareness and energy for change. "The pressures are greater today, but so is the knowledge, so young parents can balance the two for themselves. They can relive their own parenting, but also add to it. Parents today feel more empowerment because they are so aware of the struggles," he says. In his *Newsweek* article, he emphasized: "For all their doubts and fears, there is a new force in the air that I feel in my contact with young families. The parents of this generation are asking hard questions, demanding answers, and they are ready to fight for what they need for their children and for themselves."

When I began this book, I had an innocent preschooler and a cooing infant in a crib. Now the preschooler is in first grade, sporting a fanny pack and calling himself a "totally gnarly rad dude"; the infant is in preschool, carrying a lunchbox and looking rather cool himself. Last week I bought my older son his first soccer uniform and took down my baby's crib and put up his "big boy bed." Tomorrow there will be Little League and orthodontia, then all too quickly Bar Mitzvahs, graduations, weddings, and grandchildren.

I dream already of my first grandchild, a granddaughter, of course, if there is any intergenerational justice at all. She will be a mirror of my own face and my husband's, of my sons and the daughters-in-law I do not yet know (my husband's slim nose and my red hair, my sons' athletic prowess and love of words). Deeper than that, she will reflect and refine our inner lives, mirroring our strengths and giving us courage to face our insecurities. She will be a continuous affirmation of the love between the generations.

Liberated from the daily demands of parenthood, my husband and I will have unlimited time and untapped depths of attention to lavish on her. As soon as she is ready to leave her mother's and father's side, we will have her for a weekend. She will sleep in her father's old childhood bed, underneath his quilt decorated with the letters of the alphabet, its vibrant primary colors faded like his old baseball posters with the years.

In that quiet, receptive time between night and morning, she'll crawl into our bed just as her father used to do, and I'll teach her my mother's game. Her tiny back will be my slate; her arms will be ready for my messages. T, I'll tickle out between the freckles, then J and L. L for "language" and "love" and "lasting." With any luck she will pick the game up quickly, for she will already have played it with my son, her father, in the pearly morning or dusky evening at home. But still I will painstakingly write out the letters, my letters, my mother's letters, the letters I taught my sons. Just as I had to write and now must end this book, I will ensure that my own story is passed along.

— *Appendix* —

Questionnaire on Family Relationships across the Generations

1 What about parenting do you enjoy the most and the least? What do you think your own parents enjoyed most and least about parenting?

2 Which of your children's stages have been easier or more difficult for you (and have there been different ones with different kids)? Which stages do you think were easier or more difficult for your parents raising you?

3 In what ways do your children remind you of yourself, their other parent, or other members of your family of origin or your partner's family of origin? How does this influence your relationship with your kids?

4 What were two or three sensitive issues in your family of origin (for example, social or psychological problems, poor health, substance abuse)? Are these still problems in your family or have they been resolved?

5 What are three outstanding similarities and differences between your family of origin and your partner's family of origin?

6 Describe one or two parenting issues on which you and your partner disagree that grow out of these differences.

7 How has your relationship with and attitudes toward your own parents changed since becoming a parent?

8 Describe your parents' relationship with your children: how are your parents similar or different as grandparents than they were as parents?

9 How were birthdays or holidays celebrated in your family of origin, your partner's family of origin, and your present family?

10 If your parents separated or divorced or if one of them died when you were growing up, how did that experience affect you and the rest of your family?

11 If you and your children's other parent separated or divorced or if your partner died, what was the major impact of that on you and the rest of your family?

12 If you are co-parenting with someone other than your children's original other parent, describe how the parenting style of your present partner differs from that of your children's original other parent.

13 What in the way you were raised do you most want to repeat and most want to avoid?

14 What are the three most important things you have learned from becoming a parent?

WORKING

15 Describe your work history since becoming a parent: are you working now? If so, when did you go back to work (or when do you plan to return) after having children, and how many hours are you working?

16 Did your mother work while you were growing up, and if so, how did you feel about her working?

17 Compare your feelings and attitudes with your mother's about combining work and motherhood.

18 Compare the way your partner combines working and parenthood with the way his/her parents combined them.

INTIMACY AND SEPARATION

19 How was affection or intimacy expressed in your family of origin? how was it expressed in your partner's family of origin? and how is it expressed now? Give specific examples, if possible.

20 What were the major turning points in your separation from your own parents and what have been the major turning points in your children's separation from you? (For example, weaning, toilet-training, going to school or camp, moving away from home, getting married.)

ANGER AND AUTHORITY

21 How were anger, discipline, limit-setting handled in your family of origin? how were they handled in your partner's family? and how do you handle them now?

22 What things that you did or things about yourself provoked your parents and which of your kids' behavior or characteristics provokes

you? Do you and your partner have different thresholds or tolerate different behaviors?

23 Were you abused (physically, sexually, or emotionally) as a child? If so and if you wish, please elaborate.

24 Have you felt out of control or sought counseling for abuse toward your own children?

SEX

25 How do your sexual attitudes and orientation compare with or differ from your parents'?

26 How was sex education handled in your family of origin and how are you handling it in your present family?

27 If and when your children started dating, how has that affected your relationship with them?

TRUTH AND SECRETS

28 Briefly describe the communication style of your family of origin, your partner's family of origin, and your family now: for example, open, reserved, unpredictable, denying, secretive, and so on.

29 Were you aware of any important family secrets as a child? was your partner aware of any in his/her family of origin? and are you aware of any in your present family? (For example, a parent's affair, drinking problem, mental illness.)

SUCCESS AND SELF-ESTEEM

30 Which of your children's qualities or accomplishments do you value the most (for example: sense of humor, intensity, easy-goingness, athletic ability, academic success, creativity, popularity, kindness)? Are the qualities you value in your children the same or different from the ones your parents valued in you?

31 Did your parents encourage you to feel good about yourself, and if so, how? How do you encourage your children to feel good about themselves?

MONEY

32 Compare your present family financial situation with the financial situation of the family you grew up in.

33 How are your attitudes toward money similar to or different from your parents' attitudes? similar to or different from your partner's attitudes?

34 Is there anything else you would like to add about your children, your parents, yourself?

— *Notes* —

INTRODUCTION

PAGE

xv "the dependence of the older": Erik Erikson, *Childhood and Society*, pp. 226–67.

xv "it is as true": Erikson, *Identity, Youth and Crisis*, p. 96.

xix I "began to think": Margaret Atwood, *Cat's Eye*, p. 3.

I. GHOSTS IN THE NURSERY

4 "Our judge you may become": A. Wildgans, "Im Anschauen meines Kinder," in *Dichtungen* (1913), as quoted by Therese Benedek, "The Family as a Psychologic Field," in *Parenthood: Its Psychology and Psychopathology*, ed. E. James Anthony and Therese Benedek, p. 130.

5 The mirroring function of the mother's face is discussed by D. W. Winnicott in *Playing and Reality*, p. 112.

7 "I am silver and exact": Sylvia Plath, "Mirror," *Collected Poems of Sylvia Plath*, ed. Ted Hughes, pp. 173–74.

7 "The imitating child holds up a mirror" and "It can also happen": Benedek, "Family as a Psychologic Field," p. 127.

10 "In every nursery there are ghosts": Selma Fraiberg, "Ghosts in the Nursery," in *Clinical Studies in Infant Mental Health*, p. 164.

18 "How much does an environment": T. Berry Brazelton, *Toddlers and Parents*, p. x.

19 But the most striking of Chess and Thomas's theories: Stella Chess and Alexander Thomas, *Temperament in Clinical Practice*, p. 12ff.

23 "For some, confrontation": Margaret Mahler, Fred Pine, and Anni Bergman, "The Mother's Reaction to Her Toddler's Drive for Individuation," in Anthony and Benedek, *Parenthood*, pp. 262–63.

24 "I feel that a parent's": Bruno Bettelheim, *A Good Enough Parent*, p. 14.

25 "Whether or not parent and child": ibid., p. 44.

25 "The idea of empathy": Sara Ruddick, *Maternal Thinking*, p. 121.

2. BECOMING A FAMILY

31 "analogous to the discovery of the telescope": Lynn Hoffman, *Foundations of Family Therapy*, p. 3.

32 Genograms "let the calendar speak": Monica McGoldrick and Randy Gerson, *Genograms in Family Assessment*, p. 3.

33 "The genogram helps both the clinician": ibid., pp. 2–3, 76.

34 "If a person can look": Michael Kerr and Murray Bowen, *Family Evaluation*, p. 255.

41 we tend to assume the same "emotional position": Peggy Papp, Olga Silverstein, and Elizabeth Carter, "Family Sculpting in Preventive Work with 'Well Families,' " *Family Process* 12 (1973), 201.

43 "Once the emotional circuitry": Kerr and Bowen, *Family Evaluation*, p. 135.

44 "The psychodynamic family therapist": I am indebted to my sister, Anne Fishel, for these insights into family therapy as well as many others.

45 a mom who "listens so well": Marianne Walters et al., eds., *The Invisible Web*, p. 58.

47 Bowen tells the story of a family: Kerr and Bowen, *Family Evaluation*, pp. 203–6.

48 Bowen warns the father that his wife: ibid., pp. 206–7.

49 mothers "were either 'overinvolved' ": Judy Myers Avis and Cathryn Haig as quoted in Mary Sykes Wylie, "The Mother Knot," *Family Therapy Networker*, September/October 1989, p. 44.

49 But they do so "not just in any possible way": Deborah Luepnitz, *The Family Interpreted*, p. 193.

49 "Therapy can validate *his* capacity": Marianne Walters, as quoted in Wylie, "Mother Knot," p. 48.

50 As clinicians "cast their net": Wylie, "Mother Knot," p. 48.

3. FAMILY SNAPSHOTS

52 the technique of "family sculpting": Peggy Papp, Olga Silverstein, and Elizabeth Carter, "Family Sculpting in Preventive Work with 'Well Families,' " *Family Process* 12 (1973), 201, 202.

59 a new "emotional literacy": Deborah Luepnitz, *The Family Interpreted*, p. 262.

67 "[Survival skills] were necessary": Eliana Gil, *Outgrowing the Pain*, pp. 71–72.

73 Linda's appreciation of her house: Linda Weltner, *No Place Like Home*, p. xiii.

76 "The healthy family maintains a separation": Carl Whitaker with D. Keith, "Symbolic-Experiential Family Therapy," in *Handbook of Family Therapy*, ed. Alan Gurman and David Kniskern, p. 190, as quoted in Luepnitz, *Family Interpreted*, p. 92.

76 Healthy families make it "safe and acceptable": Jerry Lewis et al., *No Single Thread*, pp. 214–15.

77 Linda admits that she often "wept at these meetings": Weltner, *No Place Like Home*, p. 89.

4. CYCLES OF PAIN, STRATEGIES FOR CHANGE

80, 81 "Probably everybody has" and "Understandably, [the parent]": Alice Miller, *The Drama of the Gifted Child*, pp. 25–27.

84 Particularly when there is a history of abuse: Eliana Gil, *Outgrowing the Pain*, p. 60.

84 Identification with the aggressor is discussed by Selma Fraiberg in "Ghosts in the Nursery," in *Clinical Studies in Infant Mental Health*, pp. 194–95.

85 An unusual longitudinal study: George L. Engel et al., "Monica: Infant-Feeding Behavior of a Mother Gastric Fistula-Fed as an Infant: a 30-Year Longitudinal Study of Enduring Effects," in *Parental Influences: In Health and Disease*, ed. E. James Anthony and George Pollock, pp. 29–89.

86 "We can report that memory": Fraiberg, "Ghosts in the Nursery," p. 195.

87 "These are the parents who say explicitly": ibid.

5. FOUR PARENTING STYLES OF REPETITION AND CHANGE

105 some women assumed a "negative identity": Sampson, Messinger, and Towne, as quoted in Bertram Cohler and Henry Grunebaum, *Mothers, Grandmothers, and Daughters*, p. 29.

106 "An overfunctioning parent is often simply repeating": Norman Ackerman, "The Family with Adolescents," in *The Family Life Cycle*, ed. Elizabeth Carter and Monica McGoldrick, p. 150.

118 "[Parents] may minimize or deny their own feelings": Ivan Boszormenyi-Nagy and Geraldine Spark, *Invisible Loyalties*, p. 220.

120 holidays' "symbolic meanings are built permanently": Bruno Bettelheim, *A Good Enough Parent*, pp. 347, 349, 352.

122 Virginia Satir gives a vivid example: Virginia Satir, *The New Peoplemaking*, pp. 220–21.

124 Jack Kornfield, "Parenting as Practice," adapted from a chapter in Barry Vissel and Joyce Vissel, *Models of Love*, p. 162.

6. SEPARATION AND CLOSENESS

139 "I know he has to undergo this phase": Roberta Israeloff, *In Confidence*, p. 106.

141 "In each of the four families": Bertram Cohler and Henry Grunebaum, *Mothers, Grandmothers, and Daughters*, pp. 235–36.

141 "Parents function in ways that result": Michael Kerr and Murray Bowen, *Family Evaluation*, pp. 95–96.

141 "Did my parents resent the fact": Israeloff, *In Confidence*, p. 60.

147 "So much of what goes wrong": Bruno Bettelheim, *A Good Enough Parent*, p. 92.

148 "A complex bond was established": Cohler and Grunebaum, *Mothers, Grandmothers, and Daughters*, pp. 234–35.

152 "Psychological birth is fundamentally different": Louise Kaplan, *Oneness and Separateness: From Infant to Individual*, p. 228.

153 separation involves "the infant's emotional attachment": Louise Kaplan, *Adolescence*, p. 91.

153 interplay between "clinging and pushing away": Kaplan, *Oneness and Separateness*, p. 191.

153 "Ambivalence is at the root": T. Berry Brazelton, *Toddlers and Parents*, pp. 13–14.

154 "For example, [a mother] may suffer": Margaret Mahler, Fred Pine, and Anni Bergman, "The Mother's Reaction to Her Toddler's Drive for Individuation," in *Parenthood: Its Psychology and Psychopathology*, ed. E. James Anthony and Therese Benedek, p. 263.

156 "She believed that she must never tie": ibid., p. 266.

156 "It's a good thing to give a baby": Mary Ainsworth, as quoted in Robert Karen, "Becoming Attached," *Atlantic Monthly*, February 1990, p. 38.

158 a back door left ajar by a mother: Brazelton, *Toddlers and Parents*, p. 200.

162 it is a time of "active deconstruction": Kaplan, *Adolescence*, p. 14.

162 a search "not for separation": Terri Apter, *Altered Loves*, p. 60.

163 "We cannot but recognize," "Both periods have in common," and adolescents' "capacity to move": Peter Blos, "The Second Individuation Process of Adolescence," in *The Psychoanalytic Study of the Child*, vol. 22, 1967, pp. 173, 163, 178–79.

164 the adolescent's rebellion proceeds: Apter, *Altered Loves*, p. 51.

164 "stimulation, belongingness, loyalty": Blos, "Second Individuation Process," p. 177.

164 "Sexual maturity . . . demands some final": Kaplan, *Adolescence*, p. 164.

166 "[Parents] recall the day" ibid., p. 147.

166 "Primarily a participant-observer": Calvin Colarusso and Robert Nemiroff, "The Father in Midlife: Crisis and the Growth of Paternal Identity," in *Father and Child: Developmental and Clinical Perspectives*, ed. Stanley Cath, Alan Gurwitt, and John Munder Ross, p. 324.

168 "Could he really be so bad": ibid., p. 322.

168 suddenly "torn open with grief" and "the bittersweet paradox": Molly Layton, "The Mother Journey," *Family Therapy Networker*, September/October 1989, pp. 25–26.

169 "one of the field's most gifted therapists": Deborah Luepnitz, *The Family Interpreted*, p. xiii.

170 "fundamental attitude of protectiveness": Sara Ruddick, *Maternal Thinking*, p. 79.

173 "accommodating, observing mother of infants": Layton, "Mother Journey," p. 32.

173 "It's a hard period": ibid., p. 34.

7 . ANGER AND LIMIT SETTING

178 "rage — so easily expressed": Roberta Israeloff, "Mad Doesn't Mean Bad," *Working Mother*, February 1990, p. 57.

178 "Parents tend to punish their children": Benjamin Spock, "Have You Ever Wanted to Strike Your Child?" *Redbook*, April 1988, p. 38.

178, 179 "If we could only remember" and "It is much more difficult": Bruno Bettelheim, *A Good Enough Parent*, pp. 102, 24, 153.

179 "Under certain circumstances a child": Alice Miller, *The Drama of the Gifted Child*, p. 46.

182 "It is not simply that we displace": Harriet Goldhor Lerner, *The Dance of Anger*, p. 156.

182 *"All of us are vulnerable"*: ibid., p. 180.

183 "Even the kindest and best-intentioned parents": Bettelheim, *Good Enough Parent*, p. 116.

188 "For Annie, the relationship," "How frightening to you," "I was hurt," and "Annie was no longer afraid": Selma Fraiberg, "Ghosts in the Nursery," in *Clinical Studies in Infant Mental Health*, pp. 186, 187, 188..

189 Zigler and Kaufman analyzed some forty scholarly studies: Joan Kaufman and Edward Zigler, "Do Abused Children Become Abusive Parents?" *American Journal of Orthopsychiatry* 57, April 1987, pp. 186–192.

189 One by Egeland and Jacobvitz: study by Byron Egeland and Deb Jacobvitz, as cited by Kaufman and Zigler, "Do Abused Children," p. 189.

190 "I think one explanation": Daniel Kagan, "The Sins of My Father," *Parenting*, September 1987, pp. 126–27.

191 "that's what your soul looks like": John Bradshaw, *Bradshaw On: The Family*, p. 149.

191 "grew up in a family in which angry feelings": Israeloff, "Mad Doesn't Mean Bad," p. 57.

195 "The child realizes that he might not": T. Berry Brazelton, *Toddlers and Parents*, pp. 225–26.

196 "All of us are guilty of turning": ibid., p. 220.

196 "Punishment involves making a child feel guilty": Bananas, "Setting Limits" pamphlet pp. 1–2, in series "Growing Together."

198 "What convinced me that spanking isn't necessary": Spock, "Have You Ever Wanted," p. 38.

199 "EXPRESS YOUR FEELINGS STRONGLY," "We want to put an end," and "skills for engaging cooperation": Adele Faber and Elaine Mazlish, *How to Talk So Children Will Listen & Listen So Children Will Talk*, pp. 110, 88, 89.

207 "Abused children learn by their experiences": Eliana Gil, *Outgrowing the Pain*, p. 8.

8. SELF-ESTEEM AND SUCCESS

213 This child is "well pleased with the way": Bruno Bettelheim, *A Good Enough Parent*, p. 3.

213 "Integrity, honesty, responsibility": Virginia Satir, *The New Peoplemaking*, p. 22.

214 "This child would remain without" and "However paradoxical this may seem": Alice Miller, *The Drama of the Gifted Child*, pp. 32, 11.

215 "I understand a healthy self-feeling" and "One is free from depression": ibid., pp. 33, 39.

217 "How understandable it is, then": Bettelheim, *Good Enough Parent*, p. 28.

221 "The child who has been unable to build" and "someone at their disposal": Miller, *Gifted Child*, pp. 14, 35.

222 "I had plans of my own," "As her breasts grew," and "Between mother and daughter": Anne Roiphe, *Lovingkindness*, pp. 65–66, 104–5.

223 "My first child was born": Anne Roiphe, "Keeping Up with the Joneses," *Child*, June 1987, p. 34.

226, 227 "The booking of a five-year-old" and " 'Support' is a trigger word": Sara Davidson, "Kids in the Fast Lane," *New York Times Magazine*, October 16, 1988, pp. 74, 73.

227 "We are, I am told by educators": ibid., p. 52.

227 "The whole idea of earlier": David Elkind, as quoted in Glenn Collins, "Superbabies Aren't Happy Babies," *New York Times*, December 17, 1987, p. C6.

228 "So much emphasis has been placed": David Elkind, *The Hurried Child*, p. 129.

229 "While Gata played with detachment" and "For me, it was very strange": Fred Waitzkin, "A Father's Pawn," *New York Times Magazine*, May 13, 1990, pp. 45, 65.

230 "Each of us sees our children": Dorothy Briggs, *Your Child's Self-Esteem*, p. 45.

230 "Why do I have this expectation?" and "rapid scholastic achievement": ibid., pp. 53, 46.

237 "Feelings of worth can flourish" and "Conversely, children in troubled families": Satir, *New Peoplemaking*, pp. 26, 27.

237 "When people arrive at parenthood": ibid., p. 41.

241 "lack of interest in fatherhood" and "identity float up, away": Rafael Yglesias, *Only Children*, pp. 168, 367.

241 "do something besides be a mommy" and "Eric loved only through ownership": ibid., pp. 289, 240.

242 "Just pedal fast" and following quotes: ibid., pp. 517–21.

9. BECOMING AN EXTENDED FAMILY

246 The length of the "launching stage": Paulina McCullough, "Launching Children and Moving On," in *The Family Life Cycle: A Framework for Family Therapy*, ed. Elizabeth Carter and Monica McGoldrick, p. 171.

246 relationship between an adult daughter and her mother: Rosalind C. Barnett, "Adult Daughters and Their Mothers: Harmony or Hostility?" Wellesley College Center for Research on Women, Working Paper No. 209, p. 1.

247 midlife women may find themselves shuffling: Melinda Beck, "Trading Places," *Newsweek*, July 16, 1990, p. 49.

247 "invisible loyalties": Ivan Boszormenyi-Nagy and Geraldine M. Spark, *Invisible Loyalties*, pp. 217–18.

247 "the acceptance of one's one and only life" and "It seems possible to further paraphrase": Erik Erikson, *Childhood and Society*, pp. 268, 269.

248 "When you come to accept yourself": Barnett, "Adult Daughters," p. 4.

248 "The essence of being an adult": Donald Williamson, "Personal Authority via Termination of the Intergenerational Hierarchical Boundary: A 'New' Stage in the Family Life Cycle," *Journal of Marital and Family Therapy*, October 1981, p. 444.

249 the process helps the "older person" and following anecdote: Myrna Lewis and Robert Butler, "Life Review Therapy," *Geriatrics*, November 1974, pp. 165, 167.

250 "Thus began the slow and painful reintegration": Jeannette Kramer, *Family Interfaces: Transgenerational Patterns*, p. 168.

251, 252 "To untangle one member from another," "life as a man," "Reconnection with his siblings," and "There is no ideal way": ibid., pp. 172, 183, 185.

253 "grieving through the loss": Stanley Cath and James Herzog, "The Dying and Death of a Father," in *Father and Child*, ed. Stanley Cath, Allan Gurwitt, and John Munder Ross, p. 343.

253 "Becoming a grandparent is a second chance": Joyce Brothers quoted by Elizabeth Fishel in "It's Grand to Be a Grandparent," *McCall's*, November 1986.

253 "When you're a grandparent": Benjamin Spock, "Grandparents Can Be a Joy (and a Problem)," *Redbook*, August 1990, p. 30.

254 "The love of grandparents gives the child": Therese Benedek, "Parenthood During the Life Cycle," in *Parenthood: Its Psychology and Psychopathology*, ed. E. James Anthony and Therese Benedek, p. 201.

254 "hostages to reduce intergenerational tension": Jack O. Bradt, "The Family with Young Children," in Carter and McGoldrick, *Family Life Cycle*, p. 136.

256 "grim Irish grandfather": Fred Marchant, "A Baptismal Photograph," unpublished.

256 tells poignantly of helping her two granddaughters: Beverly Shaver, "Across the Generations," *Parents Press*, August 1990, pp. 22–23.

262 "I realize Mom is just a person": Rafael Yglesias, *Only Children*, p. 510.

264 "The reason I wrote *Working and Caring*": T. Berry Brazelton in interview by Katharine Weber, *Publishers Weekly*, November 13, 1987, pp. 57–58.

264 "enjoy[ing] the pleasures": T. Berry Brazelton, "Working Parents," *Newsweek*, February 13, 1989, p. 69.

266 "For all their doubts and fears": ibid., p. 64.

Bibliography

Anthony, E. James, and Therese Benedek, eds. *Parenthood: Its Psychology and Psychopathology*. Boston: Little, Brown, 1970.

Anthony, E. James, and George Pollock, eds. *Parental Influences in Health and Disease*. Boston: Little, Brown, 1985.

Apter, Terri. *Altered Loves: Mothers and Daughters During Adolescence*. New York: St. Martin's Press, 1990.

Atwood, Margaret. *Cat's Eye*. New York: Doubleday, 1989.

Bananas. "Setting Limits." Pamphlet in "Growing Together" series. No date.

Barnett, Rosalind. "Adult Daughters and Their Mothers: Harmony or Hostility?" Wellesley College Center for Research on Women, Working Paper No. 209, 1990.

Beck, Melinda. "Trading Places," *Newsweek*, July 16, 1990.

Bettelheim, Bruno. *A Good Enough Parent*. New York: Alfred A. Knopf, 1985.

———. "Problem of Generations," *Daedalus*, 91 (1962): 68–96.

Black, Claudia. *It Will Never Happen to Me!* New York: Ballantine Books, 1981.

———. *Repeat After Me*. Denver: M.A.C. Printing & Publications, 1985.

Block, Jack. *Lives Through Time*. Berkeley, Calif.: Bancroft Books, 1971.

Bloom, Benjamin S., ed. *Developing Talent in Young People*. New York: Ballantine Books, 1985.

Blos, Peter. *On Adolescence: A Psychoanalytic Interpretation*. New York: Free Press, 1962.

———. "The Second Individuation Process of Adolescence," *The Psychoanalytic Study of the Child*, vol. 22, pp. 162–86. New York: International Universities Press, 1967.

Boscolo, Luigi, Gianfranco Cecchin, Lynn Hoffman, and Peggy Penn. *Milan Systemic Family Therapy*. New York: Basic Books, 1987.

Boszormenyi-Nagy, Ivan, and Geraldine M. Spark. *Invisible Loyalties: Reciprocity in Intergenerational Family Therapy*. New York: Brunner/ Mazel, 1984.

Bowen, Murray. *Family Therapy: Clinical Practice*. New York: Jason Aronson, 1978.

————. "Toward the Differentiation of a Self in One's Own Family," in *Family Interaction*, ed. James Framo. New York: Springer, 1971.

Bradshaw, John. *Bradshaw On: The Family: A Revolutionary Way of Self-Discovery*. Deerfield Beach, Fla.: Health Communications, 1988.

Brazelton, T. Berry. *Infants and Mothers*. New York: Delacorte Press, 1969.

————. *On Becoming a Family: The Growth of Attachment*. New York: Dell, 1981.

————. *To Listen to a Child*. Menlo Park, Calif.: Addison-Wesley, 1984.

————. *Working and Caring*. Menlo Park, Calif.: Addison-Wesley, 1985.

————. "Working Parents," *Newsweek*, February 13, 1989, pp. 66–72.

Briggs, Dorothy C. *Your Child's Self-Esteem*. New York: Doubleday, 1975.

Bronstein, Phyllis, and Carolyn Pape Cowan, eds. *Fatherhood Today: Men's Changing Role in the Family*. New York: John Wiley & Sons, 1988.

Cable, Mary. *The Little Darlings: History of Childrearing*. New York: Charles Scribner's Sons, 1975.

Call, Justin, Eleanor Galenson, and Robert Tyson, eds. *Frontiers of Infant Psychiatry*, 2 vols. New York: Basic Books, 1984.

Carter, Elizabeth A., and Monica McGoldrick. *The Family Life Cycle: A Framework for Family Therapy*. New York: Gardner Press, 1980.

Cath, Stanley, Allan Gurwitt, and John Munder Ross, eds. *Father and Child: Developmental and Clinical Perspectives*. Boston: Little, Brown, 1982.

Chess, Stella, and Alexander Thomas. *Temperament in Clinical Practice*. New York: Guilford Press, 1986.

————. *Know Your Child*. New York: Basic Books, 1987.

Cohen, Rebecca, Bertram Cohler, and Sidney Weissman, eds. *Parenthood: A Psychodynamic Perspective*. New York: Guilford Press, 1986.

Cohler, Bertram J., and Henry V. Grunebaum. *Mothers, Grandmothers, and Daughters: Personality and Child Care in Three-Generation Families*. New York: John Wiley & Son, 1981.

Collins, Glenn. "Superbabies Aren't Happy Babies," *New York Times*, December 17, 1987.

Daniels, Pamela, and Kathy Weingarten. *Sooner or Later: The Timing of Parenthood in Adult Lives*. New York: W. W. Norton, 1982.

Davidson, Sara. "Kids in the Fast Lane," *New York Times Magazine*, October 16, 1988.

Eagan, Andrea Boroff. *The Newborn Mother: Stages of Her Growth*. Boston: Little, Brown, 1985.

Elkind, David. *The Hurried Child*. Reading, Mass.: Addison-Wesley, 1981.

Erikson, Erik H. *Childhood and Society*. New York: W. W. Norton, 1963.

———. *Identity: Youth and Crisis*. New York: W. W. Norton, 1968.

Faber, Adele, and Elaine Mazlish. *How to Talk So Kids Will Listen & Listen So Kids Will Talk*. New York: Avon Books, 1980.

Ferber, Andrew, Marilyn Mendelsohn, and Augustus Napier. *The Book of Family Therapy*. Boston: Houghton Mifflin, 1972.

Fishel, Elizabeth. "It's Grand to be a Grandparent," *McCall's*, November 1986.

Fraiberg, Selma. *Clinical Studies in Infant Mental Health: The First Year of Life*. New York: Basic Books, 1980.

———. *The Magic Years*. New York: Charles Scribner's Sons, 1959.

Gardner, Howard. *Frames of Mind: The Theory of Multiple Intelligence*. New York: Basic Books, 1983.

Gil, Eliana. *Outgrowing the Pain: A Book for and about Adults Abused as Children*. New York: Dell, 1983.

Greene, Lawrence J. *Kids Who Underachieve*. New York: Simon and Schuster, 1986.

Greenspan, Stanley. *First Feelings: Milestones in the Emotional Development of Your Baby and Child*. New York: Viking, 1985.

Guest, Judith. *The Mythic Family*. Minneapolis: Milkweed Editions, 1988.

Haley, Jay. *Uncommon Therapy: The Psychiatric Techniques of Milton H. Erickson, M.D.* New York: W. W. Norton, 1973.

Haley, Jay, ed. *Changing Families: A Family Therapy Reader*. New York: Grune & Stratton, 1971.

Haley, Jay, and Lynn Hoffman. *Techniques of Family Therapy*. New York: Basic Books, 1967.

Helfer, Ray E. *Childhood Comes First*. East Lansing, Mich.: Second Edition, 1984.

Henry, Jules. *Pathways to Madness*. New York: Vintage Books, 1973.

Hoffman, Lynn. *Foundations of Family Therapy: A Conceptual Framework of Systems Change*. New York: Basic Books, 1981.

Hovestadt, Alan J., and Marshall Fine. *Family of Origin Therapy*. Rockville, Md.: Aspen Publishers, 1987.

Imber-Black, Evan, Janine Roberts, and Robert A. Whiting. *Rituals in Families and Family Therapy*. New York: W. W. Norton, 1988.

Israeloff, Roberta. *Coming to Terms*. New York: Viking Penguin, 1984.

————. *In Confidence: Four Years of Therapy*. Boston: Houghton Mifflin, 1990.

————. "Mad Doesn't Mean Bad," *Working Mother*, February 1990.

Kagan, Daniel. "The Sins of My Father," *Parenting*, September 1987.

Kagan, Jerome. *The Nature of the Child*. New York: Basic Books, 1984.

Kahana, E., and B. Kahana. "Grandparenthood from the Perspective of the Developing Grandchild," *Developmental Psychology*, 3 (1970): 98–105.

Kaplan, Louise J. *Adolescence: The Farewell to Childhood*. New York: Simon and Schuster, 1984.

————. *Oneness and Separateness: From Infant to Individual*. New York: Simon and Schuster, 1978.

Karen, Michael. "Becoming Attached," *Atlantic Monthly*, February 1990.

Kaufman, Joan, and Edward Zigler. "Do Abused Children Become Abusive Parents?" *American Journal of Orthopsychiatry* 57, April 1987.

Kerr, Michael E., and Murray Bowen. *Family Evaluation: An Approach Based on Bowen Theory*. New York: W. W. Norton, 1988.

Klaus, Marshall. *Maternal-Infant Bonding: The Impact of Early Separation*. St. Louis: Mosby, 1976.

Konopka, Gisela. *Adolescent Girls in Conflict*. Englewood Cliffs, N.J.: Prentice Hall, 1966.

Kornhaber, Arthur. *Between Parents and Grandparents*. New York: St. Martin's Press, 1986.

Kort, Carol, and Ronnie Friedland, eds. *The Father's Book: Shared Experiences*. Boston: G. K. Hall, 1986.

Kramer, Jeannette R. *Family Interfaces: Transgenerational Patterns*. New York: Brunner/Mazel, 1985.

Layton, Molly. "The Mother Journey," *Family Therapy Networker*, September/October 1989.

Lerner, Harriet Goldhor. *The Dance of Anger*. New York: Harper & Row, 1985.

LeShan, Eda. *When Your Child Drives You Crazy*. New York: St. Martin's Press, 1985.

Levant, Ronald. *Family Therapy: A Comprehensive Overview*. Englewood Cliffs, N.J.: Prentice Hall, 1984.

Lewis, Jerry M. et al. *No Single Thread*. New York: Brunner/Mazel, 1976.

Lewis, Myrna, and Robert Butler. "Life-Review Therapy," *Geriatrics*, November 1974.

Luepnitz, Deborah A. *The Family Interpreted: Feminist Theory in Clinical Practice*. New York: Basic Books, 1988.

Mahler, M., and J. B. McDevitt. "Thoughts on the Emergence of the

Sense of Self, with Particular Emphasis on the Body Self," *Journal of the American Psychoanalytic Association* 30 (1982): 827–48.

Mahler, M., F. Pine, and A. Bergman. *The Psychological Birth of the Human Infant*. New York: Basic Books, 1975.

McBride, Angela. *The Growth and Development of Mothers*. New York: Harper & Row, 1974.

McGoldrick, Monica, and Randy Gerson. *Genograms in Family Assessment*. New York: W. W. Norton, 1985.

McGoldrick, Monica, Carol M. Anderson, and Froma Walsh, eds. *Women in Families: A Framework for Family Therapy*. New York: W. W. Norton, 1989.

Miller, Alice. *The Drama of the Gifted Child*. New York: Basic Books, 1981.

———. *For Your Own Good*. New York: Farrar, Straus, Giroux, 1983.

———. *Pictures of a Childhood*. New York: Farrar, Straus, Giroux, 1986.

Miller, Sue. *Family Pictures*. New York: Harper & Row, 1990.

Minuchin, Salvador. *Family Kaleidoscope*. Cambridge, Mass.: Harvard University Press, 1984.

———. *Families and Family Therapy*. Cambridge, Mass.: Harvard University Press, 1974.

Napier, Augustus, and Carl Whitaker. *The Family Crucible: The Intense Experience of Family Therapy*. New York: Harper & Row, 1978.

Neugarten, Bernice. "The Changing American Grandparent," *Journal of Marriage and Family* 26 (1964): 199–205.

Nichols, Michael P. *The Power of the Family: Mastering the Hidden Dance of Family Relationships*. New York: Fireside, 1988.

Oppenheim, Joanne, Betty Boegehold, and Barbara Brenner. *Raising a Confident Child*. New York: Pantheon Books, 1984.

Paley, Vivian Gussin. *Mollie Is Three*. Chicago: University of Chicago Press, 1986.

Papp, Peggy, Olga Silverstein, and Elizabeth Carter. "Family Sculpting in Preventive Work with Well Families," *Family Process* 12 (1973): 197–211.

Paul, Norman L., and Betty Byfield Paul. *A Marital Puzzle: Transgenerational Analysis in Marriage Counseling*. New York: Gardner Press, 1976.

Pincus, Lily, and Christopher Dare. *Secrets in the Family*. New York: Harper & Row, 1978.

Roiphe, Anne. "Keeping Up with the Joneses," *Child*, June 1987, pp. 33–34.

———. *Lovingkindness*. New York: Warner Books, 1987.

Ruddick, Sara. *Maternal Thinking: Toward a Politics of Peace*. Boston: Beacon Press, 1989.

Sander, Lou. "Issues in Mother-Child Interaction," *Journal of the American Academy of Child Psychiatry* 3 (1964): 231–63.

Satir, Virginia. *The New Peoplemaking*. Mountain View, Calif.: Science and Behavior Books, 1988.

Seixas, Judith S., and Geraldine Youcha. *Children of Alcoholism: A Survivor's Manual*. New York: Crown Publishers, 1985.

Shaver, Beverly. "Across the Generations," *Parents Press*, August 1990.

Simpson, Eileen. *Orphans: Real and Imaginary*. New York: New American Library, 1987.

Spock, Benjamin. "Grandparents Can Be a Joy (and a Problem)," *Redbook*, August 1990.

———. "Have You Ever Wanted to Strike Your Child?" *Redbook*, April 1988.

Stern, Daniel. *The Interpersonal World of the Infant*. New York: Basic Books, 1985.

Stinnett, Nick, and John DeFrain. *Secrets of Strong Families*. Boston: Little, Brown, 1985.

Turecki, Stanley, and Leslie Tonner. *The Difficult Child*. New York: Bantam Books, 1985.

Viorst, Judith. *Necessary Losses*. New York: Simon and Schuster, 1986.

Vissel, Barry, and Joyce Vissel. *Models of Love: The Parent-Child Journey*. Aptos, Calif.: Ramira Publishers, 1986.

Wachtel, Ellen F., and Paul Wachtel. *Family Dynamics in Individual Psychotherapy*. New York: Guilford Press, 1986.

Waitzkin, Fred. "A Father's Pawn," *New York Times Magazine*, May 13, 1990, pp. 44–73.

Wallerstein, Judith S., and Sandra Blakeslee. *Second Chances: Men, Women, & Children a Decade after Divorce*. New York: Ticknor & Fields, 1989.

Walsh, Froma, ed. *Normal Family Processes*. New York: Guilford Press, 1982.

Walters, Marianne, Betty Carter, Peggy Papp, and Olga Silverstein. *The Invisible Web*. New York: Guilford Press, 1988.

Weber, Katharine. "PW Interviews: T. Berry Brazelton," *Publishers Weekly*, November 13, 1987.

Weltner, Linda. *No Place Like Home*. New York: William Morrow, 1988.

White, Burton L. *The First Three Years of Life*. New York: Prentice Hall, 1985.

Winestine, Muriel C., Irwin M. Marcus, and Irving Sternschein, "The Experience of Separation-Individuation in Infancy and Its Reverberations for the Course of Life," *Journal of the American Psychoanalytic Association* 21 (1972): 135–54, 155–67, 633–45.

Winnicott, D. W. "The Mirror Role of Mother and Family in Child Development," in *Playing and Reality*, ed. D. W. Winnicott. Harmondsworth, England: Penguin Books, 1980.

———. *Home Is Where We Start From.* 1986.

———. *The Child, the Family, and the Outside World.* Menlo Park, Calif.: Addison-Wesley, 1964.

Wylie, Mary Sykes. "The Mother Knot," *Family Therapy Networker*, September/October 1989.

Yglesias, Rafael. *Only Children.* New York: William Morrow, 1988.

Index